YEARS OF SADNESS

The Cornell East Asia Series is published by the Cornell University East Asia Program (distinct from Cornell University Press). We publish books on a variety of scholarly topics relating to East Asia as a service to the academic community and the general public. Standing Orders, which provide for automatic notification and invoicing of each title in the series upon publication are accepted.

If after review by internal and external readers a manuscript is accepted for publication, it is published on the basis of camera-ready copy provided by the author who is responsible for any copyediting and manuscript formatting. Alternative arrangements should be made with approval of the Series. Address submission inquiries to: CEAS Editorial Board, East Asia Program, Cornell University, Ithaca, New York 14853-7601.

Number 147 in the Cornell East Asia Series
Copyright ©2009 by Wang Lingzhen and Mary Ann O'Donnell. All rights reserved.
ISSN: 1050-2955
ISBN: 978-1-933947-17-4 hc
ISBN: 978-1-933947-47-1 pb
Library of Congress Control Number: 2009925880
Printed in the United States of America

24 23 22 21 20 19 18 17 16 15 14 13 12 11 10 09   9 8 7 6 5 4 3 2 1

♾ The paper in this book meets the requirements for permanence of ISO 9706:1994.

YEARS OF SADNESS
Autobiographical Writings of Wang Anyi

TRANSLATED BY

WANG LINGZHEN AND MARY ANN O'DONNELL
WITH AN INTRODUCTION BY
WANG LINGZHEN

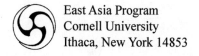

East Asia Program
Cornell University
Ithaca, New York 14853

CONTENTS

ACKNOWLEDGMENTS

I would like to thank Wang Anyi for giving me permission to translate her works into English and for discussing with me her sense of being a woman and a writer in contemporary China. Thanks also go to the three anonymous readers for the Cornell East Asia Series, who offered their great support for this translation anthology and who provided constructive and detailed suggestions for revision. I appreciate the suggestions for further revisions from Mai Shaikhanuar-Cota, the managing editor of the Cornell East Asia Series, as well as her creative design of the format of this anthology. Julia Perkins copyedited the manuscript and Zhang Xiaohong and Waverly Liu made some good suggestions on translation. I want to thank them for their important help. Last but not least, I would like to thank my co-translator, Mary Ann O'Donnell, whose patience and understanding made my impulse for endless revisions endurable and fruitful.

INTRODUCTION

Introducing the Writer

WANG ANYI is one of the most critically acclaimed writers in post-Mao China. Born in 1954 in Nanjing and brought up in Shanghai, the daughter of the noted writer Ru Zhijuan, Wang had just graduated from junior high school in 1969 when she volunteered to work and live in a commune in northern Anhui Providence. Disappointed by her peasant life in Anhui, she left in 1972 to be admitted into a local performing arts troupe in Xuzhou, Jiangsu. There she began writing and publishing short stories. In 1978 Wang returned to Shanghai to serve as an editor of a literary journal, and in 1980 her career as a professional writer began. Since then Wang has become one of the most prominent and prolific writers in China and has won many national literary prizes, including the Fifth Mao Dun Literature Prize in 2000 and the Third Lu Xun Literature Prize in 2005. She was chair of the Shanghai Writers' Association in 2001 and 2007, and was elected vice chair of the National Chinese Writers' Association in 2006.

As a leading writer in the main cultural and literary movements that have defined post-Mao China, Wang Anyi's work covers a wide range of topics from the enunciation of subjectivity to national roots-seeking literature, from an avant-garde form of literature to response to the market demand for commercialized literature. In this anthology, rather than focusing on her works that concern mostly social, historical, and changing urban and rural issues,[1] we focus on Wang's autobiographical writing, a body of work that has been less explored by English translators and scholars, thereby foregrounding a personal and emotional aspect of Wang's life and writing that is essential to a deeper understanding of the writer. In these personal narratives, Wang has persistently sought an identity that is as much constituted by public history as it is renegotiated through personal experience,

1

imagination, and writing. Her autobiographical works articulate a particular emotional trajectory of self-formation, an individual process of becoming a woman and writer in socialist and post-socialist China.

Since the late Qing period, Chinese women have continuously produced autobiographical literature in various genres.[2] Most women writers have actively engaged with dominant discourses and ideologies in their autobiographical writing; at the same time, they have also revealed and expressed gendered concerns, personal emotions, and identity negotiation in relation to the process of Chinese modernization. In socialist China, where revolutionary collectivism endorsed only those personal stories that conformed to collective and political goals, different voices disappeared. It was during the early post-Mao era that women's different and personal voices reemerged, contributing greatly to the diverse literary practice in the reform era.

Broadly speaking, Wang Anyi's autobiographical writings have played the most significant role in both continuing and developing the gendered and personal mode of writing initiated by a small group of women writers such as Zhang Jie, Zhang Xinxin, and Yu Luojin in the early post-Mao era (1979–1981). In her thirty-year writing career Wang has not only produced a significant number of autobiographical narratives but has also become known for exploring different ways of self-representation in contemporary China. The female self depicted in her autobiographical works is never a fixed identity or image, and Wang has successfully demonstrated that self-formation and transformation involve complex and continuous negotiations among history, memory, and (re)writing. In other words, Wang has pronounced through her self-centered literary practice that the female self is both constituted by historical and social forces and mediated through subjective reflection and creative writing. Wang Anyi's autobiographical practice has obviously influenced younger generations of women writers, such as Chen Ran, Lin Bai, Wei Hui, and Mian Mian, who since the 1990s have adhered to this female autobiographical tradition and further diversified this literary practice by incorporating new and different historical forces such as commercialism and post-socialist individualism. As this women's tradition of autobiographical writing both engages with and also diverges from mainstream Chinese literary production, it offers a complex as well as alternative perspective on the history of Chinese modernity.

In 1981 Wang Anyi published "And the Rain Patters On," the first short story in her Wenwen series. The series, which includes a group of short stories and Wang's first novel, *The 1969 Middle School Graduates* (1984), contains a distinctive autobiographical dimension and centers on the experiences of a young woman, Wenwen, and her perspective on life during the socialist and early postsocialist periods. "And the Rain Patters On," a fresh, poetic, and personal story of love and hope, won Wang national recognition and ushered her into the national literary scene as a promising young woman writer. She lived up to her promise and matured in her further exploration of self and society in the Wenwen series in the 1980s.

Wang Anyi's journey to the United States in 1983 redefined her career and her sense of self. With her next publication, *Baotown* (1985), she proved to be a versatile writer with serious concerns and deep thoughts about her nation and culture. As a confident and productive writer, Wang ventured in the following decade into many social, literary, and sometimes controversial areas such as rural–urban conventions and dichotomy, sexuality and desire, and avant-garde literature, surprising her readers again and again with her original and successful stories. She continued, however, to write autobiographically. In 1986, together with her mother she published a collection of essays of their travels and stay in the United States, a period that she later stated had played a critical role in transforming her as a woman writer in the ensuing years. In 1991 she published *Utopian Verses*, a significant autobiographical piece that reveals the inner and emotional source of her transformation in the mid and late 1980s. In 1993 Wang published her monumental, semi-autobiographical novel *Documentation and Fabrication: One Method of Creating the World*, a novel based on the search for a personal history and identity through both constructing and fabricating the narrator's maternal genealogy as well as connecting isolated, personal experiences with

their immediate physical environment, the city of Shanghai in socialist China. The novel contains many references to the author's life and
is also a rewriting of her earlier autobiographical stories. In the novel
Wang dispenses with the literary conventions that differentiate fiction from autobiography and creates her own distinctive world and
logic that are both independent from yet dependent on history and
reality. The power of imagination demonstrated in this novel, which
transcends but closely ties to personal experience, broke new ground
in Chinese women's autobiographical writing. In a similar approach
to history, reality, and the self, Wang published another autobiographical novel, *Sadness over the Pacific Ocean* (1994), in which the
young female narrator seeks her personal roots and identity through
discovering and constructing her paternal genealogy, the origin of
which is traced to Singapore. In the late 1990s when cultural production was commercialized in China and women's autobiographical
writing was viewed by the public more as a commodity that exposed
one's privacy for public and voyeuristic consumption, Wang Anyi
turned inward, exploring her past inner experience and emotional
growth in socialist China. In *Years of Sadness* (1998) Wang looks back
at her adolescent years through a particular emotional and aesthetic
lens, reflecting on the experience of a girl's coming-of-age, and challenging the penetrating commercial force that tends to completely
commercialize women's life stories in contemporary China.[3]

Introducing This Volume

Utopian Verses

This anthology includes Wang's two best autobiographical novellas, *Utopian Verses* (1991) and *Years of Sadness* (1998), and one
earlier essay, "A Woman Writer's Sense of Self" (1988).[4]

Utopian Verses offers a much more complex lens for understanding the significance of Wang Anyi's *Baotown*; it also depicts an
unusual historical encounter between a famous, senior, Taiwan literary figure and a young, promising, mainland woman writer in the
United States. Chen Yingzhen was a socially and politically commit-

ted Taiwan writer in the 1960s and 1970s. Greatly influenced by Lu Xun and other left-wing writers in mainland China, Chen Yingzhen was also a political activist who was imprisoned from 1968 to 1975 by the Nationalist government not only for accessing forbidden works authored by Lu Xun, Mao Zedong, and Marx, but also for starting communist and revolutionary organizations. His persistent concern for lower-class people, his patriotic passion for China, and his in-depth critique of the capitalist system and of its social ills set him, ironically, into a position opposed to 1980s young mainland Chinese writers, who had just emerged from the turmoil of the ten-year Cultural Revolution and who had just begun to engage in critical reflections on socialist China, particularly on such socialist ideas as "people," "class," and "revolution." Several mainland Chinese writers expressed surprise and disbelief when they first conversed with Chen Yingzhen, a writer from "capitalist" Taiwan, who openly and earnestly endorsed certain fundamental socialist ideals in the late 1980s.[5] Wang Anyi belonged to the younger generation of writers. As illustrated in *Utopian Verses*, she experienced a similar confrontation when discussing with Chen Yingzhen issues related to socialist collectivism and capitalist individualism. But as a woman writer, Wang was different from other mainstream, male writers of the 1980s, who were disillusioned by Chinese socialist practice but who were still obsessed with the historical motif of strengthening and modernizing China, although this time they approached the motif more through a liberal orientation and through economic reform. Like many other women writers, Wang Anyi was more concerned with the self and everyday life in the early post-Mao era. Her encounter with Chen Yingzhen in the United States, as a result, generates different and more engaging effects.

In the early 1980s Wang's self-narration showed signs of exhaustion and lethargy; Wang Anyi attempted to address this writing crisis, but to no avail.[6] Her travel to the United States in 1983, particularly her encounter with Chen Yingzhen, unexpectedly constituted a turning point in Wang's struggle to succeed as a writer. She gained a completely renewed perspective on the national, the collective, and the personal under Chen's influence in the United

States. Her next short novel, *Baotown*, published after she returned to China, transformed Wang into a successful writer who could transcend her own personal experience and produce a powerfully allegorical piece about China during the roots-seeking cultural movement.[7]

In *Baotown*, however, Wang Anyi toned down Chen Yingzhen's political passion and influence but extended his belief in universal love, the root of which, in addition to the left-wing intellectual's concern for the weak and powerless, can also be traced to the influence of Chen's father, a Christian priest in Taiwan. Chen's love contains a unique religious and utopian aspect. Wang successfully brought his utopian and humanistic concern into the mid-1980s roots-seeking movement, revising the existing roots-seeking motif and expanding the traditional Chinese concept of "benevolence" into a vernacular and humanistic ideal, a moral spirit, which, in Wang Anyi's eyes, was best embodied in Chen Yingzhen, but which has been largely endangered or even uprooted in the process of Chinese modernization.

With *Baotown* Wang Anyi's career as a successful writer who could go beyond personal experience and self-writing was established, but in *Utopian Verses* she reveals how this allegorical piece was deeply attached to personal and interpersonal elements. In *Utopian Verses* Wang discloses her internal journey and struggle during the period in which she created *Baotown*, and unveils the interpersonal, emotional source of her strong motivation to write a Chinese story (*Baotown*) after returning from the United States. While her brief sojourn in the United States played a role, it is the (inter)personal and emotional factors that contributed most to the creation of such a symbolic piece of fiction. *Utopian Verses* tells of the extraordinary relationship between the first-person narrator (Wang Anyi), a mainland Chinese female writer, and a well-known Taiwanese male writer (Chen Yingzhen). The relationship transcends political, religious, and conventional boundaries. The first-person narrator first encounters the Taiwanese writer in one of his earlier short stories, "A Race of Generals,"[8] and the relationship between Triangle Face and Skinny Little Maid in the story unexpectedly moves her. The narrator and the Taiwanese writer later meet in person at the 1983

International Writing Program at the University of Iowa and form a strong bond. Greatly touched by the writer's utopian, patriotic, and humanistic ideals for the world, the narrator, in the context of a foreign and developed capitalist country, promises him that she will write stories about "China" in the future. After they separated, the narrator's irresistible emotional longing for the writer motivates her to search for proper "Chinese" themes and material. This process culminates in her writing the story of a "benevolent" child in a Chinese village (*Baotown*). *Renyi* (benevolence) is the moral ideal the child protagonist embodies in *Baotown*, but the origin of this ideal does not come directly from the ancient Chinese meaning of the term during the roots-seeking movement, as many readers believed. Rather, the ideal grows directly from Chen Yingzhen, a modern, exemplary intellectual who has, in Wang's terms, a "loving heart" beyond any worldly restraints and who also cares deeply about this world. Wang Anyi deliberately uses "*renci*" (benevolence, with *ci* indicating seniority in age) to describe Chen in her *Utopian Verses*. The narrator's intense and unconventional love for the humanistic and idealistic or religious writer not only enables her to go through the most difficult and challenging period of her writing career, but more importantly, it reconstitutes her identity by connecting her isolated self to other human beings, China, and the world. Replete with passion and longing, the novella details five stages of the narrator's life and inner growth since she first "met" the Taiwan writer in his story, exhibiting the power of interpersonal relationships and personal imagination in recreating the self, literature, and the world.

Years of Sadness

Wang Anyi's writing of *Years of Sadness* is inseparable from the consumerist mode of nostalgia popular in 1990s China. Since the early 1990s Chinese women's writing about their private lives has played a privileged role in the expansion of consumer culture, contributing to the market as well as to state construction of private space and "private self" in contemporary China. With *Years of Sadness* Wang participates in the collective marketing of memory and women's lives, but unlike other purely market-oriented works, Wang's story also resists a total market consumption by giving voice to a particular, irreducible historical negotiation among childhood memory, writing, and self. Moreover, her meticulous and masochistic description of a young girl's lonely, uneventful, and emotionally charged experiences often diverts reader-consumers from a purely pleasure-seeking reading experience to one of disquiet caused by pressing questions regarding socialist history, emotional existence, and the formation of the gendered self.

In *Years of Sadness*, the first-person narrator tells about several seemingly trivial yet humiliating childhood episodes, revealing deep emotional scars. The narrator has unconsciously suppressed all of these experiences until one day a sobbing woman in a dark movie theater triggers their recollection. It is interesting to note how cinema and theater occupied an important part of youth life during the 1960s and how they later constituted an indispensable aspect of that generation's memory and sense of self. The narrator's experiences include losing movie tickets on two occasions before entering the theater and her consequent embarrassment, nervousness, and distress; the clash between her desire to befriend other children and her shyness; her secret admiration for and her overdone imitation of a girl in the neighborhood; her disappointment about her own appearance; a miscommunication with her math teacher and the humiliation she felt when he interrogated her; her sister's betrayal of her in front of the math teacher; her fear of loneliness and darkness; and finally the most unspeakable and shameful experience: being sent to the hospital for examination and treatment of a genital infection caused by an insect sting. Through these private and emotional episodes, we see a young, shy, and sensitive girl who in her early years is confused, ignored, unprotected, and deeply hurt. Alone and insecure among people, she lacks the means to express herself or even to communicate with her mother; she feels rejected by others and excluded from the external world, constantly feeling awkward and inadequate.

Among Wang's autobiographical works, *Years of Sadness* goes deepest in exploring her early emotional and psychic experiences, revealing an invisible, affective core of personal identity as well as the unconscious yet continuous drive to write as a way of negotiating the self. At the social level, it questions socialist gender ideology by detailing the emotional, psychic "trauma" caused mostly by the absence of the mother (a socialist revolutionary figure) at home. It also best illustrates how contemporary women writers like Wang Anyi have appropriated or worked with the market to reclaim their personal sense of self and literature. Aesthetically, the novella is beautifully written, full of nostalgic and melancholic imagery and tone.

"A Woman Writer's Sense of Self"

"A Woman Writer's Sense of Self" is an earlier piece by Wang Anyi in which she pinpoints the conjoined, important moments of gender and the personal in early post-Mao Chinese literary practice and articulates the irreplaceable significance of this personal mode of writing in her process of becoming a writer. Although from today's feminist perspective some statements may appear dated, the essay is historically true and important, revealing a critical transitional moment in Chinese women's autobiographical literature. The essay reflects on the literary practices of a group of women writers in the early post-Mao era, such as Zhang Jie, Zhang Xinxin, and Yu Luojin, emphasizing the influence of these practices on a younger generation of women writers like Wang Anyi herself. It compares male and female writers and elaborates on certain limitations of women as a socially constituted, emotional gender and on their self-obsessed writing. Wang Anyi advocates in this essay a writing attitude that requires not simply direct expression of emotions, but more importantly distanced and rational/aesthetic reflections. Self, according to Wang, has multiple layers and numerous traps; at the same time, it also contains indeterminable potential. In this early essay, Wang Anyi has already articulated her particular sense of self, which is never simply a fixed "authentic self" but a self that "improves" through imaginative search, reflection, and writing. For both general readers and literary scholars of Wang Anyi, the essay provides critical insight into the origin of Wang's writing as well as Chinese women's writing in the early post-

Mao era in general. Like many other women writers in the early 1980s, Wang began her career with autobiographical writing, a practice that questions the dominant socialist and collective mode of literary production of the time and expresses alternative and gendered perceptions. By including this essay with two of Wang's autobiographical novellas, I emphasize the importance of the historical trajectory of contemporary women's autobiographical writing and at the same time highlight Wang's conscious and continued effort from early on to articulate a self that brings together history, emotions, and creative imagination.

Notes

1. Some of Wang Anyi's (王安忆) works translated into English include *Lapse of Time* (a collection of Wang's short stories, including "And the Rain Patters On"), trans. Yu Fanqin and others (San Francisco: China Books, 1988); *Baotown*, trans. Martha Avery (London: Viking, 1989); *Love in a Small Town*, trans. Eva Huang (Hong Kong: Renditions, 1988); *Love on a Barren Mountain*, trans. Eva Huang (Hong Kong: Renditions, 1991); *Brocade Valley*, trans. Bonnie S. McDougall and Chen Maiping (New York: New Directions, 1992); "Brothers," trans. Diana B. Kingsbury, in Kingsbury, ed. *I Wish I Were a Wolf: The New Voice in Chinese Women's Literature* (London: New World Press, 1994), 158–212; and *The Song of Everlasting Sorrow*, trans. Michael Berry and Susan Chan Egan (New York: Columbia University Press, 2008).

2. For book-length studies in English and translations of modern Chinese women's autobiographically oriented writing, see Lingzhen Wang, *Personal Matters: Women's Autobiographical Practice in Twentieth Century China* (Stanford: Stanford University Press, 2004); Amy D. Dooling, *Women's Literary Feminism in Twentieth Century China* (New York: Palgrave Macmillan, 2005); Jing M. Wang, *When "I" Was Born: Women's Autobiography in Modern China* (Madison: University of Wisconsin Press, 2008); Amy D. Dooling and Kristina M. Torgeson, *Writing Women in Modern China* (New York: Columbia University Press, 1997); Jing M. Wang, *Jumping through Hoops: Autobiographical Stories by Modern Chinese Women Writers* (Hong Kong: Hong Kong University Press, 2003); and Amy D. Dooling and Kristina M. Torgeson, *Writing Women in Modern China: The Revolutionary Years, 1936–1976* (New York: Columbia University Press, 2005).

3. These are the original Chinese titles of Wang's works mentioned in this paragraph:《雨，沙沙沙》(1981),《69届初中生》(1984),《小鲍庄》(1985),《母女漫游美利坚》(1986),《乌托邦诗篇》(1991),《纪实与虚构：创造世界方法之一》(1993),《伤心太平洋》(1994),《忧伤的年代》(1998).

4. Wang Anyi, "A Woman Writer's Sense of Self" (《女作家的自我》), in *Literary Corner* (《文学角》), no. 6, 1988.

5. In Zha Jianying's interview with Ah Cheng (阿城), they discussed Chen Yingzhen, particularly his idea of "people." See Zha Jianying, The 1980s (查建英，《八十年代访谈录》) (Beijing, Shenghuo/Duzhe/Xinzhi–Sanlian Shudian, 2006), 18-19.

6. See Wang Anyi's letter to Wang Meng (王蒙) published in *Shanghai Weihui Newspaper* (《文汇报》) on April 22, 1982.

7. The roots-seeking movement (寻根运动) is often understood as a cultural reaction to the political and aesthetic values of socialist China. The major goal of the movement is to explore the various roots of the nation, of literature, and of the individual by focusing on marginalized values of the past or on those in remote, minority areas in order to revive China or to launch a critique of the previous era. The movement began in literary practice and soon expanded to other artistic areas such as cinema and painting in the mid and late 1980s. Most authors and artists of the movement were sent-down youth during the Cultural Revolution (1966–1976); members of the group are also known for their critical attention to Western modernist and magical-realist styles and for their artistic experiments.

8. "A Race of Generals" (陈映真,《将军族》) was a representative short story of Chen Yingzhen's early writing; it was published in 1964

UTOPIAN VERSES

Afterward, I knew that an islander might also hold the world in his heart.

Today, with the rapid development of transportation and printing, it is no longer difficult to know the world. Books, geography classes, and relatively limited travel all enable people to imagine the worlds on this planet. The proof of this can't get more concrete than "jet lag," which turns global theory into something that ordinary people can experience viscerally. Nevertheless, I don't think this person knew the world through these ordinary means. I think he came to know the world through Genesis 11, where the Bible says: "Now the whole earth had one language and few words."[1] Later, the people discussed building a city with a tower at its center. The top of the tower would be high enough to pierce the clouds. Like lighthouses on the ocean after the birth of seafaring, the tower would keep people on land from dispersing. In the chapter titled "Babel," it is written: "And the LORD [Yahweh] said,[2] 'Behold, they are one people, and they have all one language; and this is only the beginning of what they will do; and nothing that they propose to do will now be impossible for them. Come, let us go down, and there confuse their language, that they may not understand one another's speech.' So the LORD scattered them abroad from there over the face of all the earth, and they left off building the city." Through this chapter, this person not only understood the current state of the world in which human beings have been scattered and separated by the strength of the LORD, but also knew of the past, when it was once possible for the world's peoples to gather happily together. That sky-piercing tower called out so that they would never lose one another. This situation must have been something like a luminous party, the only form of human gathering that, being a modern degenerate, I can only imagine.

As a child living in a temperate village on that western Pacific island, this person must have repeatedly dreamt about innumerable people coming together, their hearts united in a concerted effort to build a city. These people would live and work together, just like a family. Later, grandiose scenes of the heroic mass revolution on the land across the straits made him think that his dream was being realized in one part of the world. He came to understand the situation by listening to a short-wave radio, and it wasn't long before he was jailed for this underground activity. This was before the scale of industrialization on the island could threaten his tranquil village. It was also before that powerful and prosperous country, on which the island depended, entered a recession. The crisis hadn't yet come to a head and, for that time, he could still dream a child's pleasantly soft and harmonious dreams.

I believe that he understood the world through the Bible because his father was a famous priest. This knowledge, in turn, has provided me with resources for composing these verses. I even imagine that his little head entertained thoughts like, "Why did Yahweh have to divide peoples and use language to isolate their affairs? Why was Yahweh afraid that peoples' strength would be greater than his own? Was it because Yahweh was doubtlessly good, but people doubtlessly weren't?" At this point, my ability to imagine Yahweh is exhausted. For me, the Bible seems to be both a book from heaven and a book of fairy tales. On the one hand, it is much too profound, and on the other, it is much too simplistic. What's more, this person is very far from me and I have no means of eliciting, one by one, the questions in his head.

I write these verses out of my longing for him.

It goes without saying that to long for someone far away ought to be disheartening, if only because this kind of longing cannot take root and will thus remain unrequited. Yet for me, longing for this person has become a comfort and an ideal. It matters neither how far away he is, nor for how long he remains unresponsive. This longing has created a bit of paradise in my heart, enabling me to preserve some remnants of purity, goodness, and beauty.

My longing is an invocation. When I flounder in the confusing disorder of reality, it saves me, pulling me out to see the glorious world concealed within the multihued clouds of sunrise and sunset. My longing also resembles a kind of love. It places me within the hypothetical gaze of a pair of eyes that always requires me to behave a little better. This is a very irrational kind of longing. I have never bothered with questions like, "Where is he now?" or "What is he doing now?" His image has never appeared in my mind. When I long, I never use the senses of sight and hearing. I don't even employ the capacity of thought or speculation—this longing has nothing to do with flesh. My longing seems to have an independent mode of existence through which it has become an object, or an externalization that sometimes can enter into dialogue with me. Unlike any other longing, this longing has never vexed or depressed me. Only once or twice in many years have I heard news of him. These moments have brought a happiness so great that it shines on both past and future longing, increasing their radiance.

My longing has gradually become an imaginative force that compels me to depict him. Yet this impulse to materialize my longing is also risky because it contains the danger that I might distort my longing. I write every word extremely carefully, cautiously, as if crossing thin ice. I've experienced the destructive power of language and have felt danger lurking everywhere. There is no smooth path to materialize a spiritual existence; the difficulties are many and varied. Thus, I've deployed here the word "verse." I use "poetry" to delineate literature's spiritual world, while "novel" refers to the material world. This division is my latest creative endeavor, and creating new things has always tempted my vanity. It is precisely this vanity that compels me to look for more difficult problems, which is like banging my head against a wall.

I suppose it's better to start from the beginning. I first got to know this person in a book, which included a short story by him. The story is about Triangle Face and a small, thin girl.[3] Fate had randomly brought the two together, making them depend on each other. The story moved me because the author wrote so touchingly about the condition of sharing meager resources. He made the human routines of a loving friendship appear extraordinary, combining natural strength and tenderness. I thought, "What kind of person feels this way? What kind of person could savor emotion so deeply? What is the source of this person's emotions?" At the time, I was young and ignorant and played games of amorous fantasy. Yet even in my wildest fantasies, I didn't aspire to be loved by this person. I felt that his sentiments expressed a kind of divine emotion, while romantic love belonged to this world, and this worldly love was everywhere and easily had. Yet living in this vulgar world without religious background and without belief, a child like me might, at some time, also come to long for a state of being beyond that of this world. I too might create idols and incarnations for this other state of being. This creative activity would continue until I grew up.

At first, I just followed my passion, unconscious of the process of creation. I remember that when I read the book, we were cut off from the person who wrote it.[4] We had been separated from that island for many years. During that time, we made up stories about each other to strengthen our mutual hatred. Hatred grew, flourishing in our hearts like a tree, and we relaxed in its cool shade. Nevertheless, the story of Triangle Face and the small, thin girl touched my heart. The plot of this story is difficult to recount because as soon as it is retold it seems ruined. It is immediately reduced to a vulgar and even unethical street rumor that violates traditional morality. To protect this story, I have long silenced it. When others discussed it, I always turned my head and walked away, never participating. This is how I first met this person. I met him in a book that had been read by many people, its pages worn from many years of reading.

This person had a bizarre kind of loving heart. Not until I had grown up did I gradually find the two words "loving heart." This loving heart is large and small, abstract and concrete, high and low. Pathetic creatures like Triangle Face and the small, thin girl—how could they be qualified to receive such love? Does the loving heart become so large as to be limitless precisely because it is completely unconditional? Is this state of loving so very pervasive? Even for Triangle Face and the small, thin girl, this love didn't reveal itself to be the least bit condescending. This loving heart strangely moved me and this is why the story of Triangle Face and the small, thin girl drew my attention. I only reached this conclusion after I had grown up. Only after I knew why I had been moved and was able to use the words "loving heart" did I dare retell the story of Triangle Face and the small, thin girl. Only then did I dare use this story as the muddled beginning of my longing for him.

Buried in the first phase of my experience, the story of Triangle Face and the small, thin girl was the seed of my knowing this person. During this first phase, I unguardedly accepted every kind of influence. Some of these influences were as shallow as a dragonfly skimming the water; others were so deep as to brand body and mind. At this time, my self was under construction and I had to erect the two foundational infrastructures, materiality and spirituality. I had serious thoughts about fame and fortune, and I yearned to rise above the common crowd. Not having any professional skills, I thought that by becoming a writer I could achieve my goals of fame and fortune. Writing a few words cannot be considered a professional skill, nor did writing require capital. Paper and pens were cheap, as was my time. During the day, I went to the office, and at night, I wrote and wrote.

This was a time when the outside world was undergoing myriad changes and our worldviews were constantly transforming. This situation dazzled the beholder, submerging even the understanding one had derived from personal experience. I understood extremely early on that to rise above the common crowd, you must persevere in worldviews derived from individual experience because only this perspective can be different from all others, emphasizing the self. I knew that being a writer is to erect a mountain, or rather, it is to erect one's own mountain and not to add stones and earth to somebody else's mountain. But even so, I couldn't help crumbling when faced with this proliferation of different perspectives. Fortunately, my innocence saved me. A synonym for my innocence is naiveté. Whether innocently or naively, I wrote down my experiences. I neither applied techniques nor refined my language. I didn't even employ my perspective as a prism. Unexpectedly, all this honestly expressed my perspective. Nevertheless, my thinking always rushed after the latest trend of thought, which strongly attracted me by its novelty and risk. Luckily, following the trend was merely a pleasant trip. An unadorned point of view was my actual home and when I wrote, I returned there. When I finished writing, I commenced another trip. At this time, I was frantically busy and on edge, happy one moment and dejected the next. My goal was basically clear and my will resolute. I was even presumptuous. I had completely and utterly forgotten the story of Triangle Face and the small, thin girl. I had no idea, however, that I was actually moving toward this person and my every effort to this point was in preparation to get to know him. I didn't know the meaning that the story of Triangle Face and the small, thin girl held for me, because this knowing was a future event.

Afterward, I met this person in the American Midwest, not far from the Mississippi River, where corn is produced and there is a college. Each fall, this college organizes a three-month "International Writing Program" and writers from many countries gather. That autumn was thick with red leaves. I came with my mother—an urban orphan following a People's Liberation Army soldier-writer. We sat in planes for many hours, changing planes in San Francisco and Denver. We adjusted our watches here and adjusted them there, flying in a muddle-headed state to our destination. This person was in the crowd of people who had come to meet our plane. He wore an orange shirt, was tall, and had a beer belly. His eyes were benevolent. I eventually found the word "benevolent" only after I grew up. At the time, I used the characters for "kind" as a temporary substitute.

I not only arrived muddle-headed, but also wide-eyed and dazed. This wasn't only the jet lag. The odor of some synthetic material, like plastic or rubber, mixed in with the bodily smells of make-up and the exhaust gas from vehicles. All this combined into something I called "foreign scent," which made me slip dizzily into a trance. Later, whenever I smelled this scent, I abruptly remembered arriving at my American destination, the moment when I didn't know if it was dawn or dusk. As my country has implemented modernization projects, this gaseous odor has progressively spread. Consequently, due to frequent repetitions, the circumstance this scent used to evoke has also dissolved, like the often-used fade-out effect in movies.

The horizon was fluctuating, and I didn't know if it glowed with morning's radiance or evening's. It seemed a classic painting from the romantic period. I hurriedly stumbled after the crowd to collect luggage and got into a car, where this person said to me, "I already saw the draft of your talk. My father saw it, too. After reading it, my father was moved, saying that China has hope." I neither knew who this person's father was nor which part of my talk touched on China's hope, nevertheless his compliments kindled a burst of happiness deep in my heart. This happiness even made me momentarily clear-headed. At the time, I thought that attracting the attention of an adult had caused my happiness. That's how anxious I was about being ignored, especially when accompanying a successful and famous soldier-writer-mother.

Only later did I find out about his father.

During the days his son sojourned, this father said something to him that I will never forget. "Sojourn" is a symbolic and metaphorical term that hints at the dangerous and difficult times this person underwent. It doesn't simply mean that he left home and traveled alone, but also that he left the relatively harmonious experience of his early years and entered a period of cruel learning. The ostensive referent was probably the matter of going to prison.[5] During this person's days of sojourning, his father said to him:

> Son, from now on you have to remember:
> First, you are God's child;
> Second, you are China's child;
> Only then, are you my child.

Many years later, this quotation became the marrow of my poems, the deepest part of my verse. His father was a priest. When I imagine him preaching in the church in that humid, rainy village, my heart becomes agitated and tranquil, warmed and chilled. What a happy event to have been complimented by this man!

Now it comes to me. It was dusk. The evening sun dyed red the water of that meandering river, where wild ducks quacked amid the trees along the riverbank. We came across a balloonist, a childlike old man, who, with a solemn expression, gently rose into the sky, his multicolored balloon drifting above, then past, our heads. I felt placed in a fairy-tale world. At that moment, placed in a fairy-tale world, I suddenly felt weary, old. My adulthood had abruptly begun.

Placed in that young country, those of us from the longstanding Eastern civilizations are adults from the day of our birth. Our infancy, childhood, and youth resemble the stages a silkworm undergoes when molting. Each stage merely enables our corporeal forms to change, while the inner core of our life is born complete. The silkworm becomes a chrysalis and then the chrysalis becomes a moth; this is the moment of our death. Like that moth, our death is unrestrained, beautiful, and free. It soars. We spend an entire life cultivating this moment of death, which is permeated by a sorrowfully mystical poetry.

Poetical Easterners, we walked past the blooming flowers along sidewalks that fronted the toylike and brand new houses of that country. The grass was silent and trees shaded wooden tables and chairs. In a flash, a tiny playground appeared. Tree stumps and round wood had been used to build a slide and swing set. There were no other human traces or the sound of footsteps. I imitated those mischievous children, sitting on the swing and using tiptoes to push off the ground. I wanted to fly high just once, but the swing always descended heavily. "I won't ever be a child again," I thought dejectedly. During our stay in that American town, I always wore a white dress, carried a book under my arm, and looked for a table in the green field, where I read. I didn't actually mean to read, but just to play the role of a girl reading a book in the woods. There was a time when I conceived all sorts of roles for myself, one of which was "girl reading a book in the woods." I especially wanted to render myself as a child, but my ability fell short of my desire.

Two-thirds of the residents in the town we visited were students of the college. The boys and girls walked hand in hand, back and forth on the street, while at high noon, they lay on the grass, sunning themselves. The grass seemed filled with multicolored blooms. My favorite tableau occurred at dusk when after class the students rowed boats on the river. From behind their backs, the rays of the setting sun shone, turning them into paper-cut silhouettes. As they floated past, I saw them through trees that radiated a brilliant gold. Everyday at dusk, I stood at the window facing the river and observed this picture. The moment was always unusually tranquil as all sound ceased, waiting for this moment to pass with the rowing boats. Only then did the noise rise again, like a song. The window of my temporary abode framed this picture, which made me feel rejected. It said that I would never be able to enter.

Now I remember the main point of my talk. Our generation of young, intellectual writers has started to transcend our personal experience, noticing lives more common than our own. Given the background of this larger life, we have become aware of the insignificance of our personal experience. This was the hope that this person's father saw? I am so ashamed! I'm actually far, very far away from his father's hope; indeed, I was only talking about a literary problem. All I wanted to express was: how do we make our novels represent more profound themes? My point was that because an individual's knowledge of his or her life experience is limited, we must use the broader experience of the crowd as the reference for individual experience in order to reach understanding. There's a subtle contradiction here. Individual experience is unique, but limited; the experience of the crowd can offer opportunities for limitless understanding, but it is common. How should we handle the relationship between the uniqueness of individual experience and the commonness of the crowd's experience? How should we handle the relationship between the limitless opportunity of the crowd's knowing and the limited opportunities of individual knowing? In wholeheartedly wanting to be a writer and to transform life into literary symbols, I deceived his father in his joy. Fear and sorrow that I would disillusion him gripped my heart. His hope in me had already become a symbol of honor. By disappointing him I would experience the greatest loss, at a time when I wasn't willing to endure any loss.

Actually, I was endlessly entangled in my personal experience, from which I had been using literature to liberate myself. But while sojourning in someone else's country and not writing, my personal experience returned. I discovered that literature couldn't liberate me

from my life and that my writing didn't have such strength. Its content was extremely pragmatic and demanded excessive retribution in
this life. What's more, if this demand remained unanswered, my writing would become meaningless.

Now, another memory occurs to me. I chattered constantly.
Whenever this person had a spare moment, I recounted my life experience to him. To keep him from ignoring me, I imperceptibly spiced
up my stories, as exaggeration and emphasis were my habitual tac-
tics. I don't know why I felt compelled to bother this person with my
narrow experience. After all, could he have been under any obligation to listen attentively? Why did I force this obligation on him? I
almost completely destroyed the initial good impression I had made.
If I hadn't been thoroughly honest, I would have spoiled everything.
What a mess that would have been! I think back on the look which
betrayed that he didn't have anything to say to me. For some time,
this look caused me to feel both sad and wronged. I didn't tactfully
change the subject. Instead I redoubled my efforts to tell him my life
experience, which became increasingly biased and narrow-minded
in the retelling. Why did I have to torture this person with what was
obviously my personal experience? What relationship did he have
with me?

Only much later did I finally realize that, in some dark obscurity,
I had chosen him to save me. I brought out my narrow and insipid
life to relentlessly pester him, and when he tried to stop me, my attitude became more extreme. I was in such grave danger! What would
I do if I made him tire of me? At the time, so much of my behavior
was enough to disillusion and exasperate this person. I don't think he
liked the happy way I pushed the cart in a supermarket, where I
walked beneath shelves full of commodities, as if I were on vacation.
I don't think he liked the enthusiastic way I followed the herd and
went on picnics, putting briquettes in the grill, sprinkling lighter
fluid, grilling corn on the cob, and cooking hamburgers medium-
rare. And I don't think he liked the excited way I sat among the frenzied and wild fans in those bleachers, watching American football
and screaming like an American child.

Watching American football was an important event. Although quite a long time has passed since then, the scene still vividly leaps before my eyes. The cheers endlessly rise and recede like the ocean tide. In memory, the azure sky dazzles my eyes, and a silver airplane flies back and forth above the field, resembling a giant bird. The cheerleading squad dances and jumps all over the field and the mascots outrageously provoke and encourage their respective teams. The crowd has dressed in the home team's colors, black and yellow, and the two-colored flag flutters on high. It is a bitterly cold and windy day, so people huddle in blankets, drinking. From the beginning to the end of the game, the wind blows through my flimsy body and I shiver, my teeth chattering. It really was an important day and the details drift before my eyes like tides, rising at night and receding at dawn.

I believe that thinking of the past is a good thing. It allows us to sift through our various experiences and keep those most precious, gathering them together to encourage us on gloomy days. Thinking of the past has yet another beneficial function. It reorganizes our life according to a principle truer than time and place, transforming our experiences into valuable memories. Thus, watching American football was important because it magnetized a series of scattered events and characters, attracting them to each other in the structure of a verse. In fact, one sentence this person screamed at the crazy crowd constituted the football game as an important event.

Let me explain a little more about the background of the event. In that year's International Writing Program, writers came from East and West Germany, Argentina, Palestine and Israel, Poland, and South Africa. We usually kept separate, having friends from our own ethnic groups. On the whole, our friends were foreign students and immigrants; members of every group in the entire world had migrated to that country. We met at organized events. Most of these events were parties, where we ate and drank, sang and danced. People were always dragging me along to sing, because they didn't want to see a girl from the East so silent. They thought that a girl my age visiting the United States with her Mom should be having a great time. Because I had eaten too much butter and meat, pimples broke out on my face and I looked like a college freshman in puberty. They really did their best to make me happy. They gave me pure white swan's feathers. They entered a pigsty to catch a clean piglet for me to hug. They let me ride in the driver's cabin of a combine to see corn being harvested. Who knew that the cornfield would make me cry? In my blurring vision, I saw the green curtain of sorghum, where, from age sixteen to eighteen, I had spent my young womanhood as a sent-down youth. They kept dragging me to sing. Time after time, all I could do was to perform that tune from northeastern China. The lyrics went: "Younger sister sees off her sweetheart, sees him out the village gate. A thousand teardrops fall, and they fall, keep falling. No matter where you go, you must send back a letter. Sweetheart; don't forget your little sister." Every time I finished the first line, this person struck a plate with his knife and fork to keep the beat and accompany me. To this day, I haven't forgotten the sound of that ringing plate. I think that most of our songs are songs of separation. And when we do say goodbye, we exhort one another to take care. These farewell exhortations are inexhaustible, forming an important part of our conversation.

A male writer from East Germany and a female writer from West Germany participated in our session of the "International Writing Program." Today, many years after the razing of the Berlin Wall and the establishment of free passage between East and West Germany, it is truly moving to recollect them as they were. Insignificant, temporary beings like us sometimes have the great fortune to experience the instant when, after history's long preparation, evolution occurs. The East German was tall and large, but had a pair of blue eyes that infused his face with a childlike innocence. The West German was a wan and sallow woman, who had experienced the two great events of exile and divorce. She was originally East German, but had escaped to West Germany. They were inseparable and went everywhere together. Every few days, a party was organized in our dormitory. During these parties, participants loudly recited their poems in their native language. Language of every kind and type flew through the air, becoming a totally aural thing that resembled music. One day, the

East German arrived late. All seats were taken, so he sat on the West German girl's lap. Afterward, I grew up, experiencing many separations and reunions, which wearied and distressed both body and mind. At such times, when I recalled that scene, I could not help but be moved. Love's purity showed in the way that robust man with the clear blue eyes of a child sat on the weak lap of a wan and sallow woman. This emotional love brushed aside sexual attraction and thus warmly suffused my heart.

For a long time, I detested her. That German woman was always tipsy, her eyes teary, and her voice hoarse. She once came to Shanghai and when we met, I saw that she wanted to kiss me, but I pretended I hadn't noticed. Now, I see her dejected retreat when I avoided her kiss. I also think of the cold and miserable night when, at the same time the rest of us had gathered for a party, she jumped into a river so icy cold it penetrated your bones. This is how it happened. At the "International Writing Program," groups divided according to geography and politics for weekly report sessions. She wasn't willing to participate in the western European group and the eastern European group didn't want her. Feeling rejected, she entered the dark woods and went down to the deserted riverbank. At night, even the wild ducks went home to sleep. The student dorms by the bank were lit up and blared rock music. She realized that she had neither a home to return to, nor a refuge. She also thought about how except for her, everyone else had a home, even the wild ducks. For those of us traveling, home remains the most important thing. Home is the ultimate destination of our journey, and without it our journeys cannot succeed.

So that is why watching American football became one of the important events of that trip. For the first time in my life, I saw and appreciated that frenzied scene. Such a little thing excited so many people. How could they be so happy? Could happiness be an important state of mind? I sat in the midst of the seething crowd with the person for whom I would later long. We wore insubstantial clothes, especially me, and we sat reservedly as the cold wind rustled. People in the stands batted around a giant beach ball in the shape of a football. Everyone wanted to hit it, and when they did it was like they'd hit the jackpot. The huge electronic screen showed the images of the players scoring, the stadium rocked with the jubilant crowd, and the momentum roared, swift and violent. I diligently made myself excited, echoing the crowd's emotions. Just then, the person next to me stood and screamed at the crazed crowd:

Idiots! You idiots!

Immediately, a tidal wave of blustering wind and human cheers swept away his voice. I suddenly discovered that within this ocean of happiness, we two Chinese were very alone. We had nobody and nothing to depend on. Indeed, we were clueless as to why they were this happy. Their happiness felt so close, and yet was actually very far away. Watching American football was the loneliest moment of my American sojourn. It was also the warmest because in that moment, I suddenly and with incomparable gladness discovered that this person and I actually shared a tacit understanding. This relationship was produced through a common journey of experience that had already started before either of us was born. This journey is categorically not the one I've been talking about, but is one I haven't mentioned, or perhaps, cannot articulate. What is this experience?

I remember now that my endless chattering ceased from that day on. When I think of all the nonsense I jabbered, I feel deeply ashamed and extremely upset. After that football game, I entered a peaceful stage of my foreign stay. Never again did I vainly strive to become part of someone else's happy times. I told myself that happiness and I were not destined for each other. Living abroad was peculiar and strange, and without a tranquil frame of mind, it would have been impossible to make it through even a day. I recall the night we celebrated the West German woman's birthday. We squeezed into her room shoulder to shoulder, our legs pressing against each other. It was just like being on a Shanghai bus at rush hour. We drank and chatted, each person saying her own thing regardless of whether anyone else understood. The Turkish poet was the liveliest. He said that since there were now more poets than ordinary people, who would read poetry? That sums up the scene in the West German's room; there were more speakers than listeners. Our mood was high, and we gradually forgot why we had come. The West German got drunk quickly. Her eyes filled with tears and her voice became hoarse. I also recall the party we had for an exiled Polish writer. Again, we squeezed into a room, this time eating cheese and sausages. We held that party in silence because no one could predict the Polish writer's future. He was going to New York, where his play would be produced. New York is the kind of place that resembles a revolving stage. Every day new plays are staged, and some people triumph and others fail. He seemed to have much to say to me, but in the end, all he did was grab my hair and shake my head, unable to express himself. We also held deafening dance parties in the dormitory corridors. We held hands, laughed out loud, and even ate out of each other's hands, our feet following the steps of the dance. In the time after time of remembering, I have increasingly felt that a desperate tenderness for one another's survival, as well as the equally desperate desire for happiness, suffused these parties. The eighth floor of the dorm where we lived was like Noah's Ark, with sojourners from every country in the world. There we paused on our respective journeys to lovingly care for and bless one another.

Places of sojourning are symbolic paradises, among which America comes first. Watching American football symbolizes even more—happiness, good cheer, and total relaxation, as well as idiocy. After the story of Triangle Face and the small, thin girl, the event of watching American football constitutes the second phase in my knowing this person. In this phase, I developed feelings for him that resembled but were different from love. I say they resembled love because I irrationally thought to monopolize him.

During our stay in America, this person loved to listen like a Young Pioneer to my mother's heroic stories of the war era. He longed for the life in a communist base area and derived joy from the fact that the revolutionaries had lived together like brothers and sisters. He had just written a short story about the wife of a revolutionary party member. At every critical moment, I sharply pointed out the errors of his thinking, using problems that had emerged during the socialist transition to demonstrate how the mothers' sacrifices had contributed to history's having gone awry. In the beginning, he patiently told me about the frightening crisis of human nature under industrial capitalism, where individualism was the motivational foundation sustaining the functioning of this society, but that the individual merely existed as a tool to be used. Indeed, modern society prescribed the individual to the point where there was no individual to speak of. Consequently, the individual was a false appearance. Yet I grew even angrier, feeling that he enjoyed the benefits of the very individualism that he was now criticizing. My language failed to express what I meant and I became truculent. I think he was truly angry that time. He said, "You just want to oppose your mother!" I remember after having said that, he was no longer willing to listen to what I had to say. He then left. I felt extremely wronged, angry, and broken-hearted. At that moment, I felt jilted, and tears choked me.

In addition to wanting to monopolize him, I also loved to do things for him. Before he went to Chicago, he stuffed a letter and check under my door, asking me to pay his rent for him. I was so thrilled that I immediately ran downstairs to pay. If I went someplace and he was there, I was happy, but if he wasn't I felt disappointed. When he complimented my short stories I felt exceptionally glad, and I even thought of writing better short stories for his sake. This aspect of my feeling for this person resembled love. And the aspect that differed from love was that I had not even thought of getting intimate with him. This never occurred to me, I swear. This is the first point. The second is that I never tried to guess his feelings for me. I didn't even ask myself if he liked me or not. These two aspects are fundamentally different from love. For me, it was as if he were an abstract entity.

How am I to name this abstract entity?

In fact, the name for this abstract entity is the epigram of these verses.

While I wrote my verses, longing for someone intoxicated me. I discovered that missing somebody constitutes perfect happiness in that it is a purely spiritual activity. When longing for someone, we don't seek reward or calculate fame and fortune. This spiritual activity is complete in and of itself because it immerses us in our own thoughts and does not require another's promise. In the course of life, how many opportunities do we have to miss someone? Longing for somebody is also a good, clean activity that enables us to voluntarily abandon carnal desires, enjoying excitement and joy that exceed materiality. It places the senses into a state of daydreaming, while the spirit moves about consciously. Spiritual activity is a dance. This state of longing for someone absent allows me to fabricate verses about him. I hadn't realized before that longing has these imaginative and creative functions. No one can place limits on how we long for someone. At every street corner, traffic lights direct us and there are fines for littering, but my longing is free. Whatever it wants to do, it can. So longing for somebody liberates us. But here's the rub: what do we have that can be deeply longed for? Every day, we are busier and more practical than on the previous day. We fear being the loser in zero-sum games, which makes our interactions with others stop at superficial knowledge. Meanwhile, the expansion and development of the self makes us indifferent to everything external to ourselves. Thus, we have lost almost every opportunity to construct an object for our longing. Longing for someone has become a luxury item, which is increasingly unavailable to the masses. I rejoice that I have this wealth and will especially treasure my longing to prevent it from becoming contaminated.

I remember the day we visited a farm. We were seated in the bus and he asked me what I would write after I returned home. I replied that it was hard to say. He also asked if I would write about America or still write about China? I said that of course I would write about China. He happily smacked my head with the newspaper, calling me a bright child. I was incredibly excited, even though, for the longest time, I didn't understand what in my answer proved that I was a bright child. To live up to his compliment, I persistently asked myself what made me a bright child. I did so because I wanted to further develop this brightness. I thought and thought but couldn't understand what he meant. All I could do was decide that after I returned, I would definitely outdo myself writing about China.

Nevertheless, after I returned, I couldn't write even one story. I saw that China had suddenly become a stranger and I was helpless to do anything. I believed that touring America had cut me off from my

Chinese experience. I also thought sojourning in America had made me incapable of adapting to China ever again. I felt miserable, thinking that I would fail to keep my promise to this person to write about China. It was during those days that my longing unconsciously sprouted. Sometimes, when I had failed to write a single character, I paced the streets, thinking, I am no longer a bright child. Yet how badly I wanted to be a bright child!

Being a bright child is the third phase of these verses, a phase suffused with philosophical meaning and also implying the salvation of the world. On the one hand, this person intended to use the common suffering of humanity to bury and to obliterate my experience. He asked me if I knew that the Argentine's mother was a mental patient, and that this was her lifelong prison. Of all the calamities he pointed out to me, this was the one over which I had the least control. Birth, old age, sickness, and death are eternal human calamities, and no one can avoid them. His underlying message was: is your paltry experience comparable? Yet, on the other hand, he also gained my cooperation in guarding my previous Chinese experience by appealing to my vanity in being a bright child. He kept me from discarding my Chinese experience. Why did I value his opinion so much? The problem lay in that I needed someone else's opinion; my own wasn't enough. I was situated precisely in a stage in which I wasn't all that self-confident, yet didn't acknowledge it. Thus I needed an opinion to order, to compel, and to tempt me. I chose his. I chose this person to be the object of my longing. And yet he had raised such a difficult question!

I returned to China with the aspiration of being a bright child.

Our farewell scene was so perfunctory it simply doesn't bear mentioning. We didn't share any goodbyes. I stood at the entrance to my room, which faced the elevator. A crowd of American boys and girls swelled in front of it, and before he got on, he didn't even turn around to face me. His back to me, all he did was raise his hand, wave several times, and get on the elevator. This almost wasn't a parting. It wasn't serious or earnest. Surely, when people take leave of each other they should at least share a moment of sadness. Even if you don't cry, there ought to be a period of mutual wordlessness. What's more, at this parting, a reunion together was nowhere in sight. This was another aspect of the relationship that didn't resemble love. Over a long time, as the state of longing fermented, matured, and gradually began its journey, I again reviewed the scene of separation, unexpectedly discovering its implicit significance. I realized that he waved goodbye within my field of vision, using his back to express the exhortations of separation. The worldly exhortations of separation importantly occupy the field of language, yet after being deployed for hundreds and thousands of years, they have already turned into hackneyed clichés and mere rituals. We, however, parted using a ritual that was outside of existing ritual, and exhortations that were outside of existing exhortations. Only this could be an authentic parting. Only after such a parting could an authentic separation occur. I have never once asked when I would see this person again. Seeing or not seeing this person has been irrelevant. I have no experience of the island he lived on and can't imagine the environment in which he acted. I haven't ever attempted this kind of imagining.

I lived an active life. It was a particularly busy period, as if I bore an important and urgent responsibility. I was indifferent to the matters around me. When I sat facing a stack of blank writing paper, my heart wondered, who could help me? No one! I felt solitary and lonely. I felt that my personal experience had been rejected, yet what else could I write? I began, and then it poured out. Hitting my stride, I wrote furiously. A profound sense of boredom closely followed. I dejectedly asked myself What was the point? What meaning compels me to write ceaselessly? My life was that boring and lifeless, carved up and scattered here and there by days of sojourn. The days of sojourn had been rich and varied, but they were also hasty and casual. They could be organized into many wonderful short stories. With vain thoughts of becoming an important figure, I instinctively refused small stories. This was a difficult time. Every morning, I rose early and sat in front of my desk. My desk seemed to be a destiny that I knew I could not avoid, so I obediently moved toward it. I sat from sunrise until sunset, until late frost filled the sky. What characters should I use to fill those millions of empty squares? Millions of squares formed a huge and boundless space, urgently waiting for my creation. My experience and perspective were complete blanks. The old had already gone and the new hadn't come, like a tree branch withering in winter.

I felt that during my sojourn I had probably lost myself. It had been a time when loss occurred easily. During that time, my mother lost a suitcase, this person lost his passport, a Hong Kong person's wallet was stolen, and there was also a Ghanaian who lost a case of beer. When traveling, it's always difficult to avoid chaos because you're unfamiliar with the place and people. Moreover, you want to carry many things and need to buy some souvenirs. Buying souvenirs is a large part of traveling, yet it makes it easy to make a mistake. The souvenir shops dazzle you, but as the eyes can't take it all in, more often than not this feast for the eyes causes loss. At the time, I really believed that my trouble had been created during my sojourn. I had lost myself! This is a Kafkaesque story, another version of *Metamorphosis*.

Our era causes one to sorrow. Previous generations have already occupied the territory with their mountains, and the greater a person, the greater the area he or she occupied. All we have been able to do is launch invasions. We contemptuously ignore small countries, but our strength is inadequate for conquering big countries. Our ancestors didn't leave us any room to plant our feet, so we crawl up and down other people's mountains, our hearts congested with *fin-de-siècle* feelings. As these *fin-de-siècle* feelings congest our hearts, we marvelously conceive feelings of self-satisfaction. We feel that our thoughts have converged with international trends, just like a river converges with the ocean. We thus wipe our faces clean of lonely expressions. Consequently, this *fin-de-siècle* feeling constitutes both our pride and anxiety. When I returned from my sojourn, internationalization had just become fashionable. This fad caused us to neglect our own lives, thereby exaggerating the limitations of our experience. Participating in "a common human heritage" became our goal.

Years later, a travel-stained foreigner reached into his heavy backpack and pulled out a pile of magazines, instantly lightening his load. Altogether, there were ten or so issues of *Human Worlds*. The magazine was 16 *kai* (185 x 260mm) in size and beautifully printed on fine paper. The foreigner said that he had come from that island and that this person had entrusted him to carry the magazines to me. This person and his intellectual colleagues had raised the money to launch *Human Worlds*. I pondered this title for a long time, layer by layer, dissecting its meaning. When the magazines arrived, I had already safely passed through my difficult period. My emotions had calmed down and my inner life was rich. I had travel plans and well-ordered writing plans. I placed the stack of *Human Worlds*[6] beside the head of my bed, perusing an issue each night. On one such night, my nostalgic longing rose.

Human Worlds published the story of a Cao minority youth, Tang Yingshen. One of nine indigenous peoples from that island, the Cao are a mountain people. Tang Yingshen had quit school to make his fortune in the metropolis and then he committed a shocking crime on his first night in the city. Subsequently, *Human Worlds* began its one-year mission to rescue Tang Yingshen. I saw photographs of this person engaged in rescue activities. The rescue mission thus suddenly manifested its concrete scenes. It delighted me to think that for a while during all those years this person had been doing this! Travel-stained, determined, and without regrets, this person fought so that a young man would have a new chance at life. This young man was incomparably handsome and intelligent, and his smile was pure and enthusiastic. It was unbearable that such a child would pay with his own life for those other lives.

Tang Yingshen's family faced economic difficulties because his mother had been injured in a car accident. Consequently, he had gone alone to the metropolis to earn a living. But I also imagine that he might have first become attracted to the metropolis through popular songs. He would have thought of the many opportunities there and of the rich- and colorfulness of metropolitan life. The rhythm of rock music always excites people and inflames their passions, filling them with hope for and confidence in the future. I imagine this because at this time, the space I inhabit has also become a world of popular songs. People sing and their spirits lift. On the road to and from work, people wear headsets, allowing ear-splitting sounds to excite mind and body, and dispel quotidian fatigue.

Minorities are frequently musical. These ethnic groups haven't been assimilated by the majority's rigid civilization, and in remote mountain areas, they maintain the natural instincts of primitive people. The sun, moon, and stars are their companions, while the withering and flourishing of grasses and plants have taught them life's lessons. They compose their experiences as songs, passing them from one generation to the next. Singing is frequently their most important social activity, and their primary means of communication. Later, phonographs and tape recorders broadcast the rhythm of rock. Machines and electronic instruments insured that sound had the momentum to topple the mountains and overturn the seas. In comparison, natural sounds proved inferior, weak and powerless. Popular music really is a good thing, making people forget the actual world and indulge in an imagined one. It tempts us with nameless happiness and openings. I envisage that Tang Yingshen left the mountains for the metropolis wearing a Walkman. In a photograph, I saw that Tang Yingshen had an unusually beautiful guitar hung on the wall. The essay also told me that he loved to sing. However, he didn't realize that to leave the mountain meant to step into a place of death. How did death happen?

I calculated the timeframe and discovered that I had probably gone to the countryside at the same time that the youth Tang Yingshen had stepped onto the road to the metropolis. That was my difficult period, when the blank paper on my desk compelled me every day. The countryside has given people a sense of refuge; upon reaching a dead end, they tell themselves to go to the countryside. This youth and I, distantly separated by ocean straits, rubbed shoulders and passed each other on the road connecting the country to the city. Tang Yingshen entered the city singing, his heart full of hope for success. I went to the countryside with an uncertain heart that was bright one moment and gloomy the next. Someone had told me a story about the death of a child in the countryside. There was something peculiar in this story, which called faintly to memories of my life's experience. What was called on were not purely memories, but also contained a new discovery. It was precisely for this flickering something that I went to the countryside. The countryside has many stories that inspire the heart with the breath of classic romanticism.

The child I pursued had died in the previous summer at age twelve. This occurred before the implementation of the household responsibility system redistributed land, and when his family was extremely poor. When I went, however, his family already had a large grain bin that occupied two-thirds of the house. Growing up, this child never had his picture taken and his image gradually and unstoppably faded. Afterward, a painter wanted to paint his portrait. Everyone had something to say, describing the child for the artist, who paradoxically had no way of beginning. Nor did this child leave anything behind because the country people were not only poor but also exceedingly ignorant. They thought that it was unsuitable for someone who died at age twelve to leave anything behind, as his relics would bring misfortune to other children. They burned all his things at once. Consequently, when people later organized a memorial service for this child, they couldn't find any object that could be imbued with the sad memories of him.

He had died for an old man who had no relatives and was already flickering out like a candle in the wind. A huge flood destroyed the old man's decrepit grass house. That rural area flooded frequently and there were many mysterious legends about floodwaters. All those years, the child accompanied that old man, like a grandson with his grandfather. That day and night, dirt fell from the roof in increasingly large clumps until the roof beams collapsed. As the child pushed the old person out of the way, a large beam crushed his chest. Every bit of this grass house had rotted except for that wooden beam, which was as solid as ever. The child was sent to the hospital, where he died fifteen days later.

The child's death is the prologue to the real story, which begins at this point. In this rural area was a youth who fervently loved literature. Two lines from a poem serve to illustrate his career, "Once a student has cast aside pen for country, nothing new happens, and he endures meaningless years." Now, he wrote up the child's story as a report and mailed it to the newspaper office. The child thus became a hero. The news that this rural area had produced a hero immediately spread far and wide. Children and adults walked or rode there to pay their respects at the child's grave, which was moved from beside a small river to the center of town. A memorial plaque was erected. I was among those children and adults. Given my experience, I intuited that there was, in the story, a secret, which called me in the dark. I later believed that I had had a premonition that things would change.

I want to tell this story because for a time, our actions both revolved around a child, this person's around the life of Tang Yingshen and mine around the death of the child-hero. This person has been so far away from me that sometimes I searched for something—real or imagined—to connect us and thus make my verses of longing exhibit certain logic significance.

In *Human Worlds*, this person dedicated many full pages to Tang Yingshen, making society notice this ordinary child. And even if children do not regularly commit murder, cases like this still can't be considered extraordinary. Everyday in the metropolis, felonies occur and each has its own particularity. This person and his intellectual companions cried out loudly, "Please look at this child! Look at why this child committed this crime! Before this child ever murdered anyone, each of us adults had already transgressed against him!" They seemed to have forgotten that they lived in a society that operated according to laws, hoping instead to use human principles from the natural world to resolve a capital felony in the city. They even asked people to consider the crime that the dominant ethnic group had committed against this boy's ethnic group several hundred years ago. They romanticized facts: when the youth Tang Yingshen murdered his employer's family, he was actually avenging centuries of unfair treatment. They pleaded with this unbending society of laws, "Please lash us up first, and then execute him." They also wanted this same society to heed heaven's voice, "I am called not to lose even one of all who are entrusted to me. What's more, on the last day, I will resurrect him."

This person's image was vividly present within these extreme and gentle words, bringing me incomparably close to him. This word "close" seems both too common and too bland to describe the feeling that he elicited in me, yet, that feeling was absolutely and positively one of closeness. A photo was taken after the first step in the process of securing a stay of execution for Tang Yingshen. In it, the lawyer, the pastor, Tang Yingshen's father, and this person are intently discussing the next legal move. He faces the camera squarely in customary pose: both hands propped up on his back hips. Everyone's nervous gaze is focused intently on the lawyer, a young man with an athlete's robust body, cropped hair style, and extended arms, bore the gesture for battle. At the time of the photo, the future is unknown, and life and death, unpredictable. The lawyer is the only one who can actualize their shared ideals, feelings and hopes, which they have all eagerly entrusted to him. Seeing him stand with such people, I feel very, very close to this person! Transportation and printing are really good things. That foreigner was also a good thing. An unconstrained messenger, he delivered news for people separated and thus made possible the birth of my longing.

Let me finish telling the story of our two children.

None of Tang Yingshen's urban encounters went smoothly. Everyone he met had a black heart, especially those at the employment agency. They exploited this new arrival to the city, taking advantage of his youth, his innocence and his isolated vulnerability. Within the brief span of one night, they bullied and browbeat him to such an extent that he seethed with restless anger. The murder thus occurred at dawn the following day, after a small event ignited a disagreement. It seems that Tang Yingshen wanted to leave his employer. However, his employer had already paid the employment agency a great deal of money and, unwilling to absorb the financial loss, intended to confiscate Tang Yingshen's belongings before allowing the youth to leave. This was the fuse. Already suppressed for a whole day and a night, Tang Yingshen's anger exploded like a volcano. He became prodigiously strong, summarily killing two adults and a child without thought for the consequences. Short of killing them, nothing could appease his rage. At that point, the sun rose. He dropped the weapon and then probably rubbed his hands together, as if he had just finished cleaning up. Tang Yingshen definitely would have experienced a moment of unsurpassed respite. Only later would terror and regret follow.

As I've said, my child's story actually occurred after his death. While he lived, there were hardly any stories about him and later the villagers had faint memories of him. All they could say was that the child's natural disposition had been tolerant and kind, his behavior moderate and just, and his treatment of the old man as affectionate as a grandson's. After he died, tales about the mysterious and strange connection between him and the old man circulated in the countryside. On the third seventh day after the child died, that old man peacefully passed. The dead pause in their journey and glance back on the third seventh day, and that was when the boy's spirit called the old man to come and meet him. Originally, legends about the old man and the boy could have been beautiful. However, the theory of reincarnation infused them with some ghastly trace. Later, the child became a hero. At this point the relationship between the old man and the child sparkled brightly, being transformed into a picture both of respect and love for the elderly, and of the willingness to sacrifice one's life for another's. Thereafter, that rural area became known as the hero's hometown. People came from all over to visit and a road that connected the village directly to the city was built. This child gave his life in exchange for his hometown's new prosperity.

Amateur writers strove to record the heroic deeds and biography of this child. When several young writers wrote up the child's struggle with death, it was discovered that he hadn't received responsible medical treatment for his wounds. These young writers intended to use the case to incite popular outrage so they could establish their writing career through shocking effects. However, this initiative was quietly terminated because it would have transformed a bright campaign of learning from a hero into a dark social incident. In this way, the extinction of an insignificant life was transformed into a glorious story. In addition, the more this legend was elaborated, the more excessive it became.

This person and his associates fought on behalf of Tang Yingshen, even acting to have the victim's family withdraw their complaint. They said that the world ought to offer criminals a better method than the death penalty to atone for their crimes; criminals should be given the opportunity for a new life. At the time, even women and children had heard about the Tang Yingshen case and everyone was concerned. The judgment was repeatedly postponed, giving people an inexhaustible sense of hope. Tang Yingshen's fate became the dominant preoccupation of everyday life, the focus for people's highest and most compassionate consciousness. Poets advanced the theme of "an unspeakably broad love;" educators proposed "nonvengeful methods;" politicians put forward "the advancement of civilization;" and historians raised the issue of "equality between the dominant and weak ethnic groups." People said, "Please take pity on this child and let him live!" What a heart-touching scene those pleas made.

I felt I had a strangely special relationship to this campaign because this person utterly gave himself over to it, even occupying a leadership position. I also felt that I was standing together with a young boy I never met. Yet, I learned about the Tang Yingshen case a year after it had occurred. By then, everything had been resolved and all I could do was experience this heart-wrenching process in my imagination.

Indeed, by the time I heard about the Tang Yingshen case, many memorial and study essays had been written about my child. Children solemnly passed Young Pioneer Day by going to that rural area, blowing Pioneer bugles and singing Pioneer songs. Pioneer Days had become the most common event there. As soon as they heard the sound of bugle calls, the local people would say, "The children are coming." This child's death attracted me to the countryside. I had considerable experience, which told me that this event contained a secret, an extraordinarily uncommon secret. I decided to investigate this secret, realizing that the investigation of this secret held great importance for my life. Later events proved that I had the gift of foresight. The child's death became a turning point for me, because as a prototypical incident, it evoked in me a completely new perspective on my Chinese experience. In light of this understanding, my Chinese experience became useful again, further improving my ability to observe the world. The summons of the child's death enabled my life experience to emerge out of other people's experiences, which had been drowning me. My own experience became the foreground, while their experience became the vast background. No longer an isolated event, my experience appealed to and answered some human essence. I was like a traveler, who ultimately found her lost possessions and received compensation from the relevant bureau. My experience had walked a path from fullness to emptiness, and again from emptiness to fullness, changing its appearance, and making a qualitative leap. This was precisely *Baotown*, the story which later caused my infamy.

As soon as the first line of *Baotown* appeared on the writing page, I understood that my time to be a bright and sensitive child had arrived. My desire to be a bright and sensitive child had almost faded from memory, remembering it, my heart truly exulted. The road ahead was wide open and my writer's destiny assured. Already part of my experience, my American sojourn gave my Chinese experience an international background. The very day that I left to visit Europe, the gun that executed Tang Yingshen fired, cutting open the silent dawn sky. And so ended formally the story of Tang Yingshen.

The benevolence of this person and his companions hadn't rescued the youth. Instead they had given him an additional year to feel anxious and to suffer the torture of hoping. At the time of Tang Yingshen's execution, he grasped a cross in his palm. The pastor said to him, "All those my Father in Heaven has sent to me will come to me; and all those who have come to me, I will not forsake. I am called not to lose even one of all who are entrusted to me. What's more, on the last day, I will resurrect him." These words must have comforted this person and his companions more than Tang Yingshen, so they titled the last *Human Worlds* essay, "Tang Yingshen Returns Home . . ."

In comparison, I am a realist; vain promises cannot move me. Current problems fill my head, as night and day I make plans with practicable and visible results. My trip to Europe was happy because I had traveling experience and no longer lost things. Even if I were to lose things, I wouldn't panic because I had come to deeply appreciate proverbial wisdom, "When the old man on the frontier lost his mare, who could have guessed it was a blessing in disguise?" I was mindful to absorb the things I needed and to reject the things I didn't. I also restrained inappropriately disturbing emotions, regulating my mental equilibrium. Only later did I find out that the day I began my happy trip was also the day that Tang Yingshen was executed. It was May 15, 1987, the same day that this person's hopes ended. His despair doubtlessly influenced me and I wanted to say to him, "This, this is the human world." I also understood that from then on, this person and I, writers from opposite shores of the Taiwan Strait parted company. The difference between us was that I recognized the world as it was, while he only recognized the world as it should be. I understood the world through an attitude of compliance, creating a copy of this world, while he changed the world through an attitude of resistance, wanting to create a new universe. It was obvious who would succeed and who would fail.

We both descended from the venerable Lu Xun, who had called on society to save the children. This person had tried to save one, yet failed. And I had not even tried because I knew that despite my inclination I could not have saved that child. The proof is that both our children died. Yet, this person's sadness and despair lingered in my mind. The view of his back as he walked away from me, waving his hand, provoked in me a sense of extreme sadness and solemnity. This occurred during my mature years, when it had become difficult to worship or look up to anybody. Without a spiritual leader, these years were my loneliest. I strove to eliminate all influences, wanting to establish my own unique system and denying that anyone had or would ever guide me. I couldn't avoid strutting arrogantly and feeling superior to others. I had no idea that the seed of crisis was already planted, waiting for its chance to surface. Luckily I still had the capacity to protect myself, that is, to guard my longing for this person at the bottom of my heart.

What premonition did I have that I tenaciously protected my longing for this person? Did I foresee that my success was actually a false phenomenon? Did I also foresee that this false phenomenon would be exposed and the true situation revealed? Did I foresee that when the true situation emerged, my longing for this person would enable me to bravely face the situation and transcend it? What exactly has constituted my longing for this person? Does it resemble belief, or not? And if so how is it possible that I could believe?

Belief is like the soul, it comes at birth. All I have, however, are some principles that I acquired as I grew up, telling me to behave in one way and not another. I adhere to these principles because I want to avoid missteps because missteps would distress me. My honest nature compels me to treat people candidly, and consequently other people also treat me candidly. This situation has given me some trust in the things of the human world, but this is far from saying I have belief. Relatively nimble and pragmatic, my trust varies from person to person and from event to event. It isn't all that staunch or unyielding. There are times when this kind of trust causes disillusionment, but this disillusionment needn't excessively impede us. We can adjust our direction and annotate each disillusionment with experience. In contrast to trust, belief is a more concrete thing without much room for maneuvering. Once belief has been determined, you could say that retreat is never again possible. Belief has no way of adapting and no way of compromising. It gratuitously eliminates human freedom and constantly makes people struggle in a state of dilemma. This thing called belief is too solemn, too serious, and entirely unsuited to our capricious personalities. If it didn't come with us at birth, we would have no reason whatsoever to bear its burdens. Absolute in and of itself, belief inevitably becomes vain because no object in the human world exists outside relations to other objects. Yet what object is absolute in itself? Only something metaphysical. In the vast nothingness of space we are asked to believe that someone is monitoring our every action—good or bad, beautiful or ugly—and redeeming our sins. But the question of whether or not we are sinful hasn't yet been decided. It is even more impossible to prove whether or not there is someone redeeming our sins. In fact, to make us responsible for this dubious existence exceeds the scope of our power.

I remember that during my American sojourn, I once made this person angry. It was rare for someone so self-controlled and polite to speak so harshly. In my memory, this seemed to have happened on the same day we visited the farm and he called me "a bright and sensitive child." I just wanted to discuss the question of belief with him because, academically speaking, I was still strongly interested in the question of belief and felt that this aspect of my knowledge needed to be supplemented. To develop a visceral knowledge of belief, I had attended church several times in the company of different friends. The first friend told me that the Christian god makes people believe in happiness in this life, respecting human nature and the value of human life. This is a god that understands human common emotions and needs. My friend even used family origin to prove his point: Shakyamuni Buddha was a prince, born in the Lumbini Grove in Kapilavastu, while Jesus, the son of a carpenter was born in a cowshed. One was an aristocrat, the other a common man. Therefore, the ordinary Jesus made belief something warmly accessible and quotidian. We can not only see the radiance of belief in every small matter, but we can also practice our belief. I went with him to church twice. I felt that the pastor's interpretation of the Bible was dull and ordinary, his oratory skills were commonplace, and what's more, he had a slight accent from the Shanghai suburbs of Pudong. The second friend told me that at the microcosmic level, the world was materialistic and explicable, but that at the macrocosmic level, the world was idealistic, mysterious, and inexplicable. For example, who could answer the question about the initial impetus that set the earth in motion? This friend is mystical with eyes that unpredictably flash at night. He said that a metaphysical force controls the world and that god exists. It seems to me his god was closer to the ultimate truth than the first friend's god; his god sounded more like God. Thus, over four consecutive Sundays, I returned to church with him. I even arranged to meet with a pastor for late night discussions. That pastor was both polite and warm, his attitude neither humble nor haughty, and his answer to all my questions always the same, "Come to church frequently." The only exception was when I straightforwardly and crudely asked him where his god was during the Cultural Revolution when he was forced out of church to work as a laborer in a watch factory. He said, "Please don't ask this kind of question." Both the conversation and my churchgoing ended here.

The day I made that person angry, we passed large stretches of ripe corn as the bus took us to a farm. I said, "I really don't understand what those people go to church to do." At this point, we had already reached our destination and the bus was parked alongside the road. The sun shone directly overhead and the blue sky was cloudless. He abruptly stood, saying harshly, "Go often and you will." Then he got off the bus. I felt like I had just been conked on the head and was a little confused. I asked myself what he was saying. I later learned that this person's father was a pastor and also that Jesus was his friend. I learned all this during another trip to America. We began different journeys right after this person stood with his back to me at the elevator, waving goodbye. We frequently missed each other in our traveling. He had just left a city when I arrived, or I had just departed when he turned up. In a famous Chinese bookstore in San Francisco, the owners said I could choose some books. Among those I selected was this person's volume of self-evaluation, in which he says, "Jesus, of dark complexion, suffering hardships, poor, worried, and angry, Jesus who frequently associated with sinners, the poor, and the humiliated, tender Jesus became my hero during my youth."

When you become middle-aged and want to make a friend who knows everything about you, it feels you have excessively rational but insufficient enthusiasm. At this point, I have already entered the fourth phase of these verses, which focus on Jesus and belief. In fact, by telling me to go to church often he had given me the same answer as the pastor from the Shanghai International Church. Nevertheless, I heeded and trusted his words only. To lay a good foundation for churchgoing, I respectfully read the Bible. I started on the first page of the Old Testament, *Genesis*, chapter one, "God Created Heavens and Earth": "In the beginning God created the heavens and the earth. The earth was without form and void, and darkness was upon the face of the deep; and the Spirit of God was moving over the face of the waters." I immediately thought of Marx's *Communist Manifesto*, which begins with the line, "A spectre is haunting Europe."[7] I wondered if the Bible had influenced Marx's writing. This thought was frighteningly blasphemous because everyone knows that Marx was an atheist. Fortunately I had this thought during a completely open, freethinking era. I also wondered if when "the Spirit of God was moving over the face of the waters," it resembled ice ballet, which is so unthinkingly beautiful and almost otherworldly? Too many vulgar ideas filled my head. I could only understand and accept something as abstract as this image of Spirit of God if I could find a concrete homologue. In any case, *Genesis* was very much to my taste, and it even excited me when God separated light and darkness into day and night. To my mind, the feeling of that scene resembled that of a luxurious stage, where overhead, mid-level, and footlights create the effect of light and darkness. Yet *Genesis* seemed too much like a myth. A great myth, of course, but for me, Jesus has always been a mythological character. Like Zeus in Greek mythology or Pangu in Chinese myths, Jesus is always separated from my real life by remote barrier, like that between form and spirit. This barrier is forever difficult to pass through.

For me, the difficulties of communicating with the spiritual world are myriad. For a while, my primary work was to erect a bridge that would connect the material and spiritual worlds. My tools were the Bible, some commentaries on the Bible, and literature on Jesus. I always opened the Bible diligently and conscientiously, and always began at the beginning, "In the beginning God created the heavens and the earth. The earth was without form and void, and darkness was upon the face of the deep." But over time, the matter increasingly resembled an academic research project. I understood the philosophical thought that Jesus represented. I also understood the role that this philosophical thought had played in Western modernization. I even understood the concept of Christian culture. Studying the Bible had enriched my store of knowledge, but it didn't provide any means of connecting me to the spiritual world.

For a while, I truly longed for this person. Sometimes, this mode of longing made me feel that I was approaching the spiritual world. This was purely an intuitive feeling. Each time I used inferential logic to prove and secure its existence, this feeling vanished into thin air, dispersing like smoke. My work today is actually very dangerous. I want to use real language to sketch this feeling, and failure stands right before my eyes. Yet longing for him remains my only chance of passing into the spiritual world. I yearn for that spiritual world, trudging along the traces of my longing. The road ahead is vast, and my longing, the only guide. Many hopes have been born with my longing. I hope that after the execution of Tang Yingshen he didn't become dejected and didn't grieve. I hope that he truly believed "Tang Yingshen returned home," accompanied by gentle Jesus. If a person like him no longer believed, how could I have any hope? I entrusted to him my many impractical and heavy hopes, asking him to shoulder them because I still wanted to enjoy happiness. And I could never stop wanting happiness. Year by year, I have grown older. Day by day, time and experience have accumulated. I cannot avoid feeling this considerable burden. All I wanted to do was shirk my responsibilities. Yet shirking precipitated the feeling that my very flesh and blood bound me to those hopes. Who else could carry the weight of them? And who had the duty to carry them? Was I gradually approaching the true meaning of Jesus' pain on the cross? I didn't know.

I did know one thing later, that is, I would continue to visit churches. I once traveled from the south to the north of Germany and, out of cultural interest, went into every church I saw. The southern churches were resplendent, while the northern churches were solemn and dignified. In the southern churches I felt Heaven's ardent atmosphere, while in the northern churches I experienced humanity's bitter struggle. The southern churches reminded me of Ludwig the Second, who had fervently loved art, while the northern churches made me think of Martin Luther, who had moved history.

The German churches enlightened my consciousness in several steps. The first occurred in the Bavarian countryside, when I entered a farmer's private family chapel. Its simple, gray steeple set amid blue sky and green earth harbored an unaffected sincerity. It was noon, and the quiet surrounded us. There was no one around, and we pushed opened the chapel's small wooden door to see Jesus suffering inside a small shrine. At that instant Jesus became incomparably dear. His protection of their small hopes for harvest moved my heart. The chapel's four walls had been recently whitewashed, and white and brightly clean, they smelled like limestone. I imagined that the farmer swept the chapel clean just like he swept the cattle pen clean. I also imagined that, morning or evening, this was where he called on Jesus, whom he saw as a brother. During my German travels, Jesus was first incarnate in ordinary things. He seemed to take my hand in his warm one, step-by-step, leading me onward and deeper into the spiritual world.

I arrived next in northern Germany. Church bells sounded everywhere, reverberating thunderously in a sky of hazy rain, as pigeons, like fierce sparrow hawks, took flight, their wings flapping noisily above the city. That moment terrified me, as if an invisible and intangible colossus had suffused the world with the sudden force of a thunderbolt. Desperation seized me and a voice, which was suppressed in the depths of my heart, said, "There's no place to hide, and no place to run." Innumerable church bells rang unremittingly. They pealed from a distance and nearby, some tolling forcefully, others resonantly, and still others sonorously. Rain clouds always drifted above that city and the wind roared past. Countless ships had sunk to the bottom of the sea, their debris floating on the ocean's surface. Within the enormous reverberation of those bells, I felt a profound and isolated loneliness. I also felt the endless accumulation of misfortunes. I wanted to take someone's hand, as if I were walking in a dark night. Yet there in front of the northern churches Jesus suddenly moved away from me, disappearing without a trace. I encouraged myself by imagining that he stood unseen but actually quite close before me in the dark. As a child, walking alone in the dark, I did the same thing. Speaking and singing loudly, I always created a companion to accompany me as I finished a solitary trip.

The last church I visited was in a small town in central Germany. Tulips bloomed. Weary from traveling, I rested there for seven days to recover from the long trip. Life in that small town was peaceful and while there I frequented three places. One was the central plaza, where a fountain flowed day and night. At dusk, adults brought children there to walk and eat ice cream. The second place I regularly visited was the cemetery, which resembled a beautiful garden. I walked among the gravestones, looking at the birth and death dates and thinking, "This was an old person. That was a child." I thought that the graves resembled a great and final get-together. They were probably the reason for the fresh flowers in cemetery. The third place I went to was the town church. The town's oldest and largest building, the church was an example of mid-thirteenth-century gothic. It cast a protective shadow onto the street. Women volunteered to clean the church every morning. In the afternoon, people said silent prayers there. I once unintentionally walked into their prayers and discovered that all the supplicants were women over the age of seventy. Hands clasped and placed on the pew in front of them, they looked to Jesus who hung on a cross in dimly lit depths. The long, colored-glass windowpanes transformed sunlight into undefined colors, which slowly swirled, became interweaving light-beams, and filled the space between the people and Jesus. These old women's eyes were somewhat sorrowful and melancholy, yet nevertheless at peace. In the prolonged gaze between them and Jesus, an eternal contract seemed to have been gradually established, a promise that both sides would mutually and faithfully fulfill.

The last time I entered that church was also the last time I entered any church. I haven't ever checked to find out what special holy day it was or what kind of ritual interaction that day was kept between humans and God. On my after-dinner walk that day I impulsively burst into the church. I had walked from the plaza to the cemetery, and then from the cemetery I circled back to the church. The church lights burned brightly and many people had taken seats. Curiously, I sat in one of the pews, asking myself, "What kind of drama is about to be staged?" People continued to enter, some even hurrying.

By then, I was already bored with life in the small town and had begun to anticipate some extraordinary events, which would add a touch of adventure to my travels. Seated in the church, my awareness was heightened, ready for action. People had dressed formally and their expressions were happy and earnest, as if it were a holiday celebration. In high spirits, young children ran by laughing. A clergyman in black clothing spoke from the pulpit. He seemed to be announcing the evening's program because it was obvious to me that the main attraction was still to come. The church door opened and shut as people continued to enter. I had already become relaxed and at ease in church. Indeed, my churchgoing had already become increasingly infrequent and ordinary. I no longer imagined the church to be a serious and sacred place or as a philosophical classroom. Instead I thought of it as a meeting place and a place for rest. I looked from one person to the next. This was the largest number of people that I had seen gathered together in the town. They all knew one another. Amiably smiling, they greeted each other with their eyes and then waited quietly. Soon a red-robed priest entered and a pipe organ sounded beneath the large, high dome.

Behind me sat a family of four: a father, mother, and two sons. The two sons were both crippled with twisted hands and feet, their expressions blank. They hadn't attracted much of my attention when they entered because at the time I was focused on waiting, which had caused me to become impatient. But after everything had started I suddenly felt the breath of those deformed children on my neck. "They are behind me!" I thought. Feeling a force pressing against my back, I couldn't resist turning my head. The family sat in a row with the two children in the middle and the parents on either end. When I cast a curious glance at them, their peaceful and friendly eyes met mine. Mother and Father smiled at me and I immediately became a child in their care. I was touched and also enlightened, telling myself, "Look! This is why one would want to go to church!" I understood that going to church is neither mysterious nor profound. Going to church is really quite simple. Yet, by then I had only found out why those local people attend church and where their church was located. But where was my church? And why would I want to go there?

This episode formally ended the phase of my life during which I went to church. It also fulfilled my obligation to this person to attend church a few more times. I completely understood "belief" to be a noun. I also had a basic understanding of Jesus as a person. Everything was in order, and I felt carefree. You could say that I accomplished what I had set out to do. This made me thoughtlessly presumptuous, even arrogant. It was my time to be a willful child. I did whatever I wanted and no one could stop me. When someone said to me, "Don't act so happy!" I pretended not to hear. I had absolutely no need for anyone else; on the contrary, many people came to me asking for help. There is no more beautiful feeling than the one that comes from helping others. It means that you're on top. At the time, no one realized that I was actually living a lie. No one foresaw that this false image of myself would disappear in the blink of an eye. The girl who had told me not to act so happy was jealous. She wasn't as pretty as I was. She didn't write as well as I did. She didn't have as many friends as I had. And her life was utterly lonely. I understood why she said to me, "Don't act so happy." Yet even she didn't realize that her words actually contained some inkling of what would happen.

During this period I forgot who I was. I gradually moved away from my darker experiences and accumulated happy experiences. I enjoyed the success and happiness of this world while writing about the eternal predicament of being human, which illustrates just how I remained separate from this predicament. My discovery of the predicament further enabled me to enjoy success and honors. At the same time, it showed how I benefited from other people's suffering and struggles. On the pretext of expanding my personal experience, I had abandoned my personal experience. Those were thoroughly pleasant days. I excitedly lived one day to the next, unaware that the last of the pleasant days was fast approaching. I had utterly forgotten the old maxim, "The moon wanes after it waxes" and was convinced that the good times would last forever. I thoroughly disregarded the laws of development. Consequently, the onset of despondency found me unprepared and incapacitated. I merely sat in place, feeling wronged and waiting for things to return to normal.

This despondency buried my longing for this person. In fact, occasionally I had had low spirits in the past, so I thought this time it was not necessarily that serious and it could be as peacefully navigated as previous occurrences had been. This particular eruption of low spirits, however, had been building up over many years; I became despondent just as one becomes sick from overwork. Over the years, the rhythm of my life had become regular. On any given day, I was either away traveling or at home writing. In the early stage, this lifestyle effected a series of strong contrasts between motion and stillness. Initially the periods of motion and stillness weren't in complete harmony, as they sometimes adversely influenced each other and mutually invaded the other's zones of time and energy. Later, however, I gradually calibrated my life, and the periods of motion and stillness alternated regularly. This was when my heart slowly secreted a kind of lethargy, which began to increase daily. I was unconsciously exaggerating the happiness that I felt in order to blind myself to the situation. I also intentionally created a raucous external environment to cover up my internal unhappiness. I had discovered early on that traveling had ceased to stimulate me, and the last two trips I took were rushed, as I wished to return home early. When I did return home, however, I felt bored again. Writing had gradually become homework. I felt deeply tired, yet also unusually busy. It seems as though I was already moving along an established track, unable to extricate myself from it or to control myself. I was always and everywhere busy, but my heart was incomparably desolate. Sometimes, I lost my temper for no reason. I refused to eat or sleep, and just watched television. Sometimes I did exactly the opposite. I only ate and slept, but refused to watch television. When I wasn't watching television, I didn't allow other people to watch either, and our home then became quiet like a grave. Fortunately, during those stretches of time, everything went on as scheduled. No crucial arteries were blocked. I was in a state of inertia, and was able to move in orbit as usual. My movements in turn generated new forms of inertia. In this way, things continued.

A trivial matter caused my despondency. This kind of small matter frequently occurs; it was nothing special. In the season appropriate for traveling, I went on a trip as usual. In truth, I was profoundly unwilling to take this trip and wished for a quick return home. I didn't understand why I was constantly restless. Something was pursuing me, causing me to gallop nonstop and making me unable to give up, even though I wanted to. I impatiently carried my suitcase, in which I had carelessly packed some skirts and several autographed books. This trip was delayed by fate and the cause was a traffic jam. I live in a large city where the number of vehicles is increasing, the roads are narrow, and most pedestrians don't follow traffic rules, crossing the streets whenever they like. As a result, traffic jams have become daily, normal occurrences. They are nothing to fuss about.

When I later recalled it, however, that particular traffic jam increasingly functioned as a symbol. It symbolized the obstruction and rupture that I faced in my life. It also symbolized the disruption of my previously productive rhythm of travel and writing. Inertia thrusted me off track. Like a planet that had left its orbit, I was pulverized into innumerable meteorites and scattered throughout the universe. After this, my life no longer had a track to follow or a goal to pursue. "Where should I go? What should I do?" I asked myself many times a day but received no answer.

The traffic jam was the first real and new experience that I had had in a long time. Once again, I began experiencing anxiety and irritation as a result of reality rather than from the process of creating fiction. I also began experiencing, from the real world, a confused and low state of mind. At this time, my longing for this person hadn't yet broken out of the ground. It lay buried under many vulgar things and its day to see the sun had not yet arrived. This longing waited for me to find it in the darkness. Several times I had nearly fumbled upon its warm hand, but missed by just a millimeter. My longing for this person waited patiently, tranquilly, and silently, but I was always unable to discover it. At that time, I was utterly disillusioned, thinking that nothing in the world could save me. It surprised me that I had busily and happily lived an aimless life for many years. I always thought I had a goal, but I really didn't. It also surprised me that my seemingly purposeful life of many years had disappeared as suddenly as a dream. When I opened my eyes I realized that the goal was only a dream and, when once awake, not even a memory of that dream life remained. There are times that I still don't understand why an ordinary traffic jam could have had such destructive power; it nearly disintegrated me and my situation. Could I have actually been that weak, collapsing under the first blow like an empty shell?

Given a world where the population continuously increases, public transportation continuously develops, and streets become correspondingly more crowded, an ordinary person will on average end up in one or two traffic jams. Thus, my particular traffic jam wasn't at all arbitrary, but rather inevitable. It was predestined and I could not avoid it, notwithstanding the many objective reasons I could raise as to why I should have been able to. Therefore, the traffic delay that changed my travel plans was simply in accord with the trajectory of my fate. I shouldn't have complained because there was no way I could have pushed other people into a traffic jam that had been stochastically allotted to me, thereby taking their traffic-free opportunities. That would have been not only unfair, but also arrogant. Because I had a dialectical materialist's attitude toward life, I realized that I could only overcome this crisis first by accepting the fate of being stuck in traffic and then by challenging this fate. This was the acceptable dialectical materialist attitude toward life.

It was a long process for me to understand my fate at this time and I took a long journey through China to figure things out. I decided to visit several bleak and desolate places. I rode in buses, bumping along rugged mountain roads. Coated with yellow dust, those tottering buses were run-down and packed with grimy peasants. The buses threaded through narrow mountain crevices, lurching first in one direction and then another. I went at a time when people yearned to go to the loess plateau. Urbanites who had been exhausted by all sorts of social responsibilities and everyday routines arrived with simple travel bags, blue jeans, and walking shoes, hoping to find the fundamental meaning of life. In early spring, northern Shaanxi folk songs were heard throughout the mountains and valleys. The local people were sowing the impoverished soil with one hand and driving their oxen with the other. In that moment, the singing of melodious northern Shaanxi songs reverberated in every foothill. These folk songs are composed of parallel couplets. The first line sets the mood, the second line establishes the subject, and the theme is usually love. In these songs, the lovers are called Older Brother and Younger Sister, manifesting the condition of marriage and love that characterized primitive humanity, thereby touching the hearts of these civilized urbanites.

During the first month of the lunar New Year, visitors would come upon raucous scenes of traditional festivals. On those bare mountain slopes local people sang and danced, beat waist drums and lifted umbrellas, answering and echoing each other with their lyrics. Their unaffected happiness could simplify and purify a person's soul.

In the midst of this singing, the urbanites couldn't help but think, "How far we have departed from human nature!" Artists went to the loess plateau in search of the origin of art. They collected paper cuttings, making a connection between the simple and clumsy style of the paper cuttings and the abstract and deforming tendencies of modern art. Musicians gathered folk songs and then rearranged them to the rhythms of rock and roll. By stepping artistically backward in time, these artists immediately became the leading figures of their generation. When people have lost their goals, the best solution is to return to the origin and begin the journey again. That is why the crowd making the trip to the loess plateau never diminished. I was part of that crowd. I too carried a simple travel bag and wore blue jeans. In addition to searching for an origin, I also secretly cherished the idea of being a modern person. Indeed, root-searching itself confirmed the standpoint of a modern person. A "search" can occur only after a "loss," and when we vehemently stress the search, we are above all calling attention to our loss.

At the time, I was still not very sure what I was looking for on the loess plateau, nor did I understand why I had gone there. I stepped onto that yellow earth and became depressed. This was during a period when the local people had already celebrated their festivals, but had not yet begun their spring plowing. In those silent fields, not one person, nor one ox, nor the occasion for one folk song remained. Everywhere I looked I saw yellow gullies and barren cliffs. The wind whipped up that dust, which then filled the sky and covered the sun. The bus passed quickly. Sometimes I saw sheep rolling down roadside gullies like filthy cotton balls. A shepherd stood in the whistling, gray dust, his head bound with a pitch-black wool scarf and his back bearing a small pouch, which probably held a lunch of dry grains. Eyes wide open, he woodenly watched our bus pass by. This land of gullies depressed me, especially when I stood on the banks of the Yellow River, watching hill after yellow hill spread out on the other side of the river like thick, stagnant waves or wavy fossils. This scene oppressed and suffocated me. In no way did this landscape make one happy. Rather it made sojourners feel even lonelier and more disheartened. It also made travelers feel more fearful because that yellow earth could have transformed into yellow magma at any moment, sweeping everything away without leaving any traces.

It is said that the Yellow River inevitably compels people to cherish past history and to remember successive generations of ancestors and descendants, linking past to present. Yet as I stood on those yellow banks, I felt more isolated than ever. I felt that I was the only one to have existed in the world since the beginning of time. No one had accompanied me; no one had helped me or helped me get here. Indeed, who had the power to help me? Aspects of historical truth can still be revealed in books, but on the banks of the Yellow River everything became indistinct and uncertain. In that moment, I discovered that root-searching in the loess plateau was nothing but a lie, the empty and self-centered mythology of mediocre artists. My decision to travel there also exhibited both blind and faddish tendencies. Suddenly I became rootless, like a motherless child. In searching for roots, I lost them instead. Could this have been the result of my trip to the yellow earth? Later, someone suggested that I get my fortune told. Throwing joss sticks resembles the synopsis of a performance in a playbill, likening the unfolding of one's fate to a drama. I didn't feel like I shouldn't believe, but didn't feel like I should completely believe either. Nevertheless, since it was a decent tourist attraction, I went along willingly.

I no longer have a clear memory of what happened and in what order on the day I went to Jia County. Yet despite the condition of my memory, I still want to introduce this place. According to local annals, in the fifth year of the Yuanfeng Emperor's reign, the Northern Song Dynasty built the Jialu stockade to defend against invasion by the Western Xia. That became today's Jia County. Jia County stands tall on a mountaintop, cliffs and precipices on every side, high above the Yellow River. After the establishment of the Jialu stockade, the Song, Xia, and Jin warred there fiercely for a thousand years. The surrounding landscape is truly magnificent, evoking fantasies of ancient wars, when geographical features were used for military fortification. Indeed, all ancient battlefields are majestically and dangerously steep, projecting an awesome power. Modern warfare will never take place in a theater as grand or as romantic as the ones left behind by the ancients. It was a fiercely windy day when I visited Jia County. The sound of the winds elicited thoughts of clanging weapons. In the middle of the undulating yellow dust storms, it was exciting yet risk-free to imagine ancient battlefields.

To this day, I'm not sure whether I first saw the city wall or first had my fortune told. Together, they have become the same event. All I remember is that we viewed the city wall on our way back from viewing the Yellow River. We first descended from the street of Jia County to the banks of the Yellow River. We did not notice the city wall as we exited the city through a deep, narrow, and dark tunnel. We went to view the Yellow River for the last of countless times. On our return to the city, however, at the very second that we turned from the river, the city wall appeared abruptly before our eyes. In just that instant, a forceful and infinite dirge seemed to resonate in my ears and a river of flowing blood seemed to appear before my eyes. Suddenly, the history of a thousand years of war came vividly to mind. The infinite number—one thousand—and the magnificent noun—war—flashed across my mind. I asked myself, "Who can imagine the significance of a thousand years of war?!" I gazed speech-lessly at that dark, oppressive, and towering city wall. The open sky merged with the city wall, which in turn fused with the precipice, causing intense feelings to surge through me. This dirge shook heaven and earth, endlessly.

I must have already had my fortune told because the words on those bamboo joss sticks simultaneously rang in my ear. It was in a decrepit, Song temple at a bend in the cliffs of the Yellow River that an old man had shaken the tube of joss sticks for me, murmuring, "This guest is from far away. This guest is from distant Shanghai . . ." His voice immediately made me feel like a lonely sojourner. I realized that human life was nothing but a long, long journey. In that small, remote temple by the Yellow River, as the wind whistled past, the old man had me kneel in front of a long altar. His twittering contained a fatalistic, sorrowful tone. He said, "This guest is from far away. Please forgive transgressions committed in ignorance." I suddenly felt that I was a forlorn and helpless child who had tremendous difficulty tak-ing each step on her journey through this world. Tears filled my eyes and the Jia County city wall abruptly appeared before me. At that moment, ten thousand wild birds eclipsed the sky above the city wall and the sounds of battle rose from the ground. The phrase "one thousand years of war" roared inside my head. I wondered: is this human destiny? Mountains and rivers are actually fortifications for war. Did they preordain that human beings must fight wars?

When I wrote my verses about this person, the first Gulf War had just ended. This war fulfilled the prophecy of a fifteenth-century seer: "Humanity will go to war over a black liquid." In our military landscapes, peace seems like the crevices between mountains. By then, longing suffused my being, and my mind had calmed down, returning to its quotidian routines. On the surface, everything seemed to be normal, but in fact, my situation had already changed.

During deep and quiet nights, my thoughts soared furthest, and I would remember that I had a friend who had written an epic-like story. In the epic story, he inscribed a river as his totem, and used a real-life story for its symbolic meaning. After reading the epic story, I made unwarranted comments and criticism. I was entirely focused on the real-life story, saying neither this nor that part was written correctly. Actually, whether or not the story was written in the right way was entirely beside the point. The important thing was the totem and its symbolic meaning. But as a modern person, I was completely ignorant about the meaning and use of a totem. My criticism reached him by way of a third party, who had modified my comments into something ambiguous.

Subsequently, my friend broke off relations with me. He couldn't accept that I had trampled the verses that flowed from his veins. He thought that in our pragmatic world, too many people played with words, making language a game. These colorful and fancy games buried the real verses that had flowed from our veins. On those nights when I reflected critically on my behavior, I admitted my faults, but I also felt mistreated. I thought: I wasn't one of those people who played games. I also treasured the things that flowed from our veins. But not everything that flows from our veins is always the same. Sometimes it is strong and other times weak, sometimes deep and other times superficial, sometimes plentiful and other times wanting, sometimes it blazes like fire, and other times, like water, it actually extinguishes fire. All those whose verses flow from their veins should become companions, rather than misunderstand or become angry at one another. I also thought about totems, wondering how we might actually find one. I later understood that there was only one way to search for a totem—Need. I speculated about when this friend would have first needed a totem, but it remained an enigma to me because I knew nothing about either his past or his life experience. He had already crossed the seas to a faraway place, leaving behind some epic verses and stories; he would leave behind more.

His epic verses consist of two topics, one realistic and the other nonrealistic. The nonrealistic is concealed within the realistic and is thus somewhat inexplicit. People readily appreciated the realistic topic because it was near to reason, close to daily life, and easily understood. Relatively abstruse and difficult, the nonrealistic topic surpassed the understanding of ordinary people, yet unexpectedly added a mystical beauty to the realistic. His verses provoked widespread interest. Believing their own interpretations, people argued over how to understand his verses in an inordinately lively discussion. For a while, he was a highly respected and popular poet and there were innumerable explanations and understandings for his verses. In the face of all this, he responded with two rude words, "Fuck it!" Later, he seemed somewhat unable to control himself. The realistic topic gradually simplified, while the nonrealistic one was gradually revealed. The easily understood and realistic topic finally retreated and then disappeared, leaving behind that abstruse, nonrealistic topic. His verses no longer captured people's hearts. They felt he had lost his talent, and even he also felt that he had lost his talent. But I knew that his verses revealed inexhaustible talent, and that they flew from his veins practically unadorned. These verses could burn and were therefore dangerous. They really were difficult to understand because every one of his verses emerged from his most deeply concealed personal experiences. By that time, I had made only one discovery in my study of his verses. His realistic topic was Mother, while the nonrealistic topic was Father. "Father" was the most sublime, most intimate name he gave that river. This was my only clue for understanding why he needed a totem.

Later, I also had this need. I then understood that the reason I had gone to the loess plateau was in fact to fulfill such a need. But I was a child who had grown up in the modern city of Shanghai, and pragmatic thoughts filled my head. A river or a mountain couldn't be my totem because my body and mind had little of the romantic disposition of natural humans. For my totem, I could depend only on something that could be seen, heard, and touched. I also needed real human feelings to form the basis of my worship. Consequently, I returned from my trip to the loess plateau disillusioned. Nor did my emotional state improve after my return; in fact it became worse. My depression and anxiety intensified and became more histrionic, and I became easily stirred and agitated. My moods rose and fell without warning. I later understood that being moved in this way was actually an effect of having gone to the loess plateau. Being moved was also the theme of this stage of my life.

The hardened massif of my heart was shaken. Later, I would recall that the loess plateau actually moved me profoundly and broadly. It had been a long time since I had felt moved. Living in the world of fiction, I had manufactured various emotions, emptying out my own. Sometimes I felt afloat, like an empty skin sack. Whenever I encountered fortune or misfortune in the real world, I had no inclination to share these feelings. Inventing stories had completely used up my emotions. I felt neither happiness nor sorrow, just some mood surges such as worry, vexation, delight, and sentimentality. They were merely the insignificant seasonings of life, not anything that would profoundly touch one. Now, unhappy emotions replenished my heart. At the beginning, I felt quite heavy because these unhappy emotions had great transformative power that could breach a hardened massif. I had taken it easy for so long that I was unable to bear the heavy responsibility of the first surge of transformation. Thus, I couldn't help but exaggerate my unhappiness and in exaggerating unhappy feelings, I felt sorry for myself. It was a time of despicable self-pity and narcissism. The loess plateau contributed to this stage of my life by destroying my shoddy feelings of self-pity. It deployed boundless, timeless, and inexhaustible waves of desolation and grief to beat down my self-pity, achieving victory in the end.

Now, after passing through five stages—"Triangle Face and the Small, Thin Girl," "Watching American Football," "Being a Bright and Sensitive Child," "Jesus and Belief," and "Being Moved"—the conditions that would enable me to long for this person had ripened. We arrive at the concluding verse.

This concluding verse is also the opening verse because if it hadn't happened, none of the other verses would have been written. The story seems to have started as follows. I remember it was a hazy, snowy winter day. Someone called to tell me that this person was in the Hongqiao Airport waiting room. He had been en route to Beijing, but due to the inclement weather, they had landed here and didn't know when they would depart. He had asked that person about me. That person spent a lot of time looking for my telephone number. My heart jumped violently, and suddenly the thought of speaking with him became extremely strong. I immediately tried to get the telephone number of the Hongqiao Airport waiting room, but the information hotline was busy and I almost lost hope. I called all my friends, asking if they knew the airport's telephone number. Without exception they said No, promising that they would help me dial information. All my friends simultaneously called 114, completely forgetting that the result would be like floodwaters destroying the Dragon King's temple—we were soldiers killed by friendly fire. But the moment must have been unusually grand; with several tens of friends concurrently dialing 114, the information switchboard must have boiled like a pot. I finally got the telephone number for the Hongqiao Airport waiting room and my call went through, but the person who answered said that this person's flight had just departed. I didn't know if the plane could still fly in that dark and hazy sky, perhaps the sun did shine above dark clouds.

Hanging up the phone, I was unexpectedly calm. A question suddenly occurred to me: if he had been there, what should I have said first? From then on, I wondered constantly about what I should say when I first saw him. I knew that he would return to Shanghai in ten days. What would I say first? I felt that it would be a difficult moment, and I almost retreated in the face of it. I thought it would evoke some feelings of sadness and shyness. I remembered I had once entrusted that foreigner to bring him a cassette tape, in which I said I missed him. He also wrote an essay about me titled, "Thinking about Wang Anyi." As soon as I thought of all this, I felt that the meeting would be beset with difficulties and filled with embarrassment. Nevertheless, the day closed in on me and the meeting approached.

After seven full years of separation, any reunion would be dramatic. At such a dramatic juncture, what kind of masterly performance would ensure that the reunion would not be disappointing? It was difficult to restrain my stimulated state of mind. Whenever I thought of the approaching reunion, my heart raced, and I became flustered. Whatever might happen during that moment seemed to exceed the meaning of a normal reunion. It had to be something more important. But what was it? I had no idea. None. I only felt that I had waited a long, long time for this moment, accumulating many needs and feelings. I also felt that I must not miss this moment. Even if it were beset by difficulties, I had to seize this critical juncture.

Waiting for someone is exceedingly nerve-wracking. It resembles fire, scorching dry all of a person's patience and confidence. Waiting parches your mouth and makes you fidget. There are many verses about waiting for someone and "Waiting for Godot" brings them to a close. Godot never existed and thus the bitter experience of "waiting" was elaborated to its utmost limit. Actually, the existing sense of "waiting" quietly dissipated, like multiplying two negatives to yield a positive. This self-circling or self-enclosing orientation frequently characterizes modern concepts, which return to their origin upon reaching a definitive impasse. This is analogous to the Chinese philosophical position that "having is not having, not having is having." Yet mine was classic waiting. I was waiting for an actual person and my waiting would definitely be rewarded. Therefore, I was able to wait persistently without hesitation.

It snowed hard the day he arrived in Shanghai. Shanghai is a city where it seldom snows. What's more, it had been a warm winter. The snow came unexpectedly after a stretch of ten hazy days. When I opened my eyes that morning, the world was already silver-white. High above, the sun shone in a vast, clear sky. I suddenly recalled that on the island where this person lived, every season was like spring, and it never snowed. He had to travel a long road, and climb to the peaks of a mountain to see the snow accumulated there. Fortunately, I thought happily, this person could now see fresh snow. Fresh snow is like fresh flowers, gone in the twinkling of an eye. But this person had made it just in time.

That day, I repeatedly called his hotel, from morning until late at night. This time instead of taking the strategy of telephone overkill, I deployed the military tactic of firing in bursts. I called his hotel once every three minutes. At first, he hadn't arrived. Then he had arrived, but gone to the restaurant to eat, and hadn't yet checked into his room. Next his luggage entered the room, but he had gone out. That day, he had a tight schedule: a banquet, a press conference, a tour, and an interview. Later, I successfully learned his room number and every three minutes, my calls rang in his empty room. I knew that he would leave Shanghai the next day, and every passing moment meant less time for our reunion. But I was determined. As the window of opportunity closed for a reunion, I decided to seize my chance. The importance of the moment became more and more apparent with each passing minute. In the early afternoon, a new layer of clouds covered the sun and a fresh layer of snow had floated down, covering last night's old snow. I kept my phone close, wrapped myself in a wool blanket, hugged a hot-water bottle, and dialed every three minutes. The receptionist already recognized my voice, repeatedly connecting my call to his room. Like a mischievous child, I perversely didn't stop calling his empty room. Every time I picked up the phone, my heart lurched nervously, and I thought, "What should the first words be?" Each time I listened to the phone ring in vain in that empty room, I exhaled with relief because the difficult moment had been postponed another three minutes. As I dialed repeatedly the number I had already memorized, I couldn't help thinking about the scene in which the friend, who had broken off relations with me, trekked repeatedly to view that river. It occurred to me that we were actually looking for the same thing, but that his journey was the more romantic. A wanderer, he carried a backpack and traveled on foot, roaming all over the world. But here, I dialed those seven digits again and again, no poetry at all. In this bustling, crowded city, how difficult it is to search for someone!

The moment we met up was extremely ordinary, just like the moment when we had separated. We quickly found a place to sit and he said, "Tell me, what's happened since we last parted?" The seven years of separation suddenly bulged and tears choked my throat, but I felt extraordinarily shy. I forced myself to appear calm, but nevertheless spoke incoherently. I thought, "How can the events of these seven years be described in an orderly fashion? There is no way to explain them clearly." My nostalgic longing for this person belatedly ripened at precisely that moment, suffusing my consciousness, growing into a fruit of reason. He let me finish, and then told me about his affairs of these past seven years. Most recently, he had been working on the Granite Massacre. The Cihai Dictionary says the following about the Granite Massacre:

> During the War of Resistance against Japan, the Japanese aggressors escorted to Japan many captured Chinese soldiers and forcibly conscripted Chinese workers to do bitter labor. In July 1945, the more than 900 Chinese workers in a granite mine in Akita County, Japan, revolted because they could not endure the mistreatment and were massacred in cold blood; 560 died.

This person said that some who survived the Granite Massacre were still alive and dispersed in many places. They could never forget this horrific but heroic event. Images of this event constantly disturbed their meals and rest, and they have carried those heavy memories all their lives. Yet their children and grandchildren didn't understand why they were always so joyless and anxious, like birds startled at the sound of a bow. Their experience has become more and more distanced over time. At first, they told whomever they happened to meet about what they had endured, but people's hearts gradually became tired of their story. This caused the survivors to feel like Xianglin's Wife, a character from one of Lu Xun's later stories,[8] who by incessantly repeating "A Mao," the name of her late son, turned her son's death into a hackneyed phrase. So the Granite Massacre survivors gradually sealed their lips, keeping silent even with those who were most intimate to them. No one else knew about the horrific scene in their hearts. No one else knew how arduous it was for them to endure every single day living with those dreadful memories.

This person argued that several decades of peace had turned people's heads and numbed their souls. They mistakenly thought that a perfect world would come any day now and that all misdeeds would be forgiven. It would be a sacred day when all misdeeds were forgiven, but before that day came, humanity still had to walk a long and difficult road. Only after undergoing a baptism of blood and fire would humanity wash clean the filth and mire and strike the bell that sent away an old era and welcomed a new one. The sound of that bell would resonate through heaven. He continued to say that to forgive all past misdeeds was in no way to forget those misdeeds. To conflate forgiveness with forgetting was to commit a grave error; it was to take the wrong road, delaying yet again the day when all past misdeeds would be forgiven in the true sense of the word. Forgetting was terrifying. So much shamelessness and frivolity originated in forgetting.

Taking advantage of people's forgetting, those who had committed crimes against humanity used the pretext of forgiveness to distort history in dark sewers. They approached their goal step by step. First, in children's textbooks, they quietly substituted the word "invasion" with the more neutral "war" so that children would never know the crimes of their ancestors. Then, those children erroneously thought that the world didn't even have a word for "crime" and that everything had always been bright. Yet without darkness to serve as a contrast, children had no way of knowing what brightness was. In such a state, their world could only resemble the world at the beginning: an empty and undifferentiated entity. Thus, they would again take the path of sinning and retribution that their ancestors had already walked. This was the lesson the Granite Massacre left to those survivors. Whenever one of the survivors died, the others felt they had lost a brother. Even if the incident had been recorded in our modern textbooks and the Cihai Dictionary, the words were so removed and indifferent in expression that they unintentionally diluted the truth of the matter. Case by case, words diluted all of humanity's suffering. How dangerous this situation was!

Thus, for this person the Granite Massacre became an extremely critical matter. He compiled memories of this event into a play and also performed one of the roles. They raised the money independently, and finally rehearsed and performed. From on stage, he saw older people covering their faces, crying. Their backs and shoulders twitched violently and their tears poured through the cracks between their fingers. He also saw some youths covering their faces, and at this sight he could not help but cover his face, too. He thought that this was hope. How grateful he was to these children! I don't know what kind of stage presence this person had or if he resembled his father mounting the podium in the village church. While this person's father proclaimed the Gospel, this son proclaimed catastrophe. But it doesn't matter; I long for the father and the son. This father and this son actually proclaim the same thing: when people have their eyes open in the face of catastrophe, the Gospel comes, the good news comes.

I listened to him relate his affairs, my heart at peace, emotional tears never again choking my throat. This was already in the early hours of the next day, midnight. In another six hours, his flight would depart. It suddenly occurred to me that in the final critical moment, I had realized the chance of a reunion. Like an elementary student paying attention in history class, I listened to him tell about the Granite Massacre. It didn't strike me as strange that after seven full years of separation and just before another separation, we filled the precious time of reunion by speaking about a historical event. The Granite Massacre was just a small incident in the War of Resistance against Japan. It had nothing to do with the war's beginning or end. It was also a small incident in the history of Sino–Japanese diplomatic relations. We had almost no experiential or material basis for reminiscing about this incident. Yet we neither reviewed the happy times together seven years ago, nor expressed our concerns for each other after the separation. We didn't mention the foreigner who had transmitted news between us. We didn't talk about the stories each of us had written and whether or not these stories were important. We seemed to have forgotten that we were writers from different sides of the ocean straits. All we talked about was the Granite Massacre.

After he left, I seriously looked over some materials, finding the previous quotation in the Cihai Dictionary. As I read those several dozens of words, I unexpectedly recalled how this person's father had exhorted him during the time of his long journey, "Child, from now on you must remember: first you are God's child; second, you are China's child; only then are you my child." I thought that this was probably the entire secret to how a person on an island could possibly harbor the world in his heart.

I exited the main gate. Outside it had stopped snowing and the ground had frozen: a rare, cold winter night in Shanghai. I turned to wave to him, and he suddenly raised both arms and made a two-handed fist, giving me an encouraging and happy gesture. I didn't know whether or not what he had done will influence the world. I didn't know whether or not this world could change according to his noble vision. All I knew was that a person's heart must harbor a dream, a dream for the world.

I didn't realize when the tears started to fall and freeze on my cheeks. I did know that they were tears of joy. My heart filled with a classical passion, which I did not feel to be either outdated or embarrassing. I understood that no matter how the world had changed, human hearts remained essentially classical. I finally understood the significance of my friend's search for that river, which was precisely a search for the thing that flowed endlessly from his veins. I also finally understood that I, too, was approaching something just like that friend's river. If there's any difference between us, it's simply this: the river was the past, and what I found was the future. Just like the past, the future actually gives life to people. It has a blood relationship with people and provides us with things that flow in our veins. My efforts to search for roots could not have been successful. Indeed, a child like me is without roots because my mother and father, having become citizens of a modern city, were both orphans. Instead, I can only search for my origin in the future. My origin comes from my dream for the world. Actually, this dream also existed before the world was created. This dream is thus also an origin.

The Bible says: "And God said, 'Let there be light'; and there was light." I felt that from this moment on my life would move in the opposite direction. What I mean to say is that my life had once moved from the real world toward an invented and imaginary world. From now on, my life would move from an invented and imaginary world toward the real world. I don't know if my path is the right one or not. Perhaps it's a retreat. Perhaps there's no road up ahead. Perhaps I am returning to the origin after arriving at the end. Perhaps it's merely reaching the same goal by a different route. I don't know my fate, but I know no matter what the future brings, I have already passed through one life crisis and I am able once again to continue forward. I also know, no matter what the future is, this is a path I had no choice but to take. I can only move forward and can't look back.

I am about to step onto the path and I still see him, a two-handed fist raised above his head, waving jubilantly to me. Ah, I long for him, long nostalgically for him!

Notes

1. After conducting a general comparison of several major English versions of the Bible, I found that the Chinese wording of the Bible citations in Wang Anyi's novella bears a closer relationship to the Revised Standard Version (hereafter RSV) of the Bible, which was first published in 1952. All the English translations of the Bible citations in Wang's text are therefore based on this version.

2. In Wang's text, "Yahweh" is used where LORD appears in the RSV of the Bible.

3. Wang Anyi refers to Chen's story, "A Race of Generals" (《将军族》, 1964).

4. The relationship between mainland China and Taiwan was completely cut off after the Nationalist Party fled to Taiwan and the Communist Party took power in China in 1949. The situation did not formally and officially improve until the turn of the twenty-first century.

5. Chen Yingzhen was imprisoned from 1968 to 1975 by the Nationalist government in Taiwan for promoting works by Lu Xun (鲁迅), Mao Zedong (毛泽东), and Marx and for organizing communist-oriented revolutionary groups and activities.

6. *Human Worlds* (《人间杂志》, 1985–1989) was an influential literary magazine established by Chen Yingzhen. The magazine used a realistic, documentary style and published stories and photographs that illustrated the lives of the weak and

powerless and exposed all sorts of social ills and dark problems. It was claimed as the "conscience of Taiwan society" in the late 1980s, and many regarded its closure as the fall of the human world and ideal.

7. The line is from Karl Marx, *The Communist Manifesto*, ed. John E. Toews (Bedford/St. Martins, 1999). The Chinese translation of the line reads more like, "A specter is wandering in Europe."

8. Here Wang refers to Lu Xun's short story "New Year's Sacrifice" (《祝福》), first published in 1924.

YEARS OF SADNESS

I was standing at the entrance to a pitch-dark screening room wrapped in its purple-red velvet curtain when I heard her stifled sobs. A little light seeped in from behind that curtain and I could see her silhouette. She sat in the last row next to the entrance, holding a flashlight. The woman crying was an usher. This scene didn't frighten or startle me. I didn't even wonder why she was crying. But I just couldn't help myself and started crying, too. In that instant, like a cork popping, sadness burst out and filled my heart.

The Cathay Cinema stood on the western side of the street where we lived. On the eastern side, there was another movie theater called the Huaihai. Separated by only two blocks, the theaters nevertheless differed enormously. Each represented the lives of two different urban classes. Before 1949, the Cathay Cinema specialized in foreign films. Even then, it had air-conditioning. It boasted a resplendent lobby, a marble floor, and large, framed photographs of well-known stars. After passing through the lobby and going up two steps, you arrived at the ticket-checking gate, an area cordoned off by freestanding barriers covered with red velvet sleeves and conjoined by brass balls. There was another lobby with a waxed chestnut colored floor and leather sofas on all sides just past the ticket-checking gate. Sunlight couldn't really penetrate this dim space. But precisely the sentiment associated with this dimness made it noble. Early arrivals sat on the sofas waiting for the lights in the screening room to rise. Then the purple-red velvet curtains drew back and you entered. Here, in the inner realm of the Cathay Cinema, people always remained quiet.

In comparison, the Huaihai was raucous. Its narrow lobby and entrance were only one step away from the road so that the clamor of cars and people outside mingled with the film soundtrack. Photographs of famous stars also hung in the vestibule but they seemed passé. There was no air-conditioning. At the height of summer, a basket of paper fans appeared next to the usher who checked tickets: show your ticket, grab a fan, and enter. Upon exiting, you threw the fan back into the basket. Those fans were made from gaudy-colored movie advertisements mounted on bamboo sticks and most were already tattered and torn. The rustling sound of paper fans, like silkworms chewing mulberry leaves, accompanied the entire movie. Every Sunday, the Huaihai held an early morning children's show that usually featured a war story. At the end of the film, just as our soldiers launched their final attack, the entire audience began to clap to the music. They clapped in complete synchronization as if following an invisible director. At the Cathay Cinema, a ticket cost about twice as much as at the Huaihai. Moreover, the Cathay Cinema never screened anything like a cheap morning show for children. It projected relative luxury, while the Huaihai was merely common.

My cohorts and I were a little over ten years old and the "Four Clean-ups" Movement[1] kept our parents busy. Some went into the factories while others went down to the villages. Those in the villages might come home once a week or even only once every two weeks. As for the factories, well, most were located at the city limits, at Dayangpu for example, far from the heart of the city where we lived. The trip required several bus changes so our parents left home before sunrise and only returned late at night. Meanwhile, we were already old enough to go to the movie theaters by ourselves. We used to buy our tickets with the ample allowance our parents gave us because they wanted to compensate for their frequent absence from our lives. Each of us had a change purse woven out of translucent vinyl threads in which we avidly stored small bills and loose change. When we had nothing else to do, we sorted and inventoried those notes and coins. Given our economic circumstances, going to the Cathay Cinema was a little self-indulgent. The more appropriate venue would have been the Huaihai morning show. Yet we refused to lower ourselves and rub shoulders with those little brats. Their synchronized clapping both embarrassed and disgusted us, offending our reserved dignity. Seeing a film at the Cathay Cinema made us feel wonderful. We willingly spent the extra money to go there.

We would buy our tickets to the Cathay Cinema a day in advance, arriving early on the day of the show. After checking our tickets, we strolled around the empty hall and used the waxed floor as an ice skating rink, gliding back and forth. Sometimes we skated alone. Other times, one person squatted and while someone else held her hands and dragged her across the floor. When we did this, we always proceeded gingerly, on tiptoe, swallowing our laughter in order to avoid being scolded or thrown out by the staff. We believed they had the power to do this, even though it seemed they didn't concern themselves with us.

At any rate, that day I skated to the screening room entrance, colliding into the purple-red velvet curtain. I was unable to resist wrapping myself in its downy smoothness. As I rolled myself in it once, and then again, a small corner of the pitch black screening room became visible and I heard that woman's sobs.

Many things happened before this particular event and when they happened, they didn't seem unfortunate. They were merely unnerving or startling or disappointing, but not really sad. In those days, we focused on coping, as there wasn't time to consider whether a predicament was fortunate or not. The sense of misfortune was suppressed, accumulating little by little, unconsciously, until it encountered a catalyst and burst out. Now, when I think back, I realize that so many unfortunate things occurred in this very theater, not to mention in other places.

Looking out from the dimmed screening room, the road beneath the glistening sun seemed like another world. The Cathay Cinema stood on a corner lot bordered by a bustling avenue on one side and an elegant tree-shaded boulevard on the other. The intersection of these roads constituted the city's most fashionable area, filling us with both yearning and trepidation. We knew it was kind of rather dangerous out there. In contrast, the theater's inner lobby was safe, its magnificent darkness producing a sense of security. We would clutch our theater tickets and hastily cross the street, relaxing only after we arrived. The usher first checked and then ripped our ticket in half, which amounted to issuing us an entrance permit. The screening room was dark and it would still be too early to show the movie so we played in the waiting room to our hearts' content! Because the lobby was vast and empty, our soft voices echoed. We held whispered conversations and shared opinions about the stars in the photographs. We skated after each other across the waxed floor and played hide-and-seek in the shadows. After a while, people gradually filled the waiting room. Despite the fact that we could no longer play freely, however, as the room began to buzz with excitement, we sensed ourselves returning to the world. The time to screen the film would approach and the inner lobby lights would come on, warming us further. Packed inside the crowd, we felt at ease. In comparison, our previous games seemed somewhat lonely.

Then, one day, just before it was time to enter the screening room, we couldn't find our tickets. We had been clutching those half-ripped tickets but who knows when our hands relaxed? When you're playing it's always difficult not to forget things. Both our faces turned deathly pale. In a state of disbelief, my older sister and I frantically searched our pockets, hoping that the tickets might be hidden in a corner. Then we searched the entire floor. We groped within a forest of legs, our hands becoming pitch black as we crawled. Still, we found nothing. As people slowly entered the screening room, we conferred quietly in the inner lobby. I suggested that we be truthful and tell the usher what had happened. My older sister disagreed, arguing that if we did, there was no way we would be allowed to see the film. I thought that our only option was to skip the movie and go home; if not, what else could we do? Several years my senior, my sister was not only more courageous and resourceful than I, she also had a greater desire to watch movies. In any case, she said, we had already entered the inner lobby, so no one would check our tickets again when we went into the theater. Nobody knew we didn't have tickets. The real problem was whether or not we could remember our seat numbers.

Hers was actually a dangerous plan. What if they checked our tickets halfway through the film? What if someone had picked up our

tickets and taken our seats? I didn't really want to see this film. Indeed, at this point, going home would have solved the problem.
However, without even listening to my protests, my older sister said
she knew our seat numbers and dragged me into the screening room.

We sat in the seats my sister said were ours. Everyone who looked
at us seemed to do so with suspicious eyes. As people gradually filled
the house seats, the event that I had been anxiously anticipating
didn't occur. I was waiting for a person with our tickets to approach
and say, these are our seats. And yours? But it didn't happen. No one
approached us. Instead, the lights dimmed, the screen lit up, and the
movie played. From the very beginning to the very end of the movie,
I sat anxiously. I can't explain why every detail of the movie remains
especially deep in my memory. Never before had we viewed a film so
comprehensively that nothing escaped notice. We restrained our
feelings of uneasy dread and forced ourselves to focus on the screen,
neither of which was easily accomplished. We saw "There Is a Coming Generation,"[2] which was subsequently remade as the celebrated
revolutionary model opera, "The Legend of Red Lantern."[3] Most
scenes occurred at night, in train stations and workers' shanties, even
in jails and on execution grounds, producing a somber atmosphere.
This atmosphere intensified further, thickening our current state of
mind. When the film reached its climax, we shed tears of distress.
That film truly catalyzed our sorrow and we didn't enjoy it so much
as we experienced a catastrophe. We couldn't be ourselves even after
exiting the theater. The sun shown so brightly that we couldn't open
our swollen red eyes, and tears streaked our faces. In the end, everything turned out okay. We escaped unscathed, obviously having sat
in the correct seats. My sister's judgment and memory proved first-
rate. Nevertheless, this lapse (it means "slip" or minor mistake or failure) injured us and the clarity of the memory of the film reflects our
distress.

The experience of losing of our tickets didn't end here. It happened
again, in the very same theater, but this time the outcome was more
tragic. My point is that I hadn't learned to assimilate life's lessons, and
so committed the same mistake in the same place a second time. Indeed, the Cathay Cinema's dimly lit inner lobby seemed a stage mag-
nificently set for tragedy.

The next evening show, I went with a neighbor boy my age. Our parents worked together in the same work unit, which had distributed one free ticket per family. I already had a difficult day that day, fighting with both my sister and our maid. Without my mother to mediate, these disputes never ended fairly. What's more, I was acutely sensitive to injustice, which catalyzed a sense of being wronged that in turn depressed me. No one would comfort me and I had to cheer myself up. That evening's film was undoubtedly an opportunity to reverse the course of my day. However, the documentary's title didn't appeal to me so I embellished the event where I could. The neighbor boy and I set out early. I even carried a whole azuki bean moon cake, an afternoon snack my mother had given me when she left that morning and that I had saved all day. On the way to the theater, I ate my moon cake, supplementing the happiness of this excursion. On that same street, however, harried pedestrians rushed home to dinner. It occurred to me that everyone else would soon be gathered around a dinner table, while I was walking on the street. I couldn't prevent myself from feeling desolate. It was still early but dusk was approaching. Going out alone at night suddenly seemed a feat of abnormal bravery. I unknowingly finished the whole moon cake without noticeably improving my mood.

The neighbor boy had more experience going out alone than I did. Familiar with every shop and alley on this strip of road, he frequently stopped in front of a shop, entered to check things out, or took a piss in public toilets located deep in the alley. He even suggested that we go past the movie theater to another street, which was farther away and take a walk around there. Away from home, I didn't know anyone and all I could do was follow his lead. We didn't have a destination in mind but we walked quickly, farther and farther away, finally circling back. When we returned to the movie theater, the streetlights were lit, snuffing out the once luminous twilight. More people were on the street, having come out to pass the evening after dinner. Other people's lives were so normal, so right. But ours were always just a little bit off. The shops along the street had also lit up their display windows, completing the tableau of a bustling city night. Urban sounds began to drift upward as the never-sleeping city opened its curtains. We entered the theater lobby where people stood, waited at the ticket booth to return a ticket, or admired the movie posters and star photographs. The hubbub of the street made it some-what noisy.

Once we arrived, my gloom dispersed a little and I relaxed. Noise in a movie theater brought a particular warmth. It was no longer early so the inner lobby lights were already turned on, conveying brightness, and the house seating lights were also on. People either entered the screening room or lingered in the lobby.

I don't know when it happened, but I had lost my ticket again.

The neighbor's son was seasoned at handling such matters. He went with me to negotiate with the usher who was checking tickets. In order to prove that I actually had a ticket, he took out both his ticket and the stamped letter that the work unit had sent with the ticket. What's more, this time I clearly remembered my seat number, next to his. Given my previous experience, I firmly believed in the usefulness of remembering seat numbers. The boy promised that I would give up the seat if anyone came to sit in it. A kind-hearted woman, the usher patiently listened to our explanation and proposed a solution. She said I could wait with her until the movie started. If no one sat in the seat by the start of the movie, I could go in. Thus, the neighbor boy went in to his seat, and I stood waiting at the cordoned off ticket-checking gate. The boy frequently came out to report that the seat remained empty. Threaded through the bright copper balls that topped each metal stand, the red velvet cordon formed elegant curves, appearing especially gorgeous and coldly remote. I had never seen the inner lobby from this perspective. The brown floor wax gen-tly reflected the overhead lights, while people's faint shadows criss-crossed. An incessant torrent of people surged into the screening room. The atmosphere eventually bustled and buzzed in an almost vulgar uproar. Then, the upsurge abated. Everyone had entered ex-cept for a few sporadic late arrivals. The inner lobby had been slowly deserted and the lights shining on the empty waxed floor seemed few and far between.

By then, my desire to watch the movie had already abated. I felt embarrassingly destitute standing at the ticket-checking gate. I no longer cared whether I saw the movie or not. I just waited for the matter to resolve itself, otherwise it would seem as if the entire day had been left unfinished. I didn't care how it ended, either. Whatever had to happen would happen and nothing could change it.

The boy finally brought the news: some middle-aged rascal had sat in the seat. The boy asked him where he had gotten his ticket. That rascal impudently replied that he had bought a returned ticket. At that point, even the neighbor boy who was always so sure of himself became flustered. The usher sympathetically told me that nothing else could be done. Her sympathy made me feel more destitute. The neighbor's son and I separated at the ticket-checking gate, both of us feeling sorry for each other. Alone, I walked down the platform where they checked tickets, walked out of the lobby and into the street where night had fallen. I felt wretched. This wretchedness enveloped all other problems of the day, bringing this difficult and ill-fated day to crisis and then to an end.

Once, many years later, after we had already relocated and left the area, I returned to the Cathay Cinema. In one corner of the lobby, they had opened a restaurant that served Texas steaks. A slump in the film market had forced the Cathay Cinema, like every other cinema, to expand its range of business operations. I sat down in the restaurant and ordered a steak. Lunchtime had passed and I was the only customer. The light in my corner was lit but the rest of the place was dark. Two waitresses stood on the bar platform, whispering. However, in this lonely and empty hall, their voices were quite clear, and I even heard the tone of their conversation. I sat in the deepest part of the lobby, looking out at the beautifully remote and sunlit street beyond the entrance. Unable to flood inward, the noises out there stopped at the lobby entrance. As a result, it looked like a soundless movie screen. The center of the inner lobby was dark, like a stage after a performance. The actors had exited and the set stayed silent. Yet one spotlight could bring it back to life and the play would recommence. That spotlight never came on, however. Instead, in the dark stillness, rustling sounds intimated the performance of ongoing plots.

As I ate my Texas steak, a long table in the center of the lobby was quietly set, after which some people gathered there. I heard the hushed sounds of melon-seed and candies spilling onto the table, the *kerplunk* of teacups being placed, the noise of chairs dragging across the floor, and blithe conversation. In contrast, the normal volume of human voices sounded unreal, fading in and out. Then the voices dissipated into the quiet emptiness and almost nothing remained to be heard. Consequently, the presence of that group of people didn't enliven the inner lobby but rather made it even more desolate. The rustling sounds receded, and one voice became clearly distinguishable. It gave a solemn speech. It turned out that they were giving a retirement party for two old workers. The speech recounted how they had worked a lifetime here, and had now reached the age of glorious retirement. I looked over but couldn't see the day's protagonists. I supposed they sat in the most silent corner of the table, from where the crunch-spit of melon seeds transmitted mechanically. In contrast, sounds from other directions were lively and stress-free. Those in silence must have been projectionists, ushers, and ticket takers when, long ago, I would come by myself to watch a movie. During those sad years, these people were in the prime of their lives and the masters of this theater. Steady, calm, and strong, they wouldn't have noticed a child in a melancholic stage of development.

Just then, the stage spotlight did come on, and it was as if I saw that child, a muddle-headed skater, leaving home for the first time. She found refuge from a confusingly tumultuous world here, where both the darkness and the beams of light protected her. Growing up was sad. As that tender young body gradually lost protection, every touch felt vulgarly brutal. Many years would pass before she could touch the little bit of warmth at the deepest part of brutality. This warmth didn't actually spring from an emotion like love. Instead a feeling of common humanity burst out of our mutually difficult lives. Nevertheless, at the beginning, she felt only the vulgar brutality incisively wounding her heart.

What's more, I was unconscious of all this. I neither knew what sadness was, nor understood that this precisely was sadness. Not until I wrapped myself in the red velvet curtain and heard that woman's sobs did all the unhappiness finally have a name. Only then did I open my eyes and see my predicament. As I mentioned earlier, like a cork popping, sadness burst out and filled my heart. I had already been sad for so very long, but absolutely ignorant of the fact.

I always felt injustice acutely because I had been placed in a passive position. Adults, not I, held the power to decide things, and merely by doing what they wanted, these adults determined my happiness and unhappiness. In addition, I grew up in an era when there were few satisfying opportunities. Rigorously picked over, these meager opportunities often only allowed you to experience happiness in comparison to others. These comparisons implied competition, in which I acutely felt myself always to be in the weaker position. I became angry over expected failure even before events took place. My losses then festered for a long time. Thus, a sense of injustice suffused those years, clouding the brightness of childhood.

Events always occurred in connection with movies. Nonetheless, those years began with a dance drama. My mother's work unit issued one ticket to the ballet. Naturally, the father of our neighbor boy had also received one. The tickets were issued less than an hour before the curtain rose. That summer evening, my older sister and mother were taking my little brother for a walk in the alleyway. I was home alone, completely oblivious. Suddenly, my sister rushed in, opened the dresser drawer, changed her clothes, and rushed out again. I heard her call out to the neighbor boy and his buoyant response. The event happened so abruptly that by the time I chased them out the door, all I could see were their happy backs, which disappeared around a bend in the alley. I turned to ask my mother where they had gone. My mother equivocated forever but was finally compelled to tell the truth. They had gone to see the dance drama "Raging Fury in the Coconut Grove." My anger immediately exploded and I felt profoundly wronged. Seriously enraged, I was unable to calm down for several days. I didn't talk to anyone. I sulked. Yet when I reached the edge of my anger, all I could do was find a way out of the impasse. My mother solved the problem by promising that the next ticket would definitely be mine. When tortured unbearably by my anger, I would think about her promise.

At first, however, even this promise didn't comfort me because I stubbornly held onto what had already been lost. But things already lost can never be recovered. I was acting in an unreasonable and self-defeating way but I just couldn't do anything else. Then I fell into a state of grief and indignation from which I couldn't extricate myself. My anger so frightened me that life became unbearable and every place became gloomy and dismal. Still, it was my nature to yearn for happiness. When thwarted, I could only compromise. In the end I accepted her promise, gradually calming down.

My mother definitely forgot the promise. This may be because some time had passed without an opportunity to fulfill it. That's not to say that my mother's unit never issued any more tickets, but rather, they issued two tickets at a time, preventing her from making good on her promise. Two tickets, one each for my sister and me. We went to each performance together and so she still had seen one more show than I had. The one time when they did issue only one ticket, the neighbor boy happened to be sick. His sister was too small to leave her parents to see a film so they gave that ticket to us. My sister had still seen one more show. We had yet to bring the matter to a just conclusion. The flow of tickets in and out, however, caused people to forget that they owed me a show. Only I remembered. It was no longer simply a case of seeing one more movie or performance, but to eliminate my resentment. Anxious in body and mind, I needed the promise to be realized in order to balance the scales. If not, the situation would lead to serious injury. No one else understood this. They thought that the event had already passed, that the situation had been resolved, and that everything had returned to square one. At just this moment, I got my chance.

I was always a beat slower than my sister, who, being three years older, was naturally more resourceful. This time, however, I had an opportunity. The last time, events had turned on the quicker hand. This time, the movie tickets arrived a week early. Yet the additional time didn't help matters, rather it increased my anxious misgivings.

Because the movie was part of an official reception, several short song and dance pieces would be performed before the screening. Among them, the Children's Palace Dance Troupe would perform

"Washing Clothes Song." Two girls in my sister's homeroom were part of the troupe. They usually wore wide, black belts around their waists and, during the summer, when other girls wore skirts, they wore long, staple rayon sweatpants. All of us little girls were enthralled with dancing, perhaps because of a desire to exhibit our recently awakened feminine consciousness. My own sister idolized those two girls. Every detail of their exercises, rehearsals, and performance caused my sister to admire them. Thus, even before my mother decided who would be given the ticket, my sister had already promised those girls that she would definitely watch them perform "Washing Clothes Song." Although it all occurred behind my back, it can be surmised that my sister had worked hard on my mother. The ticket was hers and she went with the neighbor boy. My mother had a week to come up with good reasons to deny me the ticket. She said I was still too young. She said she worried about the neighbor boy and me, two children of the same age, going that far down Nanjing Road to the Great Brightness Cinema.

A tragic incident, indeed. Even with time to work on another outcome, I wasn't able to change anything. Instead, I looked on helplessly as the day for watching the film came and injustice repeated itself.

Sunday morning arrived. My sister and the neighbor boy left the house overjoyed. No longer within ordinary limits, my anger depressed me. Again, I stopped talking to people. At the same time, however, I felt an intensely profound loneliness. No one knew what kind of torture my body and mind suffered in my stubborn reticence. Sometimes, when it became really unbearable, I would ask myself how the situation had reached this point. Then I would replay the entire incident in my head, increasing the fury in my heart. Those were also days when my mother left home early and returned late. No one paid any attention to my depression. Who could take notice of a small child's state of mind? I went to school depressed. I left school depressed. I watched the endless stream of traffic in the street at the alley entrance until nighttime when the street lights came on. I don't mean to imply a complete dearth of happy moments. Interesting and fun things did happen with classmates. When I played with my sister or the neighbor boy, I always laughed diligently to free myself from

depression. Yet, after all the laughter and excitement passed, my depression remained as before. I couldn't save myself.

I have already mentioned going with the neighbor boy to see a
film at the Cathay Cinema. *That* took place in this context. My sister
had magnanimously allowed that single ticket to be given to me, but
not because she remembered injustices done and wanted to compensate me. She simply wasn't interested in documentaries. But who is?
Yet all I had was this documentary or nothing. And even having
achieved compensation, I still couldn't feel happy. As I have already
mentioned above that had diligently tried to cheer myself up but the
results were pathetic. To add fuel to the fire, I lost the movie ticket. In
the end, it was as if I had been drawing water with a leaky bamboo
basket—a futile effort.

My sadness finally drew my mother's attention and after so long
a depression, she could no longer turn a deaf ear when I stated my
case. But the incident's already over. How can it be fixed, she asked
me. My mother's sincerity contained some measure of adult cunning.
In fact, she refused to accept responsibility for what had happened.
Anyway, this was how she put it: The incident's already over. How can
it be fixed? Crying, I couldn't formulate an answer. What's more, this
question hit me where I was most vulnerable. I was in terrible pain
because nothing could be done to reverse the situation. What had
been lost could never be recovered. No one could fix it. My mother's
question cut to the bone, hitting the essential point, which coinci-
dentally was also the problem that I wanted resolved right then. I
could only cooperate with my mother. Almost without thinking, I
mentioned that I wanted to see a movie. This demand wasn't refused.
My mother readily agreed and gave me more than enough money for
a movie ticket. She didn't even stipulate where I had to go.

Originally, I had intended to issue a challenge but my demand
was immediately and unexpectedly met. This resolution came too easily,
rendering me perversely dissatisfied. My mental state continued un-
relieved. In no mood to go to a cinema farther away, I went to the
closest, the Huaihai Cinema, where they were screening "Spark of
Life."[4] The film had been adapted from the novel *The Army's Daughter*,[5] which had completely engrossed me. I should say that I was

lucky. I bought the ticket in good time. I didn't lose it before entering the screening room. Moreover, the film was quietly moving and I sobbed the entire show. At three in the afternoon, I walked out of the cinema to perfect sunlight. It was Sunday, and crowds of people bustled about the city's most famous commercial street. I finally became pacified. The feeling of injustice no longer gnawed at my heart and the depression no longer oppressed me so heavily. I just felt utterly alone. Everything I had gone through had erected a wall that isolated me from the crowd. The jostling crowd and I were separated in two different worlds. Even our suns were different. We stepped on each other's shadows but that was all. And because I lacked the ability to recognize and express many feelings and impressions, they remained locked away, beyond communication. That is why I was lonely.

This was a stage of uneven development. Some parts of my being, because they received special nourishment, grew like crazy. Other parts, because they were insufficiently nourished, almost stagnated. This state of unequal nourishment lasted only a short time. Nevertheless it gave rise to unequal growth and continued to affect me. My flourishing parts used their formidable powers of incorporation to plunder available nutrients. The lack of nutrients didn't cause my weaker parts to lose their desire to grow; rather, this repression stimulated them even more. At any rate, these forces competed with one another and vied for attention, resulting in an acute inner conflict. Everything was unbalanced, ugly, and painful. Blindness caused profound hopelessness.

One emotion in particular, that of being superfluous, thrived. My sense of superfluity began from within inside and extended outward. First, my hands and feet were superfluous. I didn't know where I should put them, and this alone was enough to make me clumsy. Next, my mouth was superfluous. I wanted to express myself in an outstanding manner, to make people notice me, and to give a good impression. Instead, if I didn't emit rubbish, I spoke nonsense, or induced disdain, or effected ridicule. Once I uttered them, perfectly good words altered themselves, turning out to be unsuitable and disproportionate. Some words were too heavy, others too light. Finally,

I became a superfluous person, unable to find my place. At times, a group of people would be standing around. I longed to approach and join them, but as soon as I came close, they stopped talking and looked at me. It was as if they had been invaded. No matter how gingerly I tiptoed in, how graciously I smiled, or even if I fawned on them, the same result ensued. They stopped talking but didn't bother to turn around, just glanced sideways at me. This moment assaulted and utterly defeated my self-respect and self-confidence.

To avoid these awkward encounters, I played with smaller children, with whom I could be queen and dominate. Cowed by my age and relative strength, they were, without exception, subservient and obsequious yes-men. Yet it was precisely due to their attitude that once again I found myself superfluous. They were good company to each other. Their eyes sparkled with tacit understanding and they excluded outside invaders by giving the impression of weakness. In childhood, the line between different ages is extremely fine. Indeed, a chasm separates you from those only one year older or one year younger than you are, creating fundamental differences. Thus it was especially difficult to find companions.

Uneven inner development brings with it discordant outer relationships, making life more difficult. This is especially true if you don't realize that this stage of development will pass. When that happens, those difficult situations become your entire life. Everything magnifies.

My appearance changed dreadfully. My face grew long. Without anybody realizing it, my original child's face, lovable and round, became lost. The tenderly beautiful flesh of childhood also vanished. My complexion became both sallow and rough. I would have to wait a long time before the smooth, porcelain white skin of a young woman would emerge, to be followed by a young woman's well-proportioned and sturdy body. But then, I was just skin and bones, with a dull countenance. I became nearsighted, habitually squinting whenever I looked into the distance. Consequently, wrinkles piled up on the bridge of my nose and covered my forehead, making me appear cross-eyed with a crooked nose. My teeth were irregular. Due to a bout of tracheitis I had to breathe through my mouth for a long time, which caused my mouth to change shape. My new teeth were obviously bigger than my baby teeth, so that they jutted out, while my back teeth receded. For a time, I had to wear a retainer all day, which in turn provoked curious inquiries. To avoid these questions, I bargained again and again with my mother: I would wear the retainer one day and not the next. In the end, we settled the matter by leaving it unsettled. My hair was also a mess. From childhood, my sister had long braids and I had short hair. I looked like a Japanese doll. What's more, as my hair coarsened, it stuck out all over the place and became difficult to arrange. Hair stylists weren't interested in girls my age who were no longer adorable children and not yet beautiful young women. Several times I was given what people called a "toilet seat cover" haircut. And yet, even though the hair grew on my head, I couldn't take charge and grow braids because it was my mother who decided my sister's and my hair styles. Her authority was final. My arms and legs were thin and long so that every shirt sleeve shrank to a point between my wrist and elbow, while the legs of every pair of pants hung an inch or two above my ankle. Polyester hadn't yet been invented and cotton clothes shrank, making things worse. In addition, my waistline wasn't proportional to my height, so that even when my pants were long enough, they hung on me like a cloth sack. I was already too tall for children's clothing but women's clothing would have been the most inappropriate style imaginable. The best way to handle the situation was to have a tailor make me clothes. But even before the clothes were finished, I had grown another inch and if one part of me hadn't lengthened, then another one definitely had.

I seemed always to be situated in the midst of anxious change. Especially lively and excited, my body's growth hormones ceaselessly transformed their work of art. My reflection in a mirror frequently stunned me. My image was unstable, inconclusive. I even doubted that the me in other people's eyes and the actual me were the same.

My facial expressions, which twitched constantly yet appeared insipid, made matters worse. It was nervousness. In actuality, I always unconsciously copied other people's facial expressions. Not every child went through a period of development that was so acutely out of whack. Many children sailed through. Their perfect regulatory systems made them coolly self-composed. Their gazes were steady, while their conversational styles and facial expressions were vivid. More often than not, I admired and studied their example, involuntarily copying their every gesture and move. In effect, all that was superficial. The crux of the matter lay in something like a natural capacity for self-adjustment, which couldn't ever be achieved through imitation. This quality resembled a genetic trait, which subtly influenced their behavior. Every aspect of these children's development met average standards, guaranteeing harmonious adjustment. Usually, their intellectual prowess was middling to fair, but that didn't prevent them from achieving social success once they grew up. In contrast, those children of tortured maturation faced grave crises. Our uneven development usually resulted from some concealed personal characteristic, and the vitality of this trait destroyed any tendency toward equilibrium. This concealed trait resembled a particularly vigorous cell that rapidly divided and reproduced, becoming abnormal. Who knew if it portended a disastrous or an auspicious future?

I copied the adorable expressions of those fortunate children. In my eyes, they were all heaven's favorites. Whether at rest or in motion, they were beautiful. Their beauty arose out of laxity and carefree hearts. They were especially adept at expressing their individual personalities in a natural manner. They had an easy bearing. Consequently, they cut distinct figures, while I blurred. Much as I couldn't be convinced of my own appearance, I couldn't be sure of my own personality. I didn't know who I was or what kind of nature I had, which caused me to be dissatisfied with myself. I felt that being me was unfortunate.

At this time I met a girl from the adjacent alley. Our acquaintance benefited from the Four Clean-ups Movement. Our parents left home early and came home late, or returned home once a week, fundamentally unable to look after our social lives. This was the only reason we made friends with kids from the neighboring alley. Generally speaking, the large families of low-salaried, low-level support staff lived in that noisy alleyway. Located in large, old-style multistory buildings, their homes had uncountable numbers of large and small rooms. The numerous residents appeared to be straight out of the movie "House of Seventy-two Tenants."[6] A wall once stood between their alley and ours. During the Great Leap Forward,[7] however, it was torn down in order to have its frame removed for the steel smelting movement. From that time forward, the two alleys were connected.

The kids in that alley had been set free like a flock of sheep to graze anywhere the grass grew, while the few children in our alley were under strict parental supervision and consequently grew up timid as mice. Like turtles huddled under their shells, we holed up in the secluded back of the alley, playing quietly. In this way, we had submissively surrendered the spacious front of our alley to their occupation. Boys and girls from that alley played separately. The boys played soccer and had fights, but the girls played refreshingly novel games like doing gymnastics and dancing. These girls provoked our curiosity and jealousy. For a while, they came over every day after school. From our balcony, we watched them jump around in the alley below.

A pretty girl directed their games. She was on the gymnastics team at the district's juvenile sports school and was also a member of the school's dance troupe. Unlike our state-run school, local residents ran her school. All the children in our alley could avoid going there, attending instead a school that is now designated a key school. Our school didn't sponsor a dance troupe, although we did have one of Shanghai's most famous choruses with falsettos. But as I've said, this was a time when we all desired dance.

This girl's vigorous and nimble body, her vivacious and lovely posture, and her ability to talk—all moved us. An expert speaker, her rough voice never lost an underlying richness, and her enunciation was clear. When she narrated an event, it really did appeal to your senses and captivate you. She fascinated all of us. We initially expressed our fascination through hostility. Later, friendship grew out of our fights and she became our guest of honor. She fawned on us, more or less mollifying our egos. We reciprocated, no longer hiding our fascination. She then strove to repay us with her best performances. She danced for us. She told us about all sorts of interesting news. Her school life seemed much richer than ours, her experience, too—richer than ours. In comparison, we had wasted our time at school. Her experience consisted mostly in defiantly talking back to her teacher. Her dramatic narratives vividly described a straightforward, courageous, piquantly intrepid, and charming girl. Simply amazing. She impudently went one-on-one with the teacher, and what's more, everything turned out fine. She achieved reconciliations without making the teacher dislike her. Her teacher sounded quite democratic. We totally envied her this kind of experience. We envied her personality, too. I don't know how, but all the good things fell into her lap. We copied her walk, copied her talk, and copied her facial expressions. Our imitations never led to any independent conclusions. Her one was our one, her two our two. Whatever she did, we did. We tried too hard. In our anxiety to become people just like her, we couldn't worry about anything superfluous like exaggeration or tackiness.

Our intense yearnings gradually became hallucinatory. In our minds, we actually enjoyed the limelight. Relative to me, my older sister remained clear-headed. Whenever I got carried away and deliberately attracted attention by copying the girl's words or phrases, my sister gave me a significant look. This look needed no explanation. I would immediately feel embarrassed and would blush to the tips of my ears. But I had already succumbed, and these reminders were useless. Further down this road, an even greater embarrassment still awaited me.

I started telling people stories about my life at school. I didn't know how to pour old wine into a new bottle so I also narrated stories about challenging a teacher. The object of my challenges was a male mathematics teacher, whose pedagogy ranked relatively high in the district and was the best in our school. He dressed tastefully, brushed his hair smooth, polished his shoes till they glistened, and pressed a perfectly straight crease into his woolen slacks. He was poised, his attitude reserved. He spoke in that sonorous, high-pitched voice that seems to come out through resonating in his forehead. His only defect was forgetting himself during lectures. Then his voice would hit the highest note and would break unexpectedly as he emit-

ted a piercing screech. If other teachers had exhibited this irregular-
ity, it wouldn't have mattered. But his behavior was so meticulous, so
flawless, so almost perfect that we couldn't easily ignore his little flaw,
and so it became a great spectacle. Small children love to see people
make fools of themselves, and the less likely a person was to slip up,
the more we craved to see just what kind of fool he was. It thrilled us.
Therefore, whenever he would screech the entire classroom rumbled
with suppressed laughter. Although he neither changed his countenance nor broke his stride, lecturing through it until the end of class,
he still revealed his embarrassment.

This teacher became a character in my stories. Our every war of
words ended in his defeat as I rendered him speechless. These fabricated victories concealed the special attention I paid him. A first-rate
teacher like him frequently became a serious challenge to students,
and my superficial resistance concealed real feelings of respect, ado-
ration, and even jealousy. In point of fact, he was a liberal-minded
teacher, the kind who opened his class to a wide range of new ideas.
Once when he was explaining to us how to solve a math problem, I
raised my hand and suggested a method that had neither occurred to
him nor was it in the teacher's manual. He thought hard for a moment and then said yes, you could solve it that way. So I used my
method to complete that night's homework assignment. The next
day, he called me into the office to have me explain the thinking behind my method. I stammered, but he frequently prompted me
along, helping me improve my thought process. After I had finally
finished my explanation, he drew a star on my homework notebook
and said, "Well done." We actually could have had a really good
teacher-student relationship, but no, our relationship was filled with
anxiety. Or at least I was anxious. That's what I meant when I said
that I faced a challenge.

He was also the neighbor boy's math teacher. The neighbor boy
once told me how this teacher had used a girl in my class as a negative
example to conduct a lesson on guarding against arrogance. Listening, the boy had felt that she especially resembled me. Really, he as-
serted, she was you. In the teacher's description, this girl was an excellent but arrogant student. Accordingly, she would never achieve a

perfect score. Of course, because she was an excellent student, she'd never get a mere 80; it's just that she would always get a 97, 98, even a 99, but never reach 100. She would always fail to make that last, necessary effort. After I heard this, I was so angry my face immediately turned bright red. The me he had described was so terrible, and what's more, ill-fated. Even worse, I couldn't retaliate. After all, he hadn't said anything to my face. Pathetically, all I could do was take action behind his back.

My clumsy actions took the form of a personal attack. I told my homeroom classmates that he had a "wrapper head" hairstyle. The so-called wrapper head was also known as "rocket style." You let your hair grow out, applied pomade, and blew it high off the forehead until it flipped back over. The hair was then combed back, straight down your neck. So if you wanted to call it "wrapped," the head was "wrapped" in this way, a style that smacked of bourgeois vulgarity. I also changed one of the strokes from a character in his name; re-read it was a hilarious nickname. Busybodies brown-nosed their way into his affection by reporting both these matters to him in excruciating detail. Thus, one day, he called me again into the office. This time wasn't anything like whatwas at the last visit. It was time for a face-to-face showdown, and if I was going to counterattack, this was my chance. Instead I cried like a coward. Unable to speak a whole sentence, I bungled my opportunity. My teacher was really angry, furious, even standing up and turning around to show me his hair, asking, "Where's the wrap? Where's the wrap?" He also pointed to the name written on his lecture notebook, saying, "An older family member chose my name. It's perfectly normal for a person who came out of the old society to have feudal thinking!"

In retrospect, I see that my teacher was actually still very young, and also naive. Moreover, it was the eve of Cultural Revolution[8] and the smell of gunpowder had already saturated the political atmosphere. Although I had acted out of a personal grievance, my attack could have ruined his future. Yet I didn't even glimpse his vulnerability then, and was instead devastated by his irritable manner.

This confrontation was particularly humiliating. With no means of counterattacking, I had to endure a scolding. Although hundreds and thousands of forceful responses came to me later, they could no longer change the situation. All I did was close the barn door after the horse had run away. In light of my failure, the triumphs of the girl from the adjacent alley seemed even more glorious. How did she move from victory to victory unharmed? No matter how much I admired her, I could only play her in my dreams, where I lived vicariously through her experiences. I didn't have her guts. Thus, I came to make up stories about what went on in school.

In the beginning, all I did was exaggerate a little, remaining within acceptable limits. But I couldn't avoid being excited by my tales. As I spoke, I gradually entered a zone. I spoke more and more. And no matter how much I spoke, I basically parroted every word that girl had ever said, without editing. Eventually, my fantasies possessed me completely. I actually believed they were real, not imaginary. At first, the others didn't believe my stories but in the end they succumbed to my relentless storytelling: yet they inadvertently disclosed their indifference. You see, after she had told a story, any other story about confronting a teacher felt redundant, lacking originality. Everyone attempted to change the topic but I wouldn't allow it. I insisted on saying my piece. My maliciously fierce attitude gave them no option but to listen obediently.

And then, the humiliation commenced. My school held a meeting for all the parents of their students. My father was in the countryside and my mother left home early and returned late so the matter was entrusted to my sister. It was actually frightening to allow older children to take charge of younger children. Overly power-crazy, the older ones unavoidably abused the younger ones. We were placed at their mercy and ordered about on a whim. It was a terribly dangerous situation.

My sister represented our parents at my school meeting. Merely an eighth-grader, she thought she was all grown up. Not content to simply listen at the meeting, she wanted to discuss my situation with my homeroom teacher. She believed she had the responsibility to cooperate with my teacher to instruct me. She ostensibly reported the facts to my teacher, but in truth, she simply wanted to expose me and, at the same time, make the teachers notice her. She said that every day at home I boasted arrogantly about how I had fought with the math teacher. She said that I didn't think this was a fault but an honor. Not surprisingly, my homeroom teacher took the matter seriously, conscientiously saying that she hadn't heard about it but she would definitely investigate the matter. When she got home from the meeting, my sister immediately confronted me, saying, Your homeroom teacher said you've never fought with teachers. Her words cut me to the core. I was rendered speechless and my face burned red. She looked smugly self-satisfied. I guessed that she had never believed my heroic tales but had never been able to debunk them.

Everything that followed was embarrassingly awkward. The next day at school, my homeroom teacher came looking for me to ask about the truth of the matter. I couldn't utter a word. The homeroom teacher's perplexed gaze made me want to crawl away in shame. She said that she had already investigated the matter and nothing like this had happened. What was this all about? I couldn't answer. I didn't know what it was about, either. No one could explain. Unexpectedly, the teacher I had ridiculed didn't come looking for me. Only once, when it was my turn for class duty and I went to him to get back graded math notebooks did he say impassively, "Don't talk nonsense anymore."

This was a chaotic and oversaturated time when nothing could be clearly articulated. Indeed, clear articulation was impossible. Beneath this chaos, a simple cause lay hidden. Buried deeply, concealed, it would wait a long time before becoming apparent. At the time, however, the hidden cause of this chaos functioned as the powerful but obscure undercurrent of a river, causing boats to capsize dangerously. Unable to see the current's direction, my cohorts and I were unable to ride it out. On the contrary, we frequently went against it, which resulted in failure. In such times, life's desires are particularly vigorous, while reason has yet to awaken. Thus, in darkness, we groped for a direction in which to grow. Circumstances were disordered and, situated in confusion, we ached terribly. Yet, too preoccupied to take care of ourselves and caught in habitual patterns, we were blind to our own pain. We stumbled, groped, and crawled forward, until the wounds gradually healed themselves, forming scabs and leaving scars. We would only see this after we grew up. Our pain was often jumbled up with other ineffable feelings, preventing us from recognizing it distinctly. This wasn't all bad. It did enable us to avoid the pain, then.

We don't see our own situations clearly. Sometimes, the situation only becomes recognizable through the help of other people. Like a mirror, the specificity of their circumstances reflects ours. Just like when, wrapped in a purplish-red velvet curtain, I stood at the entrance to the screening room and heard that woman crying. It occurred fortuitously, but there will always be that kind of moment.

Another event occurred when my mother was assigned to a new work unit to participate in the Four Clean-ups Movement. The night before she left, she had a dream in which she arrived at a place she had never been to before. Surrounded by strangers, she felt terrified. My mother told me her dream. For a long time afterward, I couldn't help feeling distressed and sorrowful. Her dream touched me as my first inklings of the realm of depression, which had been locked away in obscurity, began to reveal themselves. Ominous inklings. I abruptly realized that with literally no one to rely on, we are left in cold indifference. In fact, we had always been alone, but we didn't have a clue. Slumbering reason suddenly blinked at us and fell back asleep. Yet this faint and evanescent light enabled us to see the space around us. We were and still are alone. Actually this was the primal state of independence. Naked, without armor or covering, we still might be ambushed at any time.

Independence was and is exceedingly lonely. We suddenly lose connection with the crowd, and at that moment, all communication breaks off. This is something like the agoraphobic predicament. We isolate ourselves in order to avoid and resist danger. Our terror might then erupt at any moment like a bird startled by the mere twang of a bowstring.

A park bordered one side of our alley. Every day after school, I came here alone, sat on the iron fence, and looked at the streetscape. I sat until dusk, when the streetlights were lit. There, enveloped in the dusk, I felt safe. It also separated me from people nearby. The moment when the lights came on warmed me softly. As the sun hadn't yet set, those lights appeared faint, yellowish, and utterly nonthreatening. The shapes of people on the street blurred. My shape also blurred. At that moment, I seemed to gain freedom. Body and mind liberated, I relaxed, allowing myself to twist into a strange position on the iron bar. This position made me comfortable. My mood eased. Without pressure, I became unexpectedly soft and a little melancholic, but gentle and mild, not sad at all. I truly enjoyed this moment when every worry smoothed away.

Our limited outdoor activities all took place in the back alley, which was dark and somber, like any other alley. Sunlight didn't reach this place until 3 or 4 in the afternoon, and when it did, it was quite faint. Consequently, our alley was also damp. I have already mentioned that the wall separating our alley compound and the neighboring one had been razed, so that our back alley directly faced the gable of the neighboring compound. Their gable was already old and covered by shade-loving climbing plants. Its paint peeled away to reveal dark red bricks. Like all gables, it had a triangular top, with an eternally closed wooden window just beneath the apex. The wooden frame had rotted black. The permanently stained glass was also black, but from years of accumulated ash. Beneath the gable lay a bit of empty space that hadn't been covered in concrete. Naked soil, this tiny plot grew nothing and welcomed no one, diffusing an air of desolation that drifted into our back alley. The wooden window stirred, making a depressing, hollow sound that would suddenly clamor in the lonely emptiness. If at that moment we happened to walk past this bit of empty space to turn into our back alley, we became terrified and would sprint away. In reality it was just a stairwell window and all we were hearing were footsteps on rotting, loose stairs.

The back doors in our row of houses faced a tall wall. The narrow space between the houses and the wall constituted our back alley. The Party School's campus, which was once the famous Aurora College for Women,[9] was located on the other side of the alley wall. After 1949, the College ceased to exist. A key middle school and this Party School carved up the College's dormitories and campus grounds. The section directly behind the wall of our back alley belonged to the Party School and even this section was large. The Aurora College for

Women had been a Catholic institution. From the back window upstairs, we could see a small, square arched vault containing a stone sculpture of the Virgin Mary holding her son Jesus Christ. Maybe because the carving was crude, from our distant perspective, the sculpture seemed indistinct, blurred. Nevertheless, in those evenings when the air became transparent, the edges of their tranquil silhouette, which stood in the spacious darkness, became clear. Their lonely serenity moved us.

We sometimes played badminton in the back alley. The birdie easily flew over the wall, dropping to the other side without a trace. Once, we fortified our courage and went looking for the birdie. We had to leave our alley compound, walk along the street, and finally turn into another alley compound. The Party School gate was located at the farthest section of this compound. Even today, I don't understand the geographical layout or just what the relationship was between our back alley and the Party School campus. Anyway, with great effort we convinced the School guard to admit us onto campus grounds. Once inside, however, we became confused, not knowing where to tread first. We circled around and around, searching for our particular stretch of high wall and the birdie beneath. Bushes and grass grew wildly, indeed flourished, along the wall, like a small forest. That's where our birdie had settled. The setting sun shone at a low angle on downy leaves and grass. We took off and ran straight toward it, the grass beneath our feet softly bending. Then, we saw our house. It looked unfamiliar. So was the high wall. Both appeared uncannily decrepit and gloomy. The dismissal bell of the adjacent middle school rang, the sound drifted into this large, separated courtyard, and lingered interminably.

This was our back alley. Gloomy. Lonely. Yet it had become our playground. Here we jumped rope, kicked birdies, and played house. Our various games wore it down, cracked its surface, and leveled it. The remains of every fruit we ate also clogged the sewer, causing wastewater to overflow. As a result, our back alley became rundown and filthy. But we loved to play here. The front alley, spacious and bright, abutted a road of numerous strangers and so couldn't provide the hidden safety of our back alley. That was how absurd we really were. We huddled like turtles in the alley recesses, enveloped by the high wall's protrusions. We each had a pallid face, weak limbs, and hypersensitive nerves. Afraid of our shadows, we constantly frightened ourselves, becoming scared to death for any reason at all. We didn't affect our terror, or play make-believe terror, or simply perform our terror for the adults. Our terror was absolutely real. Frequently at the bend in the back alley, we would suddenly bolt. We darted across the thresholds of our respective homes, holding back screams, our hearts pounding like drums. The heavy gloom of the back alley had already permeated our hearts, and damaged us deeply. And yet, like our bodies, this atmosphere harbored our spirits. As a mother holds a child, this ambiance embraced our spirits tightly, gently rocking us to sleep.

I don't know at which stage of development had we become so vulnerable, so afraid. For a time, we found the light from surrounding windows particularly frightening. That row of distant windows was located on the other side of the large sportsground of another middle school, facing our house. We would cover our heads with a gauze scarf, through which those lights became mysteriously elusive. Limp and scattered, these rays drifted randomly through the fibers. The strange thing was—and I don't know why—only one of the windows was lit, the rest were dark. This frightened us even more. As soon as night fell, we would pass the gauze scarf from hand-to-hand to feel that terror. We then entered sleep anxiously, allowing nightmares to disturb our rest. We indulged ourselves in the satisfying fear stimulated by that mysterious light. Of course, this was precisely the problem. Terror excited us. Indeed, we seemed to need terror in order to grow. This wasn't a very healthy requirement. Active and aroused, some gland in our bodies craved this perverse nutrient. Through nocturnal darkness, one window in that row of pitch-black windows would be lit intermittently, transmitting an obscure gloominess to us. Melancholic ambiguity permeated the dark silhouettes of the buildings and the empty spaces between. It saturated us.

Throughout that period, we obsessively explored obscure mysteries. After school, for example, we didn't take the main road home, but instead walked through long, narrow alleys. These back alleys provided alternative and unexpected paths, which led in all directions, linking the paths together to form a web. When we suddenly arrived at the quiet and secluded interstices between alleyways, we actually made unforeseen discoveries. Other times, when a back alley mysteriously disappeared and could not be traced, we had the opposite experience. We were untangling threads that came without a shadow and left without a trace. And even if it was this intricate and complex, each alley still maintained its particular clarity, some unadulterated aspect that emerged out of its different past. All this resulted in an isolated solitude, where we also dwelled.

My older sister discovered a narrow passage, about which she teased us for days. Eventually, our fierce longing pressured her into taking us there. This narrow passage couldn't actually be considered an alley. It was just a crack between two neighboring buildings, with a dried-up gutter. We had to spread our feet, straddle the gutter, balance on its edges, and, then move through, taking step by cautious step. The walls scraped our shoulders and after traversing from one end to the other, we no longer looked human. Dust from the walls stuck to our bodies while spider webs and small flying insects covered our faces. The gutter emitted a murky smell. Not exactly disgusting, that smell didn't qualify as an odor. Nevertheless, it did make us gloomy, providing obscure pleasure. A thread of sky above our heads, we squeezed back and forth like bats through this narrow crack of darkness.

I don't know what these dismally loathsome thrills pointed to, or to which parts of our bodies and souls they were connected. Our curiosity had become completely warped. We inhabited a stage of morbid and dark psyches. As night follows day, we entered a dark period of growth. On sunlit streets, we small people were like dark shadows in sunlight. We diligently moved our feet, but the shadows went wherever we walked. All the stuff from the back alley, all the murk from the cracks and corners flooded our bodies and hearts, and accumulated there, dispelling the light. When this gloom reached a certain level and our bodies and minds were in an extremely weak state, it would explode. These situations were almost tragically heroic. The kinds of torture we would endure! The sharp hormones of maturation gnawed at us, yet our anguish could not be properly named, determined, or explained. Searching for a way out was also a blind operation for us.

Such a depressing background made our back alley appear salient. Our terror sat in the corner of that bend in the back alley. Given the state of our minds, that empty space, the wooden window above the empty space, the sounds of footsteps inside the wooden window, all of which spread forth an inexhaustible desolation. After night fell, passing through the back alley was extremely difficult, ominous even. Then whatever you feared would materialize. No matter how you hid, misfortune befell you.

At the time, the Young Pioneer organization was efficient and active, especially at our school. The assistant leader of our school's Young Pioneers was outstanding. She was young, wore her hair plaited in braids that reached her waist, and had dark black eyes, inspiring awe. On every Young Pioneer holiday, she looked dignified with a red scarf tied at her throat. She had a rich imagination and was full of vitality. She thought up numerous ideas that enlivened both our school and extracurricular lives. Our school was located across from the street park that I spoke of earlier. That boulevard park in the midst of residences was our school ground. We attracted the attention of residents and people on the street through our richly vivacious activities. Who would have thought that behind this splendid park existed such a morbid alleyway?

Our school had a television room and whenever there was a good program, the school distributed tickets to each Young Pioneer brigade to allow a limited number of young pioneers to watch the television show. There weren't many tickets. Each brigade received only four, each troop, only one. The brigades were based on homeroom units. The distribution of this one ticket to our troop initiated discussions and recommendations of who should be awarded with the ticket. These discussions were seriously conscientious and took a long time. We had difficulty avoiding unpleasantness. Nevertheless, at discussion's end we still had to have a unified opinion, with everyone sincerely convinced. The ticket definitely rewarded excellence and honored the recipient.

My turn at honor finally came. That evening the television show was the movie *The Little Soccer Team*,[10] which I had already seen. I had also seen the movie's predecessor, the play *The Little Soccer Team*. But this is how it was. It wasn't simply watching television; it was an honor. I got excited for a while, and then became anxious. After watching the show, how could I pass through the back alley and make my way home? The school was no farther than the length of one alley from my home, but that back alley separated them. This problem clutched at my heart, causing a multitude of worries. Yet I could neither avoid going, nor could I give the ticket to another student. That would have been too unusual. All I could do was brace myself and go watch the television show.

It was already dark when I left for school. One or two people were still passing through the back alley, and I could hear back gates slamming. The kitchens that faced the back alley were also all lit. I hurriedly walked along the alley. There was no happiness to speak of. I was wretched. Everyone else had gone home, and I had to leave mine. No one in my family thought anything of my going out alone at night. No one stopped me. No one told me not to go. I had to go. By then, the school had also turned off its lights. Uproarious during the day, at night the school became an empty building, where footsteps echoed on the floor. Only the television room was lit, transmitting sounds that felt even more desolate. Nevertheless, the brightly lit television room generated calming effect. The teachers joked among themselves. They didn't seem as serious as during the day, but rather casual and informal. In turn, classmates acted cautiously, not speaking to one another. The situation seemed in reverse. The school at that moment seemed to be a different place. Had it been daytime, we would have felt the novelty of a television show, but the night oppressed us all. We children felt dispirited and seemed anxious. Small children didn't go out at night, and most of our experiences away from home weren't that happy. Then someone turned on the television, and *The Little Soccer Team* began. The lights in the television room went off and streetlights shone onto the windows. Neon lights flashed irregularly, some grotesque, some gaudy. *The Little Soccer Team* entranced all the others. I was the only one preoccupied by other thoughts. Indeed, as soon as the movie started I began to worry about going home.

First, I scanned the room to see which of my classmates could walk, even part way, with me. It would be great if they lived in the alley compound on that side of the wall. I could swallow my pride and ask them to take me part of the way home. At least we could walk that first section together. Then, by taking advantage of a bit of energy, I could charge through the back alley and push open our back gate. But nobody lived in the neighboring alley row houses so there wasn't anyone to walk even part way home with me. An intense mental struggle ensued.

Should I walk the back alley or the front alley? Although the front alley was the less frightening of the two, unlike the one in back alley, the gate would be locked. Separated from the house by a small courtyard, the front alley gate was fastened from inside. At night, the gate that linked the courtyard was locked. Therefore, if I took the front alley, I would have to shout for someone to open the door, and then wait. Only then could I enter the safety of my home. Now going through the back gate was simpler. Taking the back alley, I could dart directly into the house. But the back alley was so frightening! I involuntarily shivered. Taking the back alley was nearly impossible. But what about the front alley? What if my family didn't hear me shout for them? And even if they did hear me, how long would I have to wait? It was impossible for one person, alone, to wait in a dark alley. My repeated efforts to evaluate and compare these two alleys unceasingly augmented the horror I felt. Terror gripped my heart and I gradually lost the ability to decide. All through the movie and even after I had left the television room, I still didn't know which alley to take home.

Even for an adult, it would have been relatively late. There were few people on the road and the street park was darkly silent. After watching the show, we small children went our separate ways in the park. Immediately, no traces of us could be seen. I walked into the large alley where the streetlights burned farther and farther away from me. All too quickly, I couldn't see my body, only the darkness in front of me. Myopia made this dark night even deeper. My steps became faster and faster, and a decision promptly matured. I would walk home via the front alley. I turned into the front alley. As soon as I entered it, I could no longer control myself and burst into an all-out run. The ghastly darkness of the back alley surged like flood-waters behind my back, as the expansive darkness of the front alley stretched before me. Terrified, I screamed for my mother to open the door. My woeful scream rocked the entire alley, and, in a flash, all the window lights came on.

Fortunately, bodily health and purity gave us the strength to endure and resist. In the end, equilibrium naturally arose. At the very moment when an acute conflict reaches its limit, the severe pain forces you to reconcile with yourself. This isn't only compromise and weakness, but also something that enables you to grow up. The more acute a conflict, the stronger our need for self-reconciliation and the more difficult the process becomes. Yet after each inner conflict results in self-reconciliation, your body and mind radiates a peaceful glory. This deep tranquility is achieved only after experiencing cruel struggles. Extremely common, this process actually strengthens you. It occurs early in life, when body and mind have not yet suffered illness and injury, and health and purity have not yet been wounded. Throughout childhood, everything is situated in nature. Only in this way can you overcome difficulty after difficulty, moving toward self-reconciliation.

As large as the palm of your hand, our courtyard nevertheless constituted the great expanse of my world. Like when I went to Lu Xun's old home in Shaoxing and saw his famous "hundred grasses garden." It astonished me that the "hundred grasses garden" was so cramped and insipid—a far cry from his written description. Once grown up, we are never again as talented at sowing and harvesting happiness as we were during childhood. In this way, our small courtyard became my natural world.

There were two trees in the courtyard. One was a pomegranate tree that our maid and my sister had bought at the vegetable market. The other was a French parasol tree that the Forestry Bureau had planted according to the central plan. The courtyard next door flourished more visibly than ours so I'll just mention the section next to our wall, where two oleander trees, white and red, and a loquat tree grew. During the spring, heavy boughs of flowers hung over and into our courtyard, and green loquats spilled all over our ground, even as the poisonous fragrance of the oleander suffused the upper reaches of their courtyard. Our side was bleaker. Weak and sickly, flowering sparsely, our pomegranate tree never grew tall. Then, unexpectedly, it would catch the eye, shining a golden yellow. For a while, our pomegranate tree had a strange bug infestation. The bugs were brown, their bodies long, and fine scales covered them, giving them the color and shape of twigs. They stuck firmly to the tree's branches, difficult to discover. I patiently used chopsticks to peel them off, one by one, enduring disgust. Who would have thought I would successfully peel every one of them off? But this didn't help matters. The turning point of this affair emerged in an agricultural science experiment. In *One Hundred Thousand Whys*,[11] I read that if you cut a section of bark near the base of a fruit tree, it would make nutrients more effectively reach the branches and leaves, stimulating the tree to bloom. So at the base of the pomegranate tree, I cut away circles of bark. The next spring, the entire pomegranate tree unexpectedly blossomed, as if golden red lanterns had been hung on every branch. Yet still, it didn't grow tall, didn't grow big, and didn't bear fruit.

In contrast, that parasol tree grew at lightning speed. Almost no one noticed it sprout into the space above the courtyard. I don't even remember what its crown looked like. I never took care of it. It had invaded our courtyard. About seven or eight years later, already halfway through the Cultural Revolution, a typhoon blew the parasol tree over, partially uprooting it. My mother called me. We joined efforts to uproot it completely and push it over the wall. In a low voice, my mother told me that ever since that tree had grown, our family had faced difficulties. That parasol was an unlucky tree. I hadn't thought about it in those terms, yet I had never felt close to that tree, and looked at it without really seeing it. Perhaps the parasol tree was too tall for our small courtyard. Its crown blocked our view, but even so I had never paid attention to its trunk.

In addition to caring for the pomegranate tree, I planted corn, sunflowers, castor oil plants, and scallion in the courtyard. Everything I planted was a source of oil, a grain, or a vegetable simply because those seeds were relatively easy to obtain. I tended my plants scrupulously, much exceeding the level of care they needed. But the result violated the principle of "sow and you shall reap." I harvested barely a single grain. In contrast, the plantain that had never been nourished thrived. I also loved to build fences. I used scraps of bamboo to weave fences, which enclosed my fruitless crops, and lay pieces of brick to edge the plants. I even planned to dig a well in the courtyard. This engineering project went on for many days until adults halted it by filling in the well.

This courtyard buried my secrets, such as a glass paperweight that I had deliberately smashed. The small bird inside the glass paperweight always puzzled me. I asked everyone about it, and everyone replied that inside the paperweight was a piece of solid colored glass. But I firmly believed that there was a perfect glass bird inside and I was unable to rest until I had removed it. Naturally, disillusionment resulted. Besides scattering broken bits of colored glass, I feared getting into trouble. I buried the broken glass in a corner of the courtyard wall, thinking the matter finished. I also dug a field "stove" in the courtyard, just like in the movies, and then lit the fire to cook. Of course, this didn't work out either.

Even during those sad years, my sadness didn't penetrate this small courtyard, which always warmed me. With soft soil below my feet, the flourishing plantain, and the neighbor's oleander and loquats above me, this was a wonderful little world. Here, I found refuge.

During that period, plenty of soft soil was still scattered throughout the city, and if collected, it would have been a considerable amount. This soil still had sufficient nutrients to feed some trees and plants, which symbiotically existed with various kinds of insects. These insects came in different shapes and sizes. Some were beneficial and some harmful but this is precisely biological equilibrium. Of these insects, there was one caterpillar, the "Cnidocampa Flavescens" that we called "prickly fur bug." It lived on willows and parasol trees, breeding prolifically during the summer when its fine fur blew in the wind, flying up and filling the sky. This fur was so fine that it was almost invisible to the human eye. Actually it wasn't fur but extremely sharp needles, which immediately caused red welts on contact with human skin. At first those welts itched, then as soon as you scratched, they burned violently. During summers of bare legs and arms, who didn't have prickly fur bug welts? Both painful and itchy, they made you restless, not knowing how to make it stop. All you could do was wash with soap and water, hoping that the soapy water might rinse away the needles in your skin. But it's hard to say if this worked. Without a doubt, being stuck by prickly fur bug needles was one of the most unfortunate things about summer. Today, when prickly fur bugs no longer exist and the hazards of their needles no longer threaten us, our resentment has become an artifact of history.

One summer, it seemed that all my troubles were over. Already dispirited, I felt downhearted and unable to become enthusiastic about anything. My anger, fear, and depression had all dissipated amid summery indolence and the exhaustion that follows tortuous experience. Matters should have been brought to closure, but they just wouldn't end. I don't know which part of me resisted, and wouldn't let matters wind down, longing for a powerful conclusion. The place where a conclusion should have been was vacant and so this period of my life couldn't end. There was still fuel that hadn't been consumed and conflicts that hadn't been resolved. Beneath my lethargy and exhaustion was the pressure of nameless fear and blind waiting. The blow that would come did have the capacity to destroy everything. It pushed everything into the past so that nothing remained and nothing would return. Subsequent years would then constitute a new era, one with a completely different content.

Extremely mundane, the origin of that blow didn't draw anyone's attention. Some prickly fur bug needles fell onto my underpants, which were drying, inside out, in our courtyard. Those needles pricked me in a place that a child feels ashamed to mention. I had no way to tell anyone and didn't even know what had happened to me. Fear and suffering attacked me once again, but unlike previous attacks this time the attack was immediate and specific. What's more, I couldn't avoid what attacked me at every minute of every hour. At first, it was still bearable and I thought it would be over when I woke up the next day but the situation developed progressively, each day becoming more serious than the last. My underpants chaffed the welts until they bled and became infected. I didn't know what to do, and no one could help me. And during all this time, I forced myself to smile and laugh, to act just like an unaffected person, and to play with other people! My pain and fear increased each day. During the time that other people napped, I snuck out to go to the pharmacy to buy anti-inflammatory tablets.

The pharmacy stood next to the common people's movie theater, the Huaihai. At noon, few people were on the street. Cicadas chirped clearly, and the glistening sun spilled through parasol leaves, making it difficult for people to keep their eyes open. The asphalt street undulated beneath vehicle tires. Barefoot except for plastic summer shoes, I alone knew the torture beneath my knee-length, flowered skirt. I entered the pharmacy and said that I wanted to buy anti-inflammatory tablets. I nervously calculated how I would answer if someone asked me where the inflammation was. But the pharmacist didn't ask anything and just sold me the pills. I didn't dare hope that those tiny, white tablets could resolve my immense suffering. But if I didn't swallow these pills, where could I turn for help?

Other people were sweetly napping. I took a pill, the hope that I didn't dare hope. I still expected sleep to save me. I kept fantasizing that the matter would reverse its course as I slept. But by then, sleep no longer came all that easily, in part because of the prickly itching and burning pain, but also in part because of my fear and anxiety. I tossed and turned on the cool bamboo mat, silently swallowing my tears, waiting for sleep and drugs to take effect. However, all my suffering became especially acute in the dead of night. Being ill was bitter enough; worse yet, I couldn't reveal my terrible illness. I sincerely believed my illness was shameful. Inflammation and worry caused me to have a slight fever and lose weight quickly. Yet no one noticed. I still handled people in such a way that nothing slipped.

Small children have a remarkable capacity for suffering. Their endurance and toughness are simply infinite, for if they didn't have these abilities, how could they live with their sensitive feelings? Their delicate bodies and minds can feel the deepest and most subtle pain.

Without the strength to endure these consequences, how would they survive? And a child's strength implies much more than inherent delicacy and strength. Half an adult's strength lies in numbness, in the solid cocoon that has been forged around our beings and separates us from experience.

You wouldn't think that the matter could drag on like it did, but day after day I stubbornly endured the situation. I held out until late one night when my mother came home. Seeing that I was still awake, she asked what the problem was. In that instant, I weakened. My willpower collapsed. For so many days I had tenaciously maintained my self-respect and independence, and then, just like that, it all collapsed. I cried a silent river from my house all the way to the hospital. On the treatment table, exposed to that staring crowd, I cried and screamed, and wouldn't let the doctors or nurses near my body. I felt that the sky had fallen. This happened precisely during that period when your body's changes embarrass you to no end, so even you can't directly face your own body. Right then, somebody pulled the curtain open. Seven or eight doctors surrounded me, pressing on my hands and feet. What's more, patients had gathered outside the door to watch the fun. Hospital stays were boring, and a performance this good was hard to come by. All of them felt amused by my suffering.

At the height of my crying fit, a gray-haired doctor squeezed in and said to me, "Child, how can you act like this? I want you to know, my daughter is in Xinjiang . . ." For a time, I couldn't understand what her daughter being in Xinjiang had to do with me, but her serious censure shocked me and all I could do was stop crying. Afterward, the matter became simple: excision, sterilization, the application of medicine, and then in for a hospital stay. The matter actually was that simple: an injury, an infection, and the necessary medical treatment.

I was admitted to the hospital and changed into an oversized patient's smock. They placed me in the gynecology ward because of the location of my injury. The appearance of a girl my age in the gynecology ward not only made me totally conspicuous, but also invited reproaches. People frequently came to our room to peer at me curiously. Then, they whispered together. I seemed to have come right out of the lyrics to that children's song: we are all inert blockheads. I had already become unable to speak or move. I lay on the bed and ignored everyone. I didn't brush my hair and didn't bathe, waiting until my mother's afternoon visit when she did everything for me. My hair had grown long and my mother plaited it into two, tight braids. She first used translucent vinyl threads to tie two ponytails, plaited them, and then tied the braids at each end. Because they were too tight, the corners of my eyes slanted up and my sharp, pointed chin appeared even more like an awl. In my heart, I felt that these braids weren't appropriate for someone my age, but at the time, I didn't care. I just went along with whatever my mother did. When I only ate fifty grams of rice, and people complained to my mother, she urged me to eat one hundred grams without fail. The next morning, I ordered one hundred grams of rice porridge, which filled a huge bowl to the brim. Once again I earned their reproaches. This time, they complained to my mother, saying that I had actually eaten one hundred grams of rice porridge. My mother had no alternative except to give me detailed instructions: one hundred grams refers to cooked rice, but fifty grams refers to rice porridge. This is how I finally adjusted how much rice I ate.

I closed myself up tightly, separating myself from the outside world. Many people came and left the gynecology ward, which made it a noisy place. There were also lots of interesting events, but none of them had anything to do with me, nor did they provoke my curiosity. I just lay in bed all day, watching the sun move across the ceiling. Neither happy nor sad, my heart was hollow, holding nothing. The only break came at about 9 A.M., when a young nurse called on me to sit in a basin for half an hour. The nurse was very small and carried a large basin of disinfectant. She stepped nimbly through my ward without stopping, tilted her head to call me, and then continued to the bathroom. She always mispronounced one of the characters in my name, but I understood her. By the time I crawled out of bed to get to the bathroom, she had already vanished. That basin of steaming, purplish red disinfectant was placed in its frame with a clean towel next to it. In a continuing daze, I sat on the basin. Time passed without leaving a slightest trace. I didn't worry about calculating the time. I simply waited for that small nurse's tinkling voice to call me again. Then I would get up and return to the ward.

One day I had already walked to the ward door when I suddenly heard a voice behind me call out, "Hey." As there was no one else in the corridor, this "hey" was clearly directed at my back. Startled, I turned around, wondering who would call to me like an old friend. A girl stood in the door to the next ward, her hair brushed into two shoulder length braids. She pointed at me and said, At first, I was the youngest, now you're the youngest, the youngest patient. I froze, not knowing how to answer her. In a flash, she vanished.

After dinner early that evening, I walked to the balcony. Our ward was on the seventh floor and you could see places far away in the city. Uncovered and unblocked from view, the sky seemed immense and intimately close. The city didn't have as many tall buildings as it does today, and the air was cleaner, too. Sunset and evening clouds filled the sky. In the street below, I could already dimly perceive beams of yellow light through the trees. Again I saw her. The girl who had called me that morning was also on the balcony but a barrier stood between us. She played an accordion. I realized that she had been the one playing the accordion music I had heard every evening! She stared into the distance, not paying any attention to me. I crept onto the concrete balcony wall, and listened silently until night fell and enveloped us. The ward lights came on, lighting up all the windows, and the last visitors left. The ward and city were both peaceful. Deliciously cool, the breeze blew in soft gusts and swept away the summer heat. The girl had already returned to her ward and the sound of her accordion had ceased but I was still on the balcony. A thread of happiness rose in my heart; it was the happiness of tranquility. I stayed out on the balcony until an adult ward mate called me in to sleep. Because my mother had entrusted me to them, they all took care of me.

The next day at dusk, I came early to the balcony, waiting for her to appear. As expected, she came, dragging a chair, her accordion slung over her shoulder. She flashed me a smile. Before I could return her smile she had already turned away, sat down, and begun to play. She sang along with playing the accordion. In the open sky, her song and the sound of the accordion dispersed widely. The evening clouds gradually spread to the far horizon. Under these clouds the green trees and red tiles appeared beautiful. Down in the street the teeny-tiny toy-sized cars that crawled by were also beautiful. As she played her accordion, against the gradually darkening sky, her silhouette was beautiful. She had just washed her hair and it hung loosely to her shoulders. Her mouth opened and closed in song; the accordion also opened, then closed. Within the beauty of this twilight scene, voice and music dissolved into each other.

I began yearning to converse with her. I became a little vain, thinking to myself that if I could become friends with her it would be something to be proud of. Every evening at dusk, I always arrived early to wait for her, looking for an opportunity to speak with her. But after the enthusiasm of her first greeting, she ignored me. I didn't think there was anything wrong in this. She was beautiful and mature. She could play the accordion and sing. And me? Ill-favored, ugly, and not yet mature with my hair braided in that strange fashion, I was dull and uninteresting. What about me would interest her? I fawned over her so obsequiously that she later spoke several sentences to me. She told me that she was a piano student at the middle school which was associated with the music conservatory. She had come to the hospital to heal from an injury, which occurred in the following manner. One day as she was riding a boy's bicycle, a classmate suddenly called her from behind and, when she abruptly got off the bike, she rammed into the front bar. Her injury occurred in an open and forthright manner. It could be clearly narrated from start to finish and was therefore immediately accepted and affirmed. In contrast, when people came to ask me why I was in the hospital, I had no way of clearly telling them, and so remained silent. People then pursued the matter, asking, Was it caused by a bicycle? You see, gynecological injuries caused by bicycles had already been socially acknowledged. But except for bicycles, they seemed unable to come up with another reason for a girl to sustain a gynecological injury. When I shook my head, people looked at me suspiciously. Then they would walk away. I didn't care that in other people's eyes, I was already a disgrace. After experiencing all that I had, what was left to care about?

I still wasn't talking, but my inner world had become much livelier. In addition to lying on my bed watching the sunlight, I also secretly examined myself in a mirror, which was small enough to be concealed in the palm of the hand. A song sheet was imprinted on the back and the edge was wrapped in red plastic. Once when my sister came to the hospital to see me, she just left it. That day, she also ate my fruit and snacks, but watching her eat, I felt none of the usual anger. Instead, my generosity made me happy. During the day, I inspected myself in that small mirror. It only reflected part of me at a time: an eye, a nose, several loose hairs, or some facial skin. All these parts appeared so strange, as if they belonged to someone else, but if not me, then to whom? I also began paying attention to the activity in the room.

There were five sickbeds in my ward. Three had been placed side-by-side along the eastern wall, and the other two were laid head-to-toe along the western wall. I was in the first bed on the western side, next to the window. The balcony door was right next to my headboard. A peasant woman from the Chuansha area occupied the bed on the other side of the door, directly across from me. Numerous peasant-looking men and women continuously streamed in to see her, speaking that incomprehensible Chuansha language. Her illness wasn't severe and apparently she would leave soon. Nevertheless she looked distressed and sighed constantly. One day she suddenly burst into smiles. That afternoon, her daughter came to see her, also beaming smiles. The relatives and friends who came to visit all congratulated her. She couldn't speak, just smile, and was almost unable to bring her lips together. It turned out that tests had shown blood flukes had caused her illness. The local government bore responsibility for hospital costs in cases of schistosomiasis. I finally understood. All the while, she had been worried about hospital costs. Now everything was fine. The problem solved, her illness also cured, she cheerfully left the hospital. The day she left, a large group of relatives and friends came. They called from outside the door, maneuvered to stream in, and then swarmed out with her.

Her bed hadn't been empty half a day when a new patient arrived. She was a young woman, gentle and quiet, with two long braids and a pair of white-rimmed glasses. She came into the ward alone, surprisingly familiar with the place. She arranged her things and spread a white cloth on the edge of the bed. She then sat down to eat lychees. She spread a white napkin on her knees for the lychee skins and pits. She ate one after the other. After eating awhile, she stood up to inspect the white cloth she had been sitting on. Only this much exertion, and blood already stained the white clothe. She bled constantly, but was so composed. Unflustered, she changed the white cloth, sat down, and continued eating lychees.

At the time I began to pay attention to the situation around me, two women who had undergone Cesarean sections occupied the beds against the eastern wall. They seemed to me too old to be new mothers, and after coming out of the operating room they closed their eyes and slept continuously. Next to the beds, someone else, usually their husbands, kept watch. Those husbands were also frightfully old. One of them was fat and white, and wore glasses. During naptime one day, I saw him quietly wolf down the mother's watermelon. He probably wanted to get rid of the old melon so the mother could eat the fresh one without guilt, but anyway, the scene was funny. I couldn't help laughing under my breath. This was the first time I had laughed since entering the hospital.

Both mothers gave birth to girls. The head nurse frequently repeated that their daughters especially resembled them. She also frequently told one of the mothers that her uterus was inordinately ugly. This, I didn't understand. A uterus could also be good-looking or ugly? What did it matter whether it was good-looking or not? Yet the two mothers remained indifferent to whatever the head nurse said. Instead they expressed relief for having been relieved of a heavy burden. The crux of the matter seemed to have already passed, and so it didn't matter what came next. Both the mothers and their husbands appeared exhausted but relaxed. As the mothers' relief may have resembled my own, I deeply identified with them.

By this time, the girl in the ward next door had begun to ignore me completely. Naturally lively, she liked to run from ward to ward. But when she ran into ours, she didn't greet or even see me. It was as if I didn't exist. She always carried her accordion with her, playing and singing in every ward, including ours. Nevertheless, she simply ignored me. I didn't mind. I still liked to see her and listen to her voice. I adored her.

My injury was actually simple. After the uncomplicated application of medicine reduced the inflammation, my injury immediately healed. The pain and humiliation were all eliminated the first day I entered the hospital. That soul-wracking opening scene, when my wounds were cleansed, powerfully resolved my torture, and in the end something resembling happiness developed without my knowing. My body and mind became tranquil. This was an authentic, peaceful tranquility. The day I left the hospital, my mother and I got off the bus and walked past the street park at the entrance to our alley. I discovered that although my shoulder was already the same height as my mother's, I still wore those ridiculous "ox horn" braids, which threw a strange shadow on the ground.

The sun shone brilliantly, and that erstwhile era suddenly receded, submerged in dark shadows.

Notes

1. The "Four Clean-ups," also known as the Socialist Education Movement, was launched by Mao Zedong in 1963. The targets of the movement was were the "reactionary" elements within the bureaucracy of the Communist Party, and the goal was to cleanse "politics, economy, organization, and ideology." It is said that Mao's dissatisfaction over about the result of this movement set the stage for the Cultural Revolution.

2. *There Is a Coming Generation* (《自有后来人》, 1963) is a feature film directed by Yu Yanfu (于彦夫). The famous revolutionary model play, *The Legend of Red Lantern*, is based on this film.

3. *The Legend of Red Lantern* (《红灯记》, 1970) is one of the "eight revolutionary model operas" produced during the Cultural Revolution under the patronage and supervision of Jiang Qing (江青), the wife of Mao Zedong (毛泽东).

4. *Spark of Life* 《生命的火花》, 1962) is a film based on the real life story of a female soldier, Wang Mengjun (王孟筠) in the late 1960s. The screenplay was written by Deng Pu (邓普), and the film was directed by Dong Fang (东方).

5. *The Army's Daughter* (《军队的女儿》, 1963) is a short novel Deng Pu wrote modeled on his own screenplay for *Spark of Life*.

6. *House of Seventy-two Tenants* (《七十二家房客》, 1973) is a Hong Kong film directed by Yuen Chor (楚原).

7. The Great Leap Forward refers to the economic and social campaign launched in mainland China in 1958. It was the Chinese Communist Party's attempt to modernize the Chinese economy, transforming China from a primarily agrarian economy into a modern, agriculturalized, and industrialized communist society. It took

two forms: a nationwide mass steel production campaign and the formation of the people's communes. The Great Leap Forward is now widely viewed as a major economic failure and great humanitarian disaster.

8. The Cultural Revolution refers to a massive political and cultural movement that began in May, 1966, and aimed to overthrow existing political and cultural orders. The movement itself lasted about two years (1966–1968) but the effects of its radical left ideology remained until 1976. Despite its politically egalitarian rhetoric, Chinese people, especially those who had been privileged in the cultural or political realms, suffered tremendously during those ten years.

9. The Aurora College for Women (1937–1952), 震旦女子学院 in Chinese, was a division of Aurora University (*Université l'Aurore* in French), a preeminent Catholic university in Shanghai from 1903 to 1952.

10. *The Little Soccer Team* (《小足球队》, 1965) is a film directed by Yan Bili (颜碧丽).

11. *One Hundred Thousand Whys* (《十万个为什么》) is the title of a series of books that contains elementary science texts prepared for Chinese schoolchildren. The series, first published in 1961–1962, was intended to introduce to children the basic concepts of math, physics, chemistry, geology, astronomy, and meteorology through a question-and-answer format.

A WOMAN WRITER'S SENSE OF SELF

I must stress emphatically the extremely critical role that women writers have played in the literature of the new era.

The public's enthusiastic reception of "Love Must Not Be Forgotten"[1] still appears vividly before my eyes. We still remember that even before this story appeared, the question of what kind of subject matter could enter the palace of socialist literature had already been raised and vigorously resolved in the story, "The Wounded."[2]

At the same time, Liu Xinwu also eloquently articulated the position of love in human life and society. This being the case, what was the reason that this latecomer to the love story could inflame such passions among people? In no way did this tactfully beautiful story conflict with society at large; it was entirely concerned with a small matter in a personal life. It was already extraordinary that a trivial private matter could become a public short story, yet the event itself far exceeded this. What was important was that this private matter did not presuppose society and politics, but rather exclusively referred to personal emotions and feelings.

For so many years, our literature had taken "collectivization" to its most extreme. Everyone had repudiated their self and the status of the "individual" could be raised to an "ism" only as the object of criticism. We were no longer prepared to accept an emotional life that belonged solely to an individual. This was probably the first time in many years that a personal and private emotional life had appeared in literature. Now if "Love Must Not Be Forgotten" still had some aspects—such as admonitions about the selection of a spouse—that could be connected up with society's collective consciousness and public thought, then "Gleaning Wheat-heads,"[3] a short essay that appeared immediately after, more thoroughly belonged to the personal.

To be honest, it was not until I read "Gleaning Wheat-heads" that I believed it was possible for me to be a writer. Previously, I had dreaded literature. I was highly emotional and had strived to connect these feelings to social and collective consciousness. But every effort failed. At the time, the greatest portion of my literary output was di-ary- and letter-writing. Thus, I have said several times, "In the past, I wrote my diary as fiction, while today I write my fiction as a diary." Then *A Winter's Tale*[1] went to even further extremes. Even though "Love Must Not Be Forgotten" and "Gleaning Wheat-heads" had ex-pressed personal matters, we couldn't judge whether or not these matters were the authors' life story. We had to assume that these two stories were fabricated. But *A Winter's Tale* was the author's true story, a private novel, which pushed personalized literature to its fur-thest extreme. "On the Same Horizon"[2] came after this, and here the "individual" finally rose to an "ism." This was the story that truly woke up and angered a few pure collectivists. Those so angered, how-ever, didn't realize that the individualism of this work actually con-nected with the far advanced personal consciousness already ex-pressed in women's writing. They deployed "Darwinism," "existen-tialism," and other abstruse theories to criticize it. In fact, everything that had to happen had already happened.

While men writers brandished great revolutionary pens in a frontal attack against backward, decadent, and reactionary forces such as bureaucracy and feudalism, women writers quietly opened a literary path, digging their covert trench all the way to the front line. At this moment, a brand new, yet also ancient, aspect of Chinese lit-erature emerged. Literature was no longer simply an instrument of propaganda or a weapon of war. It had been granted a grace period and the distance grew between literature and what was actually hap-pening. Literature belatedly became a vehicle for individual opinions and emotions, becoming more independent with each day. Yet con-comitantly, literature also lost its fanatic support and illustrious glory, becoming increasingly lonely. Literature had returned to the place it originally belonged. What I want to say is this: women writers have made a substantive contribution to getting literature back on track.

Whether it is due to social causes, or, as is even more likely, to biological causes, women are better than men at experiencing their own emotions. They also value these emotions more. Thus, women's self-consciousness is stronger than men's, while men possess greater collective consciousness. Only a failed man indulges in love, but no matter how successful a woman is, she still yearns to sacrifice for love. Women have a greater need for personal emotions and thus have more need to reveal these emotions than men do. In fact, literature's original impulse is emotional revelation; women and literature share the same natural origin. Also, women are more concerned with the personal than men are, a fact that constitutes another fundamental alliance between women and literature. Consequently, in the literature of the new era, large numbers of women writers have emerged. Whenever one of these women writers has appeared, she has been warmly welcomed. Their descriptions of great eras, movements, adversity, and triumph always connect to their tiny, yet heavy and rich, emotions. Their natural point of departure is their self, from where they proceed to watch and observe human life and the world. This self is most important to them; it is their first created character. This character always appears onstage in a different guise, but its essence remains the same. Women writers thoroughly express their personal lives, imbuing their works with fresh and original worldviews, philosophies, emotions, and styles. Perhaps all this is especially distinctive to China because Chinese women were confined in a narrow world longer than were women from other countries, while Chinese men possess stronger political and moral ideals than do men from those countries. Thus, Chinese women's self-consciousness is stronger; likewise, Chinese men's collective consciousness is stronger.

The subsequent question is, by what means can women writers realize an authentic self on which they depend for creation and development? We all know that only the real is valuable, perfect, and truthful. We have all probably read Lu Xun's essay, "A Happy Family," and still remember how a writer in the story describes his ideal happy family: the husband and wife are married by choice; he wears Western clothing and she, Chinese clothing; and each holds a copy of "The Ideal Good Person." There is a snow-white cloth on the table, the cook serves dinner, and ". . . places a dish of 'dragon and tiger battle' in the center of the table. They pick up their chopsticks at the same time, point to the plate, and look at each other with smiling eyes . . ." Then speaking a string of some Western language, they reach for the food at the same time. Even if that poverty-stricken writer has portrayed a happy family, it is a ridiculously false one. The selves expressed in some works [by women writers] remind me of that happy family.

It is all too easy for people to imagine that they are someone other than themselves, and women are even more susceptible to taking this false road than are men. Women love their self-image more than men do. That is to say, men possess another kind of shameless courage that women don't. Because women also value and observe themselves more, they care for those selves more. They knit their image as meticulously as one knits the ideals of a lifetime, and when finished, they deceive the world and even themselves into thinking that those knitted selves are their actual selves. In fact, they're not. A simple and uneducated woman may retain some valuable authenticity because she lacks both the intelligence and the cleverness to design her self. These women lack the strength to control and suppress their jealousy, greed, fierceness, sense of inferiority, ugly selfishness, and obscene sexual desires. Ironically, they are thus able to reveal themselves directly. Yet how might an intelligent, smart, and cultivated woman, such as a woman writer, approach the image of her self? Is it possible for her not to embellish and examine that self? Here, I can't help but think of "Teibele and Her Demon" by the Jewish-American writer Isaac Bashevis Singer. In that story, a beautiful woman loves herself to the extent that even when making love she is unable to indulge herself, ultimately exhausting herself to death.

I should say that in the early period of our new era of literature, women writers instinctively expressed their self-consciousness in their works. They allowed this self-consciousness to ascend the literary stage without its being completely awakened, and thus they expressed a valuable authenticity. At the same time we should also acknowledge that because of its incomplete self-awareness, the self-consciousness of this period lacked depth and was merely superficial. The questions arise once this awareness is awakened and deepened. Women hope to be appreciated. Their need to be spoiled and admired is so fierce that they are incapable of forgetting their audience. They require that when the self makes an appearance, it makes a good showing. Whether based on deep-rooted aesthetic conventions or on a temporary fad, women unconsciously and yet soberly design themselves. What realm can this self that has been erroneously and intelligently transformed reach? Is it lofty and deep or mediocre and shallow? This is the point most worth discussing, yet also the most difficult to discuss. I've already said above that the self is the first character of a literary work, yet it is a character that either doesn't make an appearance or appears under various guises. Where then can we search for it? If we can't find it, how then can we evaluate what is authentic and what is false about it? How can we propose to further the discussion about the self after connecting the work's authenticity to its success or failure? Yet I think that we can trace back to the origin of a successful work to infer whether its self is true or false, and then how this true or false self functions in the work. Here, I can only mention a few works that I subjectively recognize as successful, including *Wuthering Heights*, "Song of the Heartbroken Café," and "The Ark."[6] Only after writing this far have I realized that I've brought myself to an impasse and can only return to the beginning again.

Given their sentimental nature, women also have an instinct to amplify their self-consciousness. The fundamental character most romantics manifest is a state of mind that comes close to narcissism, just as Liang Shiqiu incisively and sarcastically wrote in his 1930s essay, "The Romantic Tendency of Modern Chinese Literature"[7]: "Not having traveled even 100 *li*, they nevertheless describe themselves as wandering far from home." Women also have an even more romantic and fantastic character than do utilitarian men. Women participate in the outside world less frequently than do men, more often immersing themselves in their interior worlds. Once they have completely masticated their emotions and experiences and then returned to chew on them again, it is difficult for them to avoid chewing out some new taste that wasn't there previously. Once women's creativity, as vital as any man's, has been fettered in a much smaller world than men's, it is hard for women to avoid creating illusions out of nothing. And when the narrow circumstances of their lives are unable to provide more experiences for them, it is also difficult for women to avoid mixing in fillers.

Here what adds to my sorrow is that today even men writers are increasingly falling into this trap, progressively feminizing the literature of our new era. Perhaps the reasons they fall into this trap are different. For example, men don't aspire as women do to be spoiled, but they do yearn more strongly to be adored and admired, especially by women, and desire at every time and place to have their masculinity and strength confirmed. When they firmly believe that everything can be attained, they become vain. This vanity causes their fabricated illusions to approximate truth. Their lives are originally spacious, but the writer's destiny compels them to enter a study, which, even if it isn't a kitchen, is as sealed off as a kitchen and is even more dull and insipid than a kitchen, locking out even the ordinary minutiae of family life. And this sanitized study enables them to fantasize even more unreservedly. Once men transfer their fierce strength from the outside world to the inside, the creation of false selves becomes abnormally effective.

After critiquing falsities of the self, I want to direct my critique toward the lack of improvement of the self. That is to say, if we have already maintained the authenticity of the self, the next question is that of improving the self. I believe that between the true self and the improved self, there should be a rational distance, namely an aesthetic or critical distance. Liang Shiqiu has a passage from the previously mentioned essay that perhaps can help explain, "The true self is not located in the realm of the senses, but rather in rational life. Thus, in order to express the self, one must go through several steps of rational activity and cannot rely on impressions from the sensual realms." The difficulty and paradox is recognizing which is the self expressed through rational means and which is the false self. It also seems that a true self must undergo rational steps or it is not true. Then in what should our rational activity consist?

We've already heard more than one unfortunate story with the refrain, "It's hard to be a woman and even harder to be a famous woman."[8] First, we'll suppose that such a story is a true and moving piece of literary work, that the self the author expressed is true, and that the work's conclusion is also true. Next, we have to ask: Being a woman is difficult; is it difficult to be a man? Being a famous woman is difficult; is it difficult to be a woman who doesn't become famous? If we tolerantly admit that it's difficult to be a man and even more difficult to be a woman who doesn't become famous, then when we look back to inspect that difficult condition, could we discover some cause for misfortune other than gender and fame? A cause that originates in a particular self itself? Is this bad self that created its own predicament more authentic and noble? After all, the self's authenticity should subsume the meanings of truth.

From our perspective today, truth is so classical a word as to be almost decayed, whereas I believe that the principle of truth remains the same despite all apparent changes. Because classicism is closest to our origin, perhaps it more closely approaches things as they are. I am willing to maintain the concept of truth. Given this, can we say that if we don't connect with the wider world and human life outside ourselves, then our evaluation of the self will also sink into falsehood? On the one hand, this is a way of observing and experiencing the self. On the other hand, it is also a way of broadly understanding and researching the world outside oneself and humanity. This then becomes a way of establishing the aesthetic, rational, and critical distance between a true self and an improved self. This distance between a true self and a penetrating worldview should be both established and extended.

In front of the self, there should be the reflection of another self. The higher this reflecting self stands, the truer and clearer the original self will be. The improvement of this reflecting self depends on our rational activity. The great dilemma is that the self and the capacity for self-reflection both reside in the author alone.

As for women, they are too immersed in the self's emotions and are frequently unable to act for themselves. Controlled by their feelings, they cannot get outside themselves. Thus, asking them to establish a rational distance from which to calmly examine their selves would cause them once again to fall into the dilemma of falsehood.

Here I need to clarify that I am also a woman writer and cannot evade any of the above problems. I will strive to accomplish the things that I have come to understand. When I sit in front of a blank, white sheet of paper, I will strive to forget my audience, forcing myself into a solitary and isolated situation. In this way I can be free; I can tranquilly face my self.

Notes

1. Zhang Jie, "Love Must Not Be Forgotten" (张洁,《爱，是不能忘记的》), *Beijing Literature and Art* (《北京文艺》), no. 11 (1979), 9–27.

2. Lu Xinhua, "The Wounded" (卢新华,《伤痕》), *Wenhui Newspaper* (《文汇报》) (August 11, 1978).

3. Zhang Jie's essay "Gleaning Wheat-heads" (《 拾麦穗》) was first published in 1982.

4. Yu Luojin, "A Winter's Tale" (遇罗锦, 《一个冬天的童话》), *Dangdai*, vol. 1, no. 3 (1980), 58–107.

5. Zhang Xinxin, "On the Same Horizon" (张欣辛《在同一地平线上》), *Shouhuo*, no. 6 (1981), 172–233.

6. Zhang Jie, "The Ark" (《方舟》) (Beijing: Beijing Publishing House, 1983).

7. Liang Shiqiu wrote the essay (梁实秋《现代中国文学之浪漫的趋势》 in 1926 when he was studying at Harvard. The essay was included in *Liang's Romanticism and Classicism* (《浪漫的与古典的》) (Shanghai: New Moon Bookstore, 1927), 1–24.

8. This quote is from Liu Xiaoqing, a popular actress in the 1980s, who published an autobiography, "My Road" (《我的路》), in *Wenhui Monthly* (《文汇月刊》) (June 1983).

乌托邦诗篇

我后来知道，一个人在一个岛上，也是可以胸怀世界的。在交通和印刷业蓬勃发展的今天，知道世界不再是一件难事。人们可以通过书本、地理课程，以及一些相对有限的旅行，去想像这一个巨形球状的世界。时差是最具体不过的说明，它使地球的理论变成常人可感的了。但是我想，这个人却不是从这些通常的途径得知世界的，我想他是从《圣经》的那一节里得知着这一知识的。《圣经》的那一节是　　"创世纪"　的第十一章，《圣经》说："那时，天下人的口音言语，都是一样。"后来，他们商量要造一座城，城中有一个塔，塔顶高耸入云，犹如航海业诞生以后海中的灯塔，使得地上的人们不会分散。接下来的一节，题目就叫作"变乱口音"。"变乱口音"中写道："耶和华说，看哪，他们成为一样的人民，都是一样的言语，如今既做起这事来，以后他们所要做的事，就没有不成就的了，我们下去，在那里变乱他们的口音，使他们的言语，彼此不通，于是耶和华使他们从那里分散在全地上，他们就停工不造那城了。"于是，他这个人就不仅知道了现在：世上人被耶和华的力量分散与隔膜的状况；而且也知道了过去：曾经要一个可能，世上人是欢聚在一起，由一座通天的塔标作召唤，互相永不会离散，好像一个灯火通明的晚会——晚会是我们这样堕落的现代人唯一能够想像的众人聚集一处的情景。当这个人还是个孩子的时候，在那西太平洋小岛的气候温湿的乡村里，他一定做过许多次的梦，梦见许许多多的人在一起，同心协力，建造一座城。人们象一家人一样生活在一起，劳动在一起。后来，海峡对面的陆地上，那一些轰轰烈烈的群众性革命运动的壮观场面，使他以为他的梦想在世界的一部分地区实现了。他是通过收听短波这样的地下活动了解这壮观场面的，这种地下活动不久将他送进了监狱。那时侯，这个岛上的工业化程度还不足以冲击他的宁静乡村，这个岛所依附的那个大国还处在经济大萧条的繁荣的前夜，危机没有来临，这个人还可以再做上一段温馨和谐的童年的梦。我所以判断他是从《圣经》里了解世界的概况，是因为这个人的父亲是一名牧师，这给了我谱写诗篇的根据。我还想像在他小小的头脑里，会生出这样的念头：为什么耶和华要做这样的分散人们，用语言隔离人们的事情？耶和华为什么害怕人们的力量大过他自己？因为耶和华无疑是善的，而人们无疑是不善的吗？关于耶和华，我的想像力到此已经穷尽，《圣经》于我，既象是一本天书，又象是一本童话书，深的太深，浅的太浅。而他又与我相隔很远，我无法将他脑子里的问题一一套出来。我是以我对一个人的怀念来写下这一诗篇。

相隔很远很远地去怀念一个人，本来应当是一件另人沮丧的事情，因为这种怀念无着无落，没有回应。可是在我，对这一个人的怀念却变成了一个安慰，一个理想。他记我多远都不要紧，多久没有回应也不要紧。对这个人的怀念，似乎在我心里，划出了一块净土，供我保存着残余的一些纯洁的、良善的、美丽的事物；对这个人的怀念，似乎又是一个援引，当我沉湎于纷纭杂沓的现实的时候，它救我出来了望一下云彩霞光，那里隐着一个辉煌的世界；对这个人的怀念，还象是一种爱情，使我处在一双假想的眼睛的注视之下，总想努力表现得完善一些。这是一种很不切情理的怀念，我从来不用这样的问题打扰自己：比如"这个人现在在哪里"；比如"这个人现在在做什么"。他的形象从来不会浮现在脑海中。在我的怀念活动中，我从来不使用听和看这些感官，我甚至不使用思和想这样的功能，这怀念与肉体无关。这种怀念好像具有一种独立的生存状态，它成了一个客体，一个相对物，有时候可与我进行对话。这怀念从不使我苦恼过，从不曾压抑过我的心情，如同一些其他的怀念一般。当偶然的，多年中极少数一二次的偶然的机会里，传来这个人的消息，这会带来极大的愉快，这愉快照耀了在此之前和之后的怀念，使之增添了光辉。我的怀念逐渐变化成为一种想像力，驱策我去刻划这个人。这是一种要将这怀念物化的冲动，这是一个冒险的行为，因为这含有将我的怀念歪曲的危险。我写下每一个字都非常谨慎，小心翼翼，如履薄冰，我体会到语言的破坏力，觉得险象环生。要物化一种精神的存在, 没有坦途, 困难重重。所以我要选择"诗篇"这两个字, 我将"诗"划为文学的精神世界, 而"小说"则是物质世界。这是由我创导的最新的划分, 创造新发明总是诱惑我的虚荣心。就是这种虚荣心驱使我总是给自己找难题, 好像鸡蛋碰石头。

还是从头说起吧, 我和这个人最初的相识是在一本书里。这本书里有他的一篇小说, 写一个三角脸和一个小瘦丫头, 命运将他们胡乱抛在一处, 让他们相依相靠。这小说打动我的是, 作者将相濡以沫这一种情状写得感人至深, 使这一情义款款的人间常事显得非同寻常。它集浑厚与温柔于一身。我就想: 具有这样的情怀的人该是什么样的一个人呢? 这个人心中的情感源泉是什么? 来自何处? 那时候, 我年幼无知, 喜欢做爱情梦幻的游戏, 可是即使是这样异想天开, 我也不对这个人的情感有所希冀。因为我觉得这个人的情感是一种类似神灵之爱的情感, 而爱情是世俗之爱, 世俗之爱遍地皆是, 俯手可得。象我这样生活在俗世里的孩子, 没有宗教的背景, 没有信仰, 有时候却也会向往一种超于俗世之上的情境。我也会为这种情境制造偶像和化身, 这种制造活动会延续直至成年。在开始的时候, 却是情不自禁, 不知不觉。记得我当时所读的那本书是与我们隔绝的那个岛上人写的文字。我们和那个岛隔绝了多年, 多年里, 我们互相编派着对方的故事, 为了使我们彼此憎恶。憎恶的情感在我们心中滋生增长, 好像树木一样。而我们在树下乘凉。关于三角脸和小瘦丫头的故事打动了我的心, 这是一个难以言说的故事, 一说出口就要坏事似的, 立即会变成一个凡夫俗子的甚至伤天害理的有背传统伦理的街头传闻。为了保护这个故事, 我长期以来把它缄默掉。当人们议论它时, 我总是掉头走开, 从不参加。这是我和这个人最初的结识, 在一本传阅了多人, 翻得很旧的书里。这个人有一种奇异的爱心。"爱心"这两个字是我成年以后才逐渐找到的。这爱心很大, 也很小; 很抽象, 又很具体; 很高, 也很低。象三角脸和小瘦丫头这样的两个可怜虫, 要说他们有什么资格承受这样的爱心呢? 然而是否正因为它是这样不计条件, 它便可大到无限处了呢? 这种爱竟是这样无微不至的吗? 即使是对三角脸和小瘦丫头, 这爱也没有显出丝毫的俯就之感。这爱心奇异地打动了我, 这便是三角脸和小瘦丫头的故事引起我注意的原因。这原因是我成年以后总结的, 当我总结出这样的感动的原因，能够以"爱心"来为这情怀命名之后，我才敢于来复述三角脸和小瘦丫头的故事，并且将这故事作为我对这个人的怀念的懵懂的开端。

三角脸和小瘦丫头的故事是我认识这个人的一颗种子，埋在了我的经验的开初阶段。在这开初阶段，我广泛地接纳各种印象。有浅的，如蜻蜓点水；也有深的，成为一个身心的烙印。这个阶段，我的身心都处在一个建设的时期里。我要进行物质和精神的两种基本建设。我的名和利的思想都很严重，渴望出人头地。我想，于我来说，做一个作家才可名利双收，因为我没有任何技能。而书写一些文字并不能算作技能，也无须本钱，纸和笔都很廉价，我的时间也很廉价。我白天里上班，夜晚就写啊写的。那时候，外面的世界千变万化，对世界的观念日新月异，另人目眩，甚至已经将来自我们自身经验的观念淹没。虽然我及早地了解到，要想出人头地，非得坚持来自个人经验的观念不成，因为只有这样的观念才可有别于他人，突出自己；因为我知道做个作家就是立一个山头，要立自己的山头而不是去给别人的山头添石加土。尽管这样，我也不免为各种观念冲击得摇摇欲坠。幸而我的天真挽救了我，我的天真的另一个同义词是幼稚。我很天真或很幼稚地将我的一些经验写下，没有运用技巧，也不会锻炼文字，甚至不会运用我的观念以作透视，岂知这反倒诚实地表达了我的观念。可是我在思想上却总是奔赴最前列的思潮，这些思潮以其新奇与危险强烈地吸引了我。幸亏我追随这些思潮只是快乐的旅行，而我自己朴素的观念则是我真正的家园。当我写作的时候，就总是回家，写作完了，再去旅行。这时候，我忙忙碌碌，神经兮兮，一会儿快乐，一会儿苦闷，目标基本上是明确，意志也很坚决，还很狂妄。我已经把三角脸和小瘦丫头的故事忘记得一干二净，我并不知道，其实我正在走向这个人。我的一切的努力，其实都是在为认识这个人作准备。当时我并不知道，三角脸和小瘦丫头的故事对于我会有什么意味，在那时候，这是未来的事情。

后来，我在美国见到了这个人，那是在美国中西部，离密西西比河不远的，盛产玉米的地方，有一个大学。每年秋季，便举办为期三个月的"国际写作计划"，来自许多国家的作家们聚集在这里。其时，树叶一层一层地红了。我是跟随我的母亲，一个城市孤儿和解放战士出身的作家，去到那里。我们乘了许多小时的飞机，在旧金山和丹佛转乘，把钟表的指针一会儿拨到这，

一会儿拨到那，昏头涨脑地飞到了目的地。在接机的人群中，有
这个人。他穿一件橘黄的衬衫，他很高大，他有啤酒肚，他的眼
睛很"仁慈"。"仁慈"是我成年以后逐渐找到的两个字，当时我
是用"亲切"这两个字暂时替代的。当时我不仅昏头涨脑，还愣
头愣脑，不仅是时差的关系，一股人造器材，如塑料、橡胶之类
的气味，混杂着人体的化妆品气味，以及车辆的废气，合成一股
我命名为"外国味"的东西，使我眩晕，神志恍惚。后来，每当我
嗅见这股气味，我便陡然地想起到达我的美国的目的地的这一
个不知是黎明还是黄昏的时刻。后来，随了我国现代化的进程，
这股气味也逐步普及，于是，它所唤回的情景便也因为频率过密
而逐渐淡化，就象电影里时常使用的淡出的效果。天边变幻着
不知是早霞还是晚霞的光彩，好像一幅古典浪漫时期的油画。我
茫茫然，磕磕绊绊地随了人群去取行李，上车。在车上，这个人
对我说：你的发言稿我已经看了，我父亲也看了，父亲看了后很
感动，说中国有希望了。我不知道这人的父亲是谁？也不了解
我的发言稿中哪一部分联系了中国的希望，可是这个人的夸奖
却使我心底陡地升起了一阵快乐，这阵快乐甚至使我清醒了片
刻。我那时以为我的快乐是因为引起了一个成年人的注意。我
是那么担心受到漠视，尤其跟随了功成名就的战士作家母亲。后
来，我知道了这个人的父亲，这位父亲的有一段话使我永生难
忘。那是说在这个儿子远行的日子里。远行是一种象征和隐喻
的说法，它暗示了这个人的一段危险与艰辛的经历，这不仅意味
着离家的孤旅，还意味他离开他相对和谐的早期经验，走入残酷
的认识阶段。它具体的所指，大概是"入狱"这桩事吧。在这个
人远行的日子里，他的父亲对他说：

孩子，此后你要好好记得：
首先，你是上帝的孩子；
其次，你是中国的孩子；
然后，啊，你是我的孩子。

在多年以后，这成了我的诗篇的精髓，是我诗篇最核心的
部分。这个人的父亲是一位牧师，我想像他在那个湿润的多
雨的乡村礼拜堂里布道，我的心里又激动又静谧，又温暖又沁
凉。受到他的夸奖，是多么快乐的事情啊！现在我记起来了，那
是黄昏的时刻，夕阳染红了那条蜿蜒的河水，有野鸭子在河岸树

从中嘎嘎地叫，我们遇到了一个气球旅行家，一个老小孩，他表情庄严地徐徐升上天空，他的五彩气球从我们头顶飘扬而去，我觉得置身于一个童话的世界。当我觉得置身于一个童话的世界的时候，我陡然地觉出了身心的疲惫和苍老，我的成年时期陡然地开始了。

在这个年轻的国度里我们文明悠久的东方人从出生那一天起就是成年人了。我们的婴儿时期以及少年时期和青年时期是象蚕蜕那样的东西，只是使我们的形体有所变化，而内中的生命之核则生来俱成，待到蚕做成了蛹，待到蛹做成了蛾子，便是我们的死亡。我们的死亡就象蛾子那样洒脱、美丽、自由，有飞翔之感。我们花尽了一生去培养这个死亡的时刻，充满了感伤神秘的诗意。我们这些诗意的东方人，走在这个国度的玩具般的簇新的房屋前的甬道上，鲜花盛开。绿地静悄悄，树木沿着木桌木椅。忽然间，出现了一个小小的儿童乐园，树桩和圆木搭成滑梯和秋千架，没有人迹和足音。我学着那些调皮的儿童样，坐在秋千上，用脚尖急猝地点地，想作一次高昂的起飞。可是秋千总是沉重地落下，我沮丧地想，我再作不成一个孩子了。那时候我总是穿一条白色的连衣裙，夹着书本，到绿地里去找一张桌子，读书。我其实并不真的去读书，只是为了冒充一个树林子里读书的女孩。我曾经为自己设计过多种角色，林子里读书的女孩便是其中的一个。我特别想做一个孩子，做一个孩子，做一个孩子，而我力不从心。在我们作客的这个城市里，有三分之二的居民是大学里的学生。男孩和女孩们手拉着手，从街上走来走去，在太阳当头的正午，躺在草地上晒太阳，草地上就好像开满了五色的花朵。我最喜爱的图画，是黄昏时分，下课的孩子们在河上荡桨，落日的逆行的光辉将他们照成剪影，从金光灿灿的树丛后面滑行过去。每天这个时刻，我都站在我的面朝河流的大楼的窗前，观看这一幅图画。这时刻又总是宁静异常，所有的声音都为这一时刻偃息着，等这个时刻随了小艇滑行而过，再重新噪然而起，好像一个歌咏。我的临时栖宿的窗户，框下了这幅图画，使我感觉到一个排斥，告诉我：你永远进入不了。

现在我想起来了，我的发言稿的内容大意是：象我们这一代知识青年作家，开始从自身的经验里超脱出来，注意到了比我们更具普通性的人生，在这大人生的背景之下，我们意识到自身经验的微不足道。这个人的父亲所看到的希望是这个吗？我多么惭愧啊！我其实距离这个父亲的希望很远很远，我其实只是在谈一个文学的问题, 我想表达的只是: 如何使我们的小说表现得更深刻。我的意思是: 个人的对其经验的认识是有限的, 要以大众的广阔的经验去参照个人的经验, 从而产生认识。我觉得其中有一个微妙的矛盾, 那就是, 个人的经验是独特的, 却是有限的, 大众的经验可提供无限认识的机会, 可却是普遍的。怎样处理好个人经验的独特性和大众经验的普遍性关系; 怎样处理好大众认识的无限机会和个人认识的有限机会的关系。我一心要做一个作家, 　　我将人生的内容全演化为文学的象征性符号。我欺骗了这个人的父亲的喜悦, 我将要使他失望了。要使他失望的恐惧和悲哀抓住了我的心, 他的喜悦和希望于我已成了一种光荣的象征, 辜负了他会使我遭到莫大的损失, 我不愿受损失。

　　我其实被我的经验纠缠个不休。　我曾经用文学来将自己从这些经验中解救出来。　可是在人家的国度里作客的日子里, 在这些不写作的日子里, 我的经验又回来了。我发现文学无从将我从经验中解救, 我的文学没有这样的力量, 我的文学充满了急功竞利的内容, 它刻求现世现报, 得不到回应它便失去了意义。现在我又记起来, 我是那样喋喋不休, 抓住空子就向这个人诉说我的经验。为了不使他忽视, 我无形中加油添酱, 夸张与强调是我惯用的手法。我不知道我为什么要这样地用自己狭隘的经验去麻烦这个人, 　这个人难道对倾听我的经验有什么义务吗? 我为什么要把这个义务强加给他? 我几乎把我给这个人最初的好印象全砸了, 如不是我是彻底的诚实, 我就要把事情全弄砸了。要是事情全弄砸了, 那是多么糟糕啊! 我现在回想起他那时脸上流露出的、对我无话可说的表情, 这表情曾经使我又伤心又委屈。我非但没有知趣地改变话题, 反而加倍地诉说我的经验, 我的经验在我反复的叙述中越来越偏狭。我为什么要把明明是我自己的经验去折磨这个人呢? 这个人与我有什么关系呢? 很久很久以后, 我才发现, 冥冥之中, 我选择了这个人作解救我的力量, 　我觉得他能够解救我。我拿我狭隘的乏味的经验无休止地去麻烦他, 当他试图制止我时, 我的态度就越发激烈。我那时是多么危险啊! 我如要使这个人心生厌烦, 可怎么办呢? 那时侯, 　我有多少地方足以使他对我失望与厌烦的啊。我想, 他不喜欢我在超级市场推了小车, 情绪昂扬地走在满架的货物之下, 好像在做一次游行; 我想, 他不喜欢我热情地随了大流去野餐, 将煤球装进烤炉, 浇上酒精, 一点即着, 烤着半生不熟的肉饼和玉米棒子; 我想, 他不喜欢我坐在沸腾如开了锅似的看台上, 观看美国足球, 象那些美国佬小孩一样大声疾呼。

看美国足球是一个重要的事件。 虽然于今相隔了很多日子, 那日的情景却历历在目。观众的呼声如同海潮, 此起彼伏, 无休无止。碧晴的天空在我的回想中眩着眼目, 一架银色的飞机在足球场的上方飞来飞去, 好像一只大鸟。啦啦队在球场四周舞蹈跳跃, 敌我双方的吉祥物作着种种挑衅和鼓舞的表演。人们身着黄黑两色的衣帽, 黄黑两色是本城队伍的标志, 两色旗高高飘扬。那是一个寒冷的大风天, 人们裹着毯子, 喝着饮料。风吹透了我单薄的身体, 我从头至尾打着寒战, 牙齿格格响。那真是一个重要的日子, 许多细节在此时此刻浮起眼前, 又退下去, 好象潮汐, 夜涨日消。怀念是一件很好的事情, 它可筛选我们的繁杂的经验, 留出那些最最宝贵的, 聚集在一起, 在我们时常经历的暗淡的日子里, 鼓舞我们。怀念还具有一种很好的功能, 它可使我们的经验, 按照比时间空间更真实的原则, 重新组织, 让这些经验得到转变, 成为最有益的记忆。看美国足球所以是一个重要的事件, 是因为它好像一块磁石, 将一系列松散的事情和人物, 吸引到一起, 组成一个诗篇的结构。构成这个重要事件的, 其实仅只是一句话。

在我们那一期的"国际写作计划"里, 有东德和西德的作家, 有阿根廷的作家, 有巴勒斯坦和以色列的作家, 有波兰的作家, 有南非的作家。我们平时各管各的, 我们各有自己民族的朋友, 这些朋友大多是留学生和移民, 几乎全世界的民族都有自己的移民在这个国家里。举行活动的时候, 我们就聚在一起。这些活动以晚会为多, 我们吃, 喝, 唱歌, 跳舞。人们总是拉我唱歌, 他们不愿意看到一个东方女孩沉默不语。他们以为我这样年纪的女孩, 跟了母亲来旅行美国应当玩得高高兴兴。由于吃黄油与肉类过多的缘故, 我脸上起了许多疙瘩, 这使我看上去就好像一个青春期的大一女生。人们为了使我开心, 真是想尽了办法。他们找来天鹅的洁白的羽毛送我, 他们到猪圈里捉一只干净的小猪塞在我怀里, 他们把我送上康拜因的驾驶室, 让我观看收割玉米, 岂不知玉米地使我热泪盈眶。我泪眼婆娑地看到了我的青纱帐, 在那里我度过了从十六岁到十八岁的少女时光。他们大声地拉我唱歌, 我只得唱一支东北小调, 我唱来唱去只会唱这一支东北小调, 歌词是: 小妹妹送情郎; 送到大门外, 泪珠几千行; 掉呀掉下来, 天南地北你可要捎封信, 莫把小妹妹忘呀忘心怀。每当我唱完第一句, 这个人就用刀叉敲打着碟子, 合上我的节拍,为我伴奏,我至今不忘那叮淙的碟声。我想我们的许多歌都是关于离别的, 关于离别的歌占了我们歌曲的大部分。离别的时候, 要叮咛的话是说也说不完的。离别时的叮咛是我们说话中的一个重要的部分。

在我们那一期的 "国际写作计划" 里,有一个来自东德的男作家,和一个来自西德的女作家。多年之后的今天, 柏林墙已经拆除, 人们自由来往于东西德间, 回述这段往事是多么动人心魄。而象我们这样短暂的微小的生命, 却经历了历史长期准备后形成演变的伟大瞬间, 又是多么幸运。那一个东德人高高大大, 却有一双蓝眼睛, 这双蓝眼睛使他脸上有一种童真的神情。来自西德的则是一个憔悴的女人, 她一生中经历了逃亡和离婚两个大事件。她本是东德人, 后来逃到了西德。他们这两个德国人形影不离, 同进同出。那时候, 每隔几日, 在我们住的公寓里就要举行晚会。在晚会上, 诗人们就用自己的语言朗诵自己的诗歌,各种各样的语言在空中飞行, 变成一种仅仅是听觉的东西, 好像音乐。有一天, 东德人来晚了, 没了座位, 于是他便坐在西德女人的膝上。当我成年以后, 经历了许多离别与重逢的事件, 身心又疲惫又感伤, 再回想那一个场面, 不由怦然心动。那个有着大男孩一样纯洁蓝眼睛的强壮男人, 坐在那憔悴的、早衰的、神经质的、 面目丑陋的、 身心交瘁的女人的脆弱的膝上, 有一股屏除男欢女爱的纯粹的情爱之感, 一股暖流注满我心中。在那很长一段时间里,我一直厌恶这女人, 她总是那样醉醺醺, 泪汪汪, 声音嘶哑。后来她曾经有一次来到上海,当我们见面时, 我明明看见她想要吻我, 可我装作不知道回避了。现在,我的眼前出现了当我回避她的亲吻, 她黯然退之的神情。我还想起那个寒冷的悲惨的夜晚, 当我们大多数人聚在一处举行晚会的时候, 她跳进了冰冷彻骨的河水。事情是这样发生的。在 "国际写作计划" 期间, 每个星期要举行一次报告会,根据地理和行政分成小组。她不愿参加西欧组, 而东欧组不要她参加。她是怀了被抛弃的心情蜇进黑压压的树丛, 走下河岸。夜晚的河岸没有人, 野鸭子也回家睡觉了, 沿河的学生公寓亮着灯, 响着震耳欲聋的摇滚。她想: 她无家可归, 无所归依; 她想: 人人都有家, 野鸭子也有家, 而她没有家。家是我们出门在外的人最重要的东西, 是我们旅行的终极目标, 没有家我们哪儿也去不成。

看美国足球是我那 一次旅行中的 一个重要事件。那沸腾的景象是我有生以来头一次领略。那么多的人, 为了这样一件小事激动和高兴。一个人怎么会这样高兴？高兴竟是一个人的很重要的心情？我和这个后来我所怀念的人坐在沸腾的人群里，我们穿得很单薄，尤其是我，寒风瑟瑟，我们矜持地坐着。有一个吹气的巨大的美国足球在看台上空被人们传来传去。每个人都要去拍打它，拍打了它就好像中了彩似的，欢快无比。巨型的电子屏幕上打出进球的球员的形象，场内一片欢腾，山呼海啸。我努力使自己兴奋，去附和人们的情绪。就在这时，我身边的这个人，忽然站起身，向着狂欢的人群大声叫道：

傻瓜！你们这些傻瓜！

他的声音刹那间被风声和人声的浪潮席卷而去。我忽然发现，我们这两个中国人在这欢乐的海洋中是多么的寂寞，我们无依无靠，我们其实一点都没弄明白他们为什么这样高兴，他们的高兴与我们相距甚远，有咫尺天涯之感。看美国足球是我美国之行中最寂寞的时刻，又是最温暖的时刻，因为在这一刻里，我忽然无比欣喜地发现，我与这个人之间，其实是有一个宛如默契一样的联系，这联系产生于我们各自出生之前就已开始的经验的旅途之间。这经验的旅途恰恰不是我说出来的那些，而是我没有说，或者说不出来的那些，这经验是什么呢？

我现在回想，我的喋喋不休是从那一天中止的。想到我曾说了那么多的废话，我便深觉惭愧，懊恼万分。我现在觉得自从看美国足球以后，我度过了一段心情宁静的旅居生活，我不再去做那种徒然的努力：要参加进人家的快乐时光。快乐是与我无缘的，我对自己说。在人家的国度里活动是一件特异的事情，假如没有宁和的心境几乎一天也过不下来。我想起我们大家为西德女人庆祝生日的晚上，那么多的人挤在她的房间里，肩并着肩，腿挨着腿，就象我们中国上海高峰时间的公共汽车。我们喝酒，聊天，各人说各人的，也不管别人是否听懂。我们中间最活跃的是那个土耳其人，他写诗，他说如今诗人比普通的人多，谁来读诗呢？这情景颇象我们在西德人房间里的情景，说的人比听的人多。我们兴致很高，渐渐忘记我们是为什么而来。西德人很快就醉得差不多了，泪眼汪汪，声音嘶哑。我还想起，我们为波兰的流亡作家送行的那个晚会，也是挤了一屋子，吃着奶酪和香肠。那是一个沉默的晚会，人人言语不多，因为波兰作家前途叵测。他要去的地方是纽约，纽约将上演他的戏剧。纽约这样的地方，每一天都有新的戏剧上演，有人成功，有人失败，好像一个旋转舞台。他好像有无穷的话要与我说，可最终却只是揪住我的头发摇了摇，欲语还休。我们那时还经常在走廊上开舞会，音响震耳欲聋。我们手拉手跳着舞，哈哈大笑，我们还很亲热地你在我手里咬一口，我在你手里咬一口的吃东西，脚下走着舞步。在后来的一次又一次的回想中，我越来越觉得我们这些来自全世界各国的人们的晚会，具有一种相濡以沫和苟且偷欢的味道。我们所居住的公寓八楼，就象洪水中的方舟。我们停留在我们短暂的旅居中，互相悉心照顾、呵护。

旅居之地是象征性的乐园，而所有的旅居之地之中，又首推美国。看美国足球更是一个象征，象征快乐、高兴、无忧无虑、无牵无绊、一身轻松，还象征"傻瓜"。看美国足球是我认识这个人的，继三角脸和小瘦丫头的故事之后的第二个段落。在这个段落里，我对他产生了一种类似于爱情又不同于爱情的心情。说它类似于爱情，是因为我很无理的生出一种要垄断他的念头。那时侯，他象个少先队员似的，喜欢听我母亲讲述战争年代里的英雄故事。根据地的生活令他向往，人们象兄弟姐妹一样生活在一起，另他心旷神怡。那时他刚写作了一篇小说，关于一个革命党人的妻子。而我总是在最关键的时刻尖锐地指出他思想的弊病，以社会主义过渡时期中出现的问题为例证，说明母亲们的牺牲反使历史走上了歧途。他起先还耐心地告诉我，一个工业化资本化的现代社会中人性的可怕危机，个人主义是维持此种社会机能的动力基础，个人是一种被使用的工具，个人其实已经被社会限定到一无个人可言，个人只是一个假象。而我却越发火起，觉得他享了个人主义的好处，却来卖乖。我词不达意，且气势汹汹。那一次我想他是真正的火了。他说：你是要故意反对妈妈！记得他说完这话不愿再听我的分辩，当他走出门去后，我委屈难言，愤怒难言，且又伤心难言。这一刻的心情非常象是失恋，眼泪噎住了我的喉咙。我还很乐意为他办事，有一次他去芝加哥，走之前将一封信和一张支票塞进我房门，请我帮他去交这一月的房租。我是那么兴高采烈，赶紧跑下楼去交房租。去什么地方，有他在场我就高兴，没他在场则有一点儿扫兴。他夸奖我的小说也会使我欣喜万分，我甚至还有这样的想法，为了他我要把小说写得更好。这就是类似于爱情地方。而不同于爱情地方则是我连想都没有想过，要与他去亲热一下，亲热的念头从来不曾有过，千真万确。这是第一点，第二点是我从来不去揣测他对我的心情，我甚至从来没有想过这样的问题：他喜欢我还是不喜欢我。这些地方都与爱情有着本质的区别。他于我，好像是一个抽象的存在，我如何为这抽象的存在命名呢？为这个抽象存在的命名其实就是这诗篇的末尾的警句。

当我写着我的诗篇的时候，怀念一个人使我陶醉。我发现怀念原来是这样完美的一种幸福。这是一种不求回报、不计名利的纯粹的精神生活，这是完全只与自己有关的精神活动，它不需要任何别人的承诺，它使人彻底地沉浸在自我的思想里。一个人的一生中，能够有多少次怀念的机会呢？怀念还是一种很卫生的良好活动，它可使人自动地放弃肉身的欲念，享受超然物质的激动和喜悦，它使感官处在梦幻的状态，而灵魂清醒地行动，灵魂的活动是一场歌舞。我用怀念来虚构这个人的诗篇，怀念具有想像和创造的能力，这也是我的新发现。没有人可以制止我的怀念。在这个城市里，动辄得咎，过马路有红绿灯指挥你，随地乱仍纸屑要罚款，而我的怀念很自由，它想怎么就能怎么。怀念可使我们获得自由，问题是我们有什么可去深深怀念的？我们日益繁忙，并且实用，怕吃亏的思想使我们和人交往浅尝辄止，作我的扩张与发扬使我们对身外一切漠不关心，我们几乎失去所有的建设一个怀念的对象的机会，怀念变成奢侈品一样，开始从大众生活中退出。我庆幸我拥有怀念这一桩财富，我要倍加珍爱，不使我的怀念受到一些儿玷污。

我想起有一日我们去参观农庄，坐在大客车上，他问我回去之后准备写些什么。我回答很难说。他又问，写美国还是写中国？我说，当然写中国。他很高兴地用握在手里的一卷报纸在我的头上敲了一下，说：好聪敏的孩子。我心中激动万分，虽然我用很长久的时间也没弄明白，我的回答中哪一点证明我是聪敏的孩子。为了不辜负他的夸奖，我苦苦地思想：为什么我是个聪敏的孩子。想明白我是聪敏的孩子的原因，是为了使聪敏发扬光大。我思来想去也没有想明白，只是坚定了一条，那就是：回来以后，一定好好地写中国。可是回来之后，我却一篇也写不出来了。我看见中国忽然变成了一个陌生人，我对它毫不认识，我束手无措。我以为去美国旅行中断了我对中国的经验，我还以为旅居美国使我不再适应中国。我苦恼地想：我要对这个人爽约了，我无法写中国了。我这个人的爽约使我难过，这就是怀念在无意识里萌芽的日子。有时候，我因为写不出一个字，在马路上走来走去，心里就想：我做不成聪敏的孩子了。可是我多么想做成一个聪敏的孩子啊！做聪敏的孩子是诗篇的第三段落。这个人一方面要用人类的普遍的苦难，掩埋我的经验，他消灭我的经验，他对我说：看见吗？那阿根廷人，她的母亲是一个精神病患者，那是她终身的监狱。这是他所提示于我的最令我无可奈何的一种灾难，生老病死是人们永远的灾难，谁也规避不了。他的言下之意是：你那一点点经验算得上什么呢？可是另一方，他又以做聪敏的孩子的虚荣心笼络我，去守住我的中国经验，不让我舍弃我的中国经验。我为什么这样重视他的意见？问题在于我需要一个意见，光有我自己的还不够，我正处在一个不那么自信却又不承认的时期里，于是我需要一个意见作驱策，作逼迫，作诱惑，我选择了这个人的意见。我选择中国人作我怀念的对象。可是他给我出了多大的难题啊！

　　怀了做一个聪敏孩子的心愿回到了中国。　分手的情景是那样的草率，简直不值得一提。我们没有说一句告别的话，我站在我的对了电梯的房门口，电梯前涌了一大群美国男孩和女孩，他走进电梯之前连身体都没有转向我。他只是背对着我，伸出胳膊，对着空中挥舞几下，然后就走进了电梯。这几乎不象是分别，一点不严肃，一点不郑重，分手总归要难过一下吧，就算不掉眼泪，也应当相对无言一会，况且，这一分手，聚首的日子遥遥无期，这也就是不象爱情的地方。过了许多许多日子，当怀念这一桩心情酝酿成熟，渐渐地开始了它的旅程，我再回顾这一离别的场景，却发现了其中的意味。我想：他是在向我目送挥别，他是在用他的背影与我告辞。世界上关于分别的叮咛是那么重要地占据了语言的领域，而所有的叮咛在运用了几百年几千年后，已变为陈词滥调，仅仅成为一个仪式。而我们是用仪式之外的仪式，叮咛之外的叮咛来作告别，这才是真正的告别。在这告别之后是真正的分离。我从来不曾想过这样的问题：什么时候再能见到这个人呢？见到不见到这个人是无所谓的事。他所居住的那个岛是我从来没有经验的，我想像不出他在什么样的环境里活动，那是一个特别忙碌的时期，似乎背负着很要紧的责任。我对周遭事物漠不关心。当我坐在我的书桌前，面对一叠空白的稿纸，心里便想：谁能帮助我呢？谁也帮不了我啊！我觉得又孤独又寂寞。我感到我的经验已经被排斥了，我还能在我的稿纸上写什么呢？我常常开了头，然后一泻千里，写得热火朝天。热火朝天后面紧跟着就是深刻的无聊之感。我颓然想到：这有什么意义呢？是什么意义驱使我这样不停地写，不停地写？个人的经验显得那样无聊，那样苍白，被旅居的日子分割地七零八落，断断续续。旅居的日子丰富多彩，而又浮光掠影，可以组织成一个又一个的美妙的小故事。我的做一个大人物的妄想，本能地拒绝小故事。这是一个困难的时期，我每天早晨起来，坐在我的书桌前面。我的书桌好像是我的宿命，我知道逃避不了，于是就乖乖地迎上前去。我从早上太阳升起，直坐到黄昏日落，晚霞满天。我应当拿什么去填满那成万上亿的空格，成万上亿的空格形成一个巨大的茫茫空间，逼迫地等待着我的创造物。我的经验和观念全成了空白，旧的已去，新的不来，好像冬日凋零的树干。我想我大概在我的旅居中，将自己遗失了，那是一个容易发生遗失的地方。在我们的旅行中，妈妈遗失了一个箱子，这个人遗失了护照，一个香港人被抢劫了钱包，还有一个加纳人遗失了一箱啤酒。旅行总难免有些混乱，人生地不熟，又想携带很多东西，还要购买一些纪念品。购买纪念品是旅行的一大内容，也是最容易出错的时刻。纪念品商店是那样琳琅满目，叫人眼花缭乱，目不暇接，往往顾此失彼。这时我越发相信我的困难是造成于旅居之中，我把自己丢了啦！这是一个卡夫卡式的故事，一个"变形记"的翻版。我们的时代多么叫人悲哀，前人已将他们的山头占满了地盘，越是伟大的人，占地面积越大。我们只好去进行侵略，小国我们不屑一顾，大国又实力不够。前人们没有给我们留下一点插脚之地，我们在人家的山头爬上爬下的，世纪末的情绪充斥我们心头，当世纪末的情绪充斥我们心头的时候，我们很奇妙地会生出一股自得的情绪，我们觉得我们已经汇入了国际性的思潮，就象河流汇入了大海，我们因此而在我们脸上抹去了孤寂的表情。于是，世纪末的情绪成了我们又骄傲又焦灼的心情。在我结束旅居回来的时候，这里正流行着国际化的趋势，这趋势使我们轻视我们的经验，夸大了我们经验的局限性，"人类的背景"是我们追求的目标。

　　多年之后，有一个外国人，风尘仆仆，肩了一个沉重的背囊，他找到我后，倾囊而出的一堆杂志，他的背囊转眼间轻飘无比。这杂志的名字叫作《人间》。总共有十来本。大十六开的版面，印刷精美，纸张优良。外国人说，他是从这个人的岛上来，这个人托他带来这些给我。《人间》杂志是这个人和他的知识分子同伴们自筹资金创办的杂志，这杂志的名字让我琢磨了很久，《人间》的含义被我一层一层地释剖。这时候，我的困难时期已经渡过，我情绪平定、内心充实，我有旅行计划和写作计划，有条不紊。我把这堆《人间》放在我的床头，夜晚时分我就翻上一本，怀念的情绪就是在这样的晚上升起。《人间》里有一个曹族少年汤英伸的故事。曹族是一个山地民族，是那岛上的原住民之一。汤英伸退学去都市闯荡，一夜之间犯下了骇世惊俗的杀人罪。从此后，《人间》就开始了整整一年的救援汤英伸的行动。我看见了这个人在这救援活动中的照片，于是，这场救援便忽然地呈现出活动的场面。 这些年的有一个时间里，这个人原来在做这个啊！我欢欣地想。他风尘仆仆地九死而不悔地，在为一个少年争取一个新生的机会，汤英伸少年英俊无比，聪慧无比，笑容清纯而热忱，这样一个少年要偿命，令人心不忍。于是他的母亲车祸受伤，家中经济状况面临困难，于是他只身一人来到都市谋生。但是，我还设想，他可能是从流行歌曲里开始了对都市的向往，他觉得那里机会很多，生活丰富多彩。摇滚的节奏总是使人兴奋无比，热血沸腾，对前途充满希望和信心。因为这时候，我们这里也成了流行歌曲的世界，人们唱着歌，心情就很欢畅。人们在上下班的路上，戴着耳机，让那震耳欲聋的音响，激励我们的身心，驱散日常的疲乏。少数民族通常是能歌善舞的民族，他们没有被大民族整肃的文明同化，在偏远的山地， 保持了原始人的自然的天性。日月星辰是他们的伙伴，草木枯荣教给他们生命的课程。他们将他们的经验编成歌曲，一代传给一代。唱歌往往是他们最重要的社会活动，是他们交往的主要方式。后来，留声机和录音机，多声道的音响传播了摇滚的节奏，机械和电子的作用使得声音具有排山倒海之势，自然之声相形见绌，软弱无力。流行歌曲真是个好东西，它使人忘记现实世界，沉湎在一个假想世界，以未名的快乐和出路来诱惑我们，我设想汤英伸是戴着"walkman"的耳机离开山地，去到大都市。我从照片里看汤英伸有一个吉他，挂在墙上，线条异常优美，文章也告诉我，这是一个热爱唱歌的少年。而他没有想到，离开山地就意味着踏上了死亡之地。死亡是怎样来临的呢？

　　我核算了一下时间，发现大约在汤英伸少年踏上走向城市的旅途时，我正去往乡间。那是我的困难时期，书桌上的空白稿纸天天逼迫我。乡间总是使人想起规避之地，人走投无路时，就说："到乡间去。"我与这个少年隔了遥远的海峡，在连接乡村城市的道路上交臂而过。汤英伸唱着歌儿进城了，他满心都是成功的希望。我去乡间的心情飘摇不定，忽明忽暗。有人告诉我那乡间的关于一个孩子死亡的故事，这故事里有一种奇异的东西，隐隐约约的，呼唤着对我的经验的回忆，受到呼唤的这一种回忆似乎不仅仅是单纯的回忆，还包含有一种新的发现。我就是为了这一点闪烁不定的东西去了乡间，乡间里总是有着许多故事，这些故事带着古典浪漫主义的气息，鼓舞人心。我去追踪的孩子死在前一个夏天，死去的那年他十二岁。他的家庭非常贫穷，那是在农村责任制分田到户实行之前。在我去的日子，他家已经有了一个巨大的粮食囤，占去住房三分之二的面积。这孩子从小到大，没有照过一张相片，他的形象就渐渐地不可阻挡地淡化。后来，有一个画家要为他画像，人们你一言我一语，描绘给那画家听，画家反无从下手了。他还没有留下一件遗物，因为那乡间不仅贫穷还极其愚昧，认为十二岁的死者不宜留下任何东西，留下任何东西将会给其他孩子带来厄运。人们将他的东西一把火烧光。于是，但人们要对他进行纪念活动的时候，就找不到一件实物，可寄托对他的哀思。他是为一个老人而死，这老人无亲无故，已到了风烛残年，一场特大洪水冲垮了他的破旧的草屋。那乡间是个洪水频发的乡间，关于洪水，那里有许多神奇的传说。长年来，孩子一直陪伴老人，好比一祖一孙。这天夜里，屋顶开始落土，土块越落越大，屋梁塌下了。孩子推开老人，木梁砸在他的腹部。这间草屋的所有部分都已朽烂，唯有这根木梁，坚硬如故。孩子被送往医院，十五天之后死去。孩子死去仅是故事的引子，正篇这时才开了头。在这乡间，有一个热爱文学的青年，关于他的生涯他有两句诗可作写照，那就是，"学生为国曾投比笔，粪土经年无消息"。这一回，他将孩子的事迹写成报告，寄到报社，孩子因此而成为一名英雄。那乡间出了一名英雄的消息，顿时传遍了四面八方。许多孩子和大人，步行或者坐车到那乡间去瞻仰孩子的坟墓从小河边迁到村庄的中央，竖起了纪念碑。我就是这些孩子和大人中的一个，以我的经验，我预感到这里面有一个秘密，这秘密在暗中召唤着我。后来，我相信我是有预感的。我预感到事情要有变化了。

现在，我所以要叙述这个故事，是因为在某个时期里，我和这个人的活动都是围绕着一个孩子：他是为了那一个孩子的生，我则是为了这孩子的死。这个人距离我是那样遥远，有时候我也想寻找一些或虚或实的东西，作为我与这个人的联系，好使我的怀念的诗篇有一些逻辑的意义。他在他的刊物《人间》里，开辟了偌大的版面，描述汤英伸少年，使得全社会都注意到一个普通的孩子。孩子杀人虽不算是太平常的事，可却也不算太稀奇。都市里每天都发生许多案件，每个案件都有特别之处。他和他的知识分子伙伴们大声地疾呼：请你们看看这个孩子！看看这个孩子为什么犯罪！当这个孩子犯罪的时候，我们每一个大人都已经对他犯了罪！他们似乎忘记了他们身置一个法制社会，　他们企望以自然世界的人道原则去裁决这一桩城市的命案。他们甚至提请人们注意到几百年前，一个大民族对这个少年所属的小族所犯下的罪行。他们提请人们注意这样一个带有浪漫的诗化倾向的事实：当汤英伸少年向那雇主一家行凶的时候，其实是在向几百年不公平的待遇复仇。他们向这个严厉的法制社会讲情，说："请先把我们都绑起来，再枪毙他。"他们还要这个法制社会注意到天国里的声音："凡他交给我的，叫我连一个也不丢失，并且在末日，我要使他复活。"这个人的身影活跃在这些激越而温存的话语里，使我觉得无比亲切。亲切的心情是他时常给予的，"亲切"二字似乎太平凡且太平淡了，然而千真万确就是亲切。有一张照片，是在汤英伸的父亲，以及这个人，正密切讨论下一步的法律行为。他正面站着，以他习惯的双手撑着后腰的姿势。所有人的视线都紧张，兴奋地看着律师，律师是个身材健壮、运动员形的年轻人，剃着平头，伸出手臂，做出战斗的姿态。这时候，前途叵知，生死未卜。律师是他们中间唯一能够将所有人的理想、感情、愿望付于行动的人。他们所以人都殷切地、热烈地期望于他。这个人在他们中间，使我感到多么多么的亲切啊！交通和印刷业真是个好东西，外国人也是个好东西，他是自信的信使，为分离的人们传递消息，使怀念由此诞生。

让我把那两个孩子的故事说完，汤英伸在城市里的遭遇很不顺利，他没有遇到好人，他遇到的人都黑了心肠，那个职业介绍所首当其冲。他们压榨这个初到城市的山地少年，　欺他年少、单纯、人生地不熟。他们在一夜之间，就将这少年欺压得怒火中烧，焦灼不安，杀人的事情就是在黎明时分发生的。争执是从很小的一件事开始的，似乎是汤英伸要离开他的雇主，而雇主由于已经付了佣工介绍所许多钱，不肯吃这个亏，要扣下汤英伸的行李，这是一个导火线式的事件，汤英伸在一昼夜间积压的怒火如火山一样爆发了。他变得力大无穷，不计后果，他一口气杀了两个大人，一个小孩。他不杀人不足以解气，太阳这时候才升起。他丢下手里的凶器，大约还拍了拍手，好像刚干完一件清扫的劳动。他肯定会有片刻觉得轻松无比，骇怕与懊悔是后来的事情。如前所说，　我那个孩子的故事其实发生在他死亡之后。他活着的时候，几乎没有故事，村人们对他记忆淡薄，只是说这孩子秉性宽厚，为人中义，待那老人亲如儿孙。在他死后，有关于他与老人神秘的奇缘之说在乡间流传，在孩子死后第三个七天，那老人安然城长逝，三七是死者回眸之时，召唤了老人前去会合。老人和孩子的传说本可以很优美，　可是轮回之说却平添一段阴森之气。后来，孩子成为一名英雄，老人和孩子的关系才有了明亮的色彩，　成为一副尊老爱幼、舍身救人的图画。从此，乡间成了英雄的故乡，人们从四面八方来到这里，村庄有了直通城镇的公路。这孩子以他的生命换来了乡间的繁荣景象。　为孩子树碑立传成为热爱文学的青年们争先恐后的事情，当有人去采写孩子与死亡作斗争的一页时，才发现孩子的创口在当时没有受到负责的治疗。这几个人很想以此掀起一场轩然大波，好立惊世骇俗之说。可这个念头被悄然制止，这将使一个光辉的学习英雄运动变成一个阴暗的社会事件。就这样，这小草般的生命的冥灭，演绎出辉煌的故事，而且越演越烈。

　　这个人和他的同伴们，为汤英伸奔走呼号，他们甚至活动到使苦主撤诉。他们说，世间应当有一种比死刑更好的赎罪的方式，要给罪人们新生的机会。在那些日子里，汤英伸的案件妇孺皆知，人人关心。关于案件的判决一拖再拖，给予人们不尽的希望，汤英伸的命运成为了一个悬念，寄托着人们心中最良善的知觉。诗人们提出"难以言说的宽爱"；教育家提出"不以报复的方式"；政治家提出"人文的进步"；历史家提出"优势民族与劣势民族的平等"，人们说：可怜可怜孩子，枪下留人！这是一幅如何激动人心的场面。由于这个人投身其间，甚至处于领先的位置，使得这场运动与我有了一种奇妙的关系。我与这个从未谋面的少年似乎有了一种类乎休戚与共的情感。而我是在一年之后才得知关于汤英伸的消息，这时候一切都有了结局，我只能在想像中体验这另人心悬的过程。这时候，关于我的孩子已有了许多纪念与学习的文章。孩子们吹着队号唱着歌来到乡间，过一个庄严的少年队队日。队日已成为乡间最经常的事件，一听到号角声声，人们便说：孩子们来了。这孩子的死亡事件把我吸引到了乡间，我已经有了相当的阅历，我的阅历告诉我，这事件中有秘密，我意识到调查着秘于我事关重大。后来的事情证明我颇具先见之明，孩子的死亡事件于我恰成契机，它以一个极典型的事例，唤起了我对我的中国经验的全新认识。我的中国经验在此认识之光的照耀下重新变成有用之物，使我对世界的体察更上了一曾楼。我的经验由于孩子的死亡事件的召唤，从那些淹没了我的别人的经验中突现出来，成为前景，别人的经验则成了广阔的背景。我的经验不再是孤立的事件，而是有了人类性质的呼吁和回应。我就象个旅行中人，最终找回了我的失物，还附带有部门的赔偿。我的经验走过那一个从有到无，再从无到有的路程，改变了模样，有了质的飞跃。这就是后来使我名声大噪的《小鲍庄》。

《小鲍庄》的故事刚刚在稿纸上开始了头一行的时候，我就明白做一个聪敏孩子的时候到了。关于做聪敏孩子的愿望几乎被我淡忘，这时想起它来，心里真是无比欢喜。以后的道路一直很通畅，做一个作家的命运几乎不容怀疑。旅居美国已成为我经验的一部分，使我的中国经验有了国际性的背景。就是在我踏上访问欧洲的旅途的这一天，枪毙汤英伸的枪声划破了寂静的黎明的天空，汤英伸的故事正式结束。这个人和他的伙伴们的善心，没有为这少年挽回生命，只给他整整一年焦灼和受尽希望折磨的时间。汤英伸受毙时掌心里紧握着十字架，神父曾对他说："凡他交给我的人，必到我这里来。而我连一个也不丢失，并且在末日，我要使他复活。"这与其是安慰汤英伸，毋宁说是安慰这个人和他的伙伴，因此，他们以"汤英伸回家了……"作最终的文章的标题。我是个现实主义者，任何虚妄的许诺都不会使我动心。现时的问题缠绕着我的头脑，日里夜里我都在作一些可行而见效的计划。访问欧洲是快乐的旅行，我已具备旅行的经验，不再会发生遗失的事件，即使发生我也不会惊慌失措，我深知"塞翁失马，安知非福"的道理。我很注意吸取我所需要的东西，舍弃我不需要的东西。我还会约束不适应带给我的骚动的心情，调节心里的平衡。我过后才知道，在我他踏上快乐旅途的那一日，是汤英伸的死日，那是一九八七年五月十五日，这个人的希望在这一天告终。他的失望无疑对我也是有影响的，我很想对他说：这，就是人间。我还明白了一个事实，从此以后，我与他这两个海峡两岸的作家便分道扬镳。我与他的区别在于：我承认世界本来是什么样的，而他却只承认世界应该是什么样的。我以顺应的态度认识世界，创造这世界的一个摹本，而他以抗拒的态度改造世界，想要创造一个新天地。谁成谁败，可以一目了然。

我们同是号召要救救孩子的鲁迅先生的后辈，他去救了却没有救成，而我压根儿就没有去救，因我知道我想救也救不了。我们俩的孩子都死了，这就是证明。可是，这个人的哀绝却缠绕在我心头。他的告别的那一个挥手的背影，令我有一股哀绝的悲壮之感。这是在我成熟的年头，这样的年头，已很难崇拜谁或者仰慕谁，这年头缺乏精神领袖，是最孤独的年头。我力图排除一切影响，要建立自己独一无二的体系，我否定有谁曾经或者要指导我。我不免有写趾高气扬，目中无人。我一点点没有意识到危险已经潜伏下来，正伺机待发。只是我尚有自卫的本能，那便是在我心底的深处，卫护着对这个人的怀念。我所以冥冥的卫护着对这个人的怀念，是因为我预感到了什么吗？我预感到我所身处的那一个成功之圈，其实是一个假象？我还预感到假象终会拆穿，真象就要来临？我预感到当真相来临的时候，对这个人的怀念可以使我勇敢地直面并超越？我对这个人的怀念究竟是什么呢？是不是有些信仰类似呢？而我有怎么可能会有信仰呢？

　　信仰这样的东西，是如灵魂一样，与生俱来，而我只有一些后天的原则，告诉我这样做，而不是那样做。我所以遵循的原则，是为了避免遭到损失，损失会令我痛心。我的诚实的天性，使我对人坦率，因而也使人对我坦率，这保留了我对人间事物的一些儿信任，然而说有信仰是远远不够的。我的信任是因人而易，因事而易，比较灵活，也比较现实。它不是那么确定无疑，不屈不挠。它有时难免回带给我们失望，但这失望也不会太使我们受挫，我们可以调整方向，并以我们的阅历为这失望做一个注解。而信任却是比较坚固的东西，它没有那么多的回旋之地，一旦它被决定，可说就不再有退路。它无法变通，无法折中，它平白地取消人的自由，使人常常处于两难境地。信仰这东西太庄严，太郑重，于我们轻浮的个性很不合适，如果不是与生俱来，我们就完全没有必要再去背负起它来。因为它是那样绝对，不由就虚妄起来，因人间事物没有一桩不是相当存在，有什么事物是绝对的呢？那只可能是形而上的事物。　在茫茫无一物的空间里，要我们相信有一个人正俯瞰我们的善恶美丑，有一个人正为我们赎罪，我们是否有罪还是一桩说不定的事情，是否有那为我们赎罪的人就更无法确证。　要我们做事为这可疑的存在负责，实在勉为其难。记得在旅居美国的日子里，我曾有一次叫这个人生气。如他这样的涵养与礼貌，这样生硬的语气是罕有的事情。在回想中，似乎就是在他称我"聪敏孩子"的访问农场的一日。其实我是想与他讨论一下信仰这个问题，因为从学术上来说，我对信仰这问题还是有着浓厚的兴趣，我自觉得在这方面的知识很不够，需要补充。为了培养对信仰的感性认识，我几次三番去过教堂，跟随不同的朋友。第一个朋友对我说，基督教中的上帝使人们相信现世的快乐，他尊重人性及人生的价值，这是一个颇通人之常情的上帝。他还举其出身的例子进行证实：佛教的释迦牟尼是迦毗罗卫国的生于蓝毗园的王子，基督则是木匠的生于牛棚的儿子，一是贵族，一是平民。因此，平凡的基督就使信仰这一桩事变得平易近人，成为一桩日常的事情，我们每天都可在每一桩琐细的小事里看到信仰的光辉，并且实践我们的信仰。我跟了他去了两次教堂，牧师对"圣经"的释解使我觉得乏味而平庸，演讲的才能也很一般，并且带有上海郊县浦东的口音。我第二个朋友对我说，世界从微观上说是唯物的，可解的，宏观上则是唯心的，神秘不可知的，比如，谁能回答出地球的第一次推动呢？这朋友是个神秘人物，他的眼睛叵测地在黑夜的灯光下闪烁。他说控制着世界的是一种形而上的力量，因此，上帝是存在的。我想，他的上帝似乎比第一个朋友的上帝要更接近真义，似乎他这个上帝更象上帝。于是，我又跟他重新进入教堂，一连去了四个礼拜日，甚至还安排了与一位牧师的深夜谈话。那牧师很礼貌也很温和，态度不卑不亢，对我所有的问题，他的回答只是一句：你可常来教堂。唯一的例外，是我直率而粗鲁地问他，在我们的文化革命中，他被赶出教堂，去做一名钟表厂工人的时候，他是如何安置他的上帝，他说："请不要问这样的问题。"谈话就此结束，去教堂的生涯就此结束。那一日，在去往某一个农庄的大客车上，窗户外是大片大片的成熟的玉米地，我说："我实在是不懂那些人上教堂是去做什么。"这时候，汽车已达目的地，停在路边，太阳当头，蓝天无云。他忽然站起来，粗声对我说："你多去几趟就懂了"。然后他就下了车，而我就象当头挨了一棒，有点发懵。这是什么话？我在心里对自己说，后来我知道，，这个人的父亲是一个牧师。后来我还知道，耶稣是这个人的朋友。那是在旅行的途中，就是在这个人站在电梯口背身向我挥别之后，我们各自踏上不同的旅途。我们在旅途中常常交臂而过，他刚离开这个城市，我就到了，或者我刚离开这个城市，他就到了。在旧金山的著名中国书店里，董事们说，我可以挑选几本书。在我挑选的书中就有这个人的一本自评，书中说:"面目熏黑的,饱受风霜的,贫穷的,忧愁的,愤怒的,经常和罪人、穷人和被凌辱的人们为伍的,温柔的耶稣,成了我青年时代的偶像。"

人近中年的时候,要交一个彻心彻肺的朋友,显得热情不足,理智有余。这时候,我已进入了诗篇的第四段落,段落大意是耶稣和信仰。其实他让我多去几趟教堂,和那上海国际礼拜教堂的牧师对我的回答是同样的,可是我却对这个人偏听偏信。为了给去教堂打好基础,我就拜读《圣经》。我打开新旧全约第一页,"创世纪"的第一章"神创造天地";"起初,神创造天地,地是空虚混沌的,渊面黑暗。神的灵运行在水面上。"我一下子想到马克思的《共产主义宣言》,起首一句就是:"一个幽灵在欧洲游荡。"我想,马克思的写作手法会不会受到"圣经"的影响,这想法亵渎得吓人,因为大家都知道马克思是个无神论者,幸而那是在一个全面开放,思想自由的时代,我还想像"神的灵运行在水面上"的姿态是否有些接近冰上芭蕾,冰上芭蕾简直美得不可思议,不象人间的形态。我头脑中的俗念过多,象这样抽象的东西,必须找到具体的对应物,才可被我理解并接受,无论如何,"创世纪"还是比较对我的胃口,神将光和暗分开为昼与夜的那一行甚至使我激动。那情那景在我脑海中,象是一个豪华的舞台,用顶灯、耳灯、脚灯,造成光和暗的效果。但是,"创世纪"过于象一则神话,当然是伟大的神话,耶稣其人于我永远是神话人物,好比希腊神话中的宙斯,中国神话中的盘古,于我的现实生活远远相隔了一个迢迢的隔障,好比形神之间,永难通行。要与那个神灵的世界交往,于我是困难重重。建设一个连接形神两界的桥梁是我有一个时期的主要工作,我的工具就是《圣经》,还有一些解释《圣经》和耶稣其人的书籍。我总是勤勤恳恳地打开《圣经》,每一次都从头读起:"起初,神创造天地,地是空虚混沌的,渊面黑暗。"然而,事情越来越接近于学术的研究。我弄清了耶稣所代表的哲学思想,以及其哲学思想对于西方现代化的作用,我还弄清了基督教文化的这一个概念。研究《圣经》丰富了我的知识的库藏,可是,通往神灵世界连门都没有。

有一段时间里,我真的很怀念他,怀念他的这一种心情,有时会使我觉得,开始往那个神灵世界接近了。这纯粹是一种感觉,待我要以逻辑的推理去证实和挽留其存在,这感觉便不翼而飞,烟消云散。我如今的工作实在是一桩危险的工作,我要想以现实的语言去描绘这一种感觉, 失败就在眼前, 可是怀念他是唯一的通往神灵世界的可能。那神灵世界使我向往, 我试图沿了对他的怀念跋涉。前途茫茫, 对他的怀念是唯一的指引。在我对他怀念之际, 还生出许多希望, 我希望他在曹族少年汤英伸受毙之后, 不要消沉, 不要悲伤, 我希望他真的相信: "汤英伸回家了", 而且旁边伴有温柔的耶稣。假如连他都不再相信了, 我还有什么希望可言呢? 我把我的很多的不切实际的沉重的希望交托给他的背上, 请他为我负着, 我还没快乐够呢! 我要快乐是要个没够的! 我一年一年的长成, 时间与经历日积月累。我无法不感觉出这重荷, 我只是想脱卸掉。一旦脱卸, 又觉出它与我血肉相连。谁能承得起呢? 谁又有承起它的义务呢? 现在, 我算不算渐渐接近于耶稣钉在十字架上受难的真义了? 我不知道。

但是有一点后来我却知道了, 那就是我去教堂的生涯还将延续。那是在德国的日子里, 我从南部走到北部, 看见教堂我就要进, 那是出于文化的兴趣。南部的教堂金碧辉煌, 北部的教堂肃穆庄严; 南部的教堂使人感受到天堂里的热烈气氛, 北部的教堂使人体验到人世的艰苦卓绝; 南部的教堂使人想到热爱艺术的路德维希二世, 北部的教堂使人想起推动历史的马丁·路德。德国的教堂以几个步骤来启迪我的觉悟, 第一步是在巴伐利亚的乡间。我走进一个农人自家的小教堂, 灰色的朴素的尖顶在蓝天绿地之间, 含有一股天真的诚挚。是正午的时间, 四下里静悄悄的, 没有一个人, 我们推开教堂的小木门, 看见基督在前方的神龛里受难。耶稣霎那间变得无比亲近, 他佑护着人们小小的丰收的希望, 令人心动。教堂的四壁是新近粉刷的, 白而光洁, 散发出石灰水的气息。我想像那一个农人就象打扫他的牛栏一样, 打扫着这个教堂, 他还在早晨或者傍晚来看望一下耶稣, 他望着耶稣就好像望着他的兄弟。耶稣在我旅行德国的日子, 先化身于平凡之中, 似乎向我伸出了暖和的手, 以他的手牵住我的手, 一步一步向前深入。然后我到了德国的北方, 教堂的钟声从四面八方响起, 在阴雨霏霏的天空中回荡轰鸣。紧接着鸽子飞了起来, 如同凶恶的鹞鹰, 扑啦啦啦地腾起在这城市上空, 这是令人惊惧的一刻, 似乎有一样看不见又触摸不着的庞然大物, 以迅雷不及掩耳之势, 铺天盖地而来。一股绝望掠过心头, 一个声音被压抑在心底, 那声音是: 无处可藏, 无处可逃啦! 教堂的无数的钟声在每时每刻共同响起, 有的由远及近, 有的由近及远, 有的雄浑, 有的嘹亮, 有的高亢, 有的低沉。那城市的天空永远有着雨云的游行, 风声浩荡而过, 无数的船只沉没海底,　船的残骸在海面飘荡。在这巨大的钟声里,　我感到孤独无依, 且厄运重重,　很想牵拉一个人的手,　就象黑夜里的行路人。可是耶稣忽又远去, 他消失在北方教堂深远的前方, 他无影无踪。我只可想像他在伸手不见五指的前面,　其实离我很近很近, 我尽可以放大胆子。我就象小时候,　一个人在夜里走路, 我总是大声地说话和唱歌, 制造一个伙伴, 陪我走完孤旅。最后的去教堂是在中部的一个小镇, 郁金香盛开。我在小镇住了七日, 为了消除旅行的疲劳。小镇的生活很安宁,　我常去的地方有三处: 一处是中心广场, 广场上有日夜不息的喷泉, 傍晚时, 大人就带着孩子来散步, 吃着冰激凌。我常去的第二处地方是坟地, 坟地象一座美丽的花园, 我在墓地走来走去, 看着大理石墓碑上的生日与卒日, 心里想: 这是一个老人, 那是一个孩子, 我想墓地就象生命终点盛大的聚会,　大约这就是墓地鲜花的由来。我去的第三处地方是小镇的教堂。　教堂是小镇上最古老最庞大的建筑, 风格属于十三世纪中叶的哥特式, 在小镇的街道上投下了大片的荫庇。每天早晨有妇女在那里作义务的清扫,　下午则有人在那里默祷, 我曾经无意地闯入人们的默祷, 见那都是一些年过七旬的女人。她们双手紧握, 搁在前排的背椅上, 望着教堂深处的耶稣。耶稣悬挂在深远而幽暗的十字架上,　长窗上的彩色玻璃将天光变幻成混沌的光色, 缓缓地旋转, 成为光柱, 纵横相交, 充斥于人们与耶稣之间。她们的眼睛有些哀愁, 有些忧伤, 却很安宁。她们与耶稣长久的凝望中, 似乎渐渐地立下了某种契约, 他们都将彼此忠诚地践约。我最后一次进那教堂, 也是我最后一次进所有的教堂。　至今我也没有去考察那是一个什么日子, 是一个什么样的人神之间的约期。我冒冒然闯进教堂, 是出于饭后百步走, 活到九十九的习俗。我从广场走到墓地, 又从墓地绕到教堂。教堂里灯火通明, 坐了好些人。我好奇地在长椅上坐去一个位子, 心想: 将有什么好戏要开场呢？人们陆陆续续进场, 有的还脚步匆匆。这时节, 小镇的生活已使我深感无聊, 开始期待这里能发生一些离奇的事情,　好使我的旅行增添历险的色彩。这时, 我的兴致勃然而起, 蠢蠢欲动。人们穿了整齐的服装, 表情愉快而郑重其事, 就象度一个节日。有年轻的孩子兴高采烈地跑来, 嘻嘻笑着。一个黑衣的神职人员在讲台上说话, 象是预报节目, 因为显然话剧还在后头, 他也显然是一个龙套的角色。教堂的门一会儿开, 一会儿关, 进来的人不断。现在我在教堂里已经很轻松也很自在, 去教堂已变得稀松平常, 我不再把教堂想像成庄严的圣地, 或者哲学的课堂, 我将它当作聚会的场所, 歇脚的地方。我看看这个人, 又看看那个人, 这里聚集的人是我在小镇上所见过的最多的人。他们彼此都熟识, 笑容满面, 待人和气。他们互相有眼睛打着招呼, 安安静静地等待。后来, 红衣神父出来了, 管风琴响起在高大的穹顶之下。在我身后坐有一个四口之家, 一父一母和两个儿子, 两个儿子都是畸形, 手脚扭曲, 表情呆滞。但他们初进来的时候, 并没引起我的注意, 我的注意力全在等待上, 我正等得有些不耐烦。可是, 当一切开始以后, 我忽觉得那两个畸形孩子的鼻息吹拂在我的后颈窝, 他们在我身后呢! 我想到。我感到背上有一股力量在压迫, 我忍不住回过头去。那一家四口肩挨肩坐成一排, 两个孩子在中间, 父亲和母亲在两边。当我回过头去, 投向他们好奇的目光, 得到的回答则是他们安详与友爱的眼神, 那父亲和母亲向我微微笑着, 我顿时也成了他们呵护下的孩子。这时, 有一种感动在我心里升起, 同时还有一种恍悟, 我告诉我自己: 看哪! 这就是为什么要去教堂! 去教堂的事情其实并不神秘, 也不深奥, 去教堂的事情其实很简单。可是, 事情到此, 我只弄明白了, 人家为什么去教堂, 我还弄明白了, 人家的教堂在哪里。可是, 我的呢? 我又为什么要去呢?

去教堂的生涯这时候正式结束, 这个人让我多去几趟的任务似已圆满完成。信仰作为一个名词, 我已彻底了解, 耶稣其人, 我也大概了解。所有的准备都已做好了, 而那时候, 我无忧无愁, 一帆风顺。我这样努力都有回报, 可谓种瓜得瓜, 种豆得豆。这使得我轻薄狂妄, 目中无人。那是一个任性孩子的快乐时光, 我想怎么就怎么, 谁也拿我没办法。有人对我说: 你不要太开心了! 我听见也装没听见。我完全不需别人的支援, 倒有许多人要我对他们作支援, 支援别人的感觉无比美好, 高高在上。那时候, 没有人能够想到我其实生活在一个假象中, 没有人预料到那假象转瞬即逝。叫我"不要太开心了"的是个女孩, 她的话里充满了妒嫉, 她长得没我好, 写得没我好, 朋友没我多, 她的生活很寂寞, 她让我"不要太开心了"完全话出有因, 情有可原。连她自己也没有想到, 她的话里其实含有先知先觉。这是一个忘本的时期, 我渐渐远离我那些较为沉重的经验, 而获取了快乐的经验。我享受现世的成功与快乐, 宣扬人的永恒的困境, 这带有隔岸观火的味道。 由于我关于人和世界的困境的新发现，便又享有了一次成功与光荣，这带有鹬蚌相争，渔翁得利的味道。我在开拓个人经验的旗帜下，放弃了我个人的经验。那日子是十分的好过，我兴冲冲地过了一日又一日，好不知晓这日子已临界终点。我完全记不起"月满则亏，水满则盈"的古训，深信不疑好景长在，好宴不散，彻底违背了事物发展的规律。于是，当那消沉的日子来临，我一无准备，束手无措，我不知道该做什么。我只是坐在那里，赌气什么都不干，等待着事有转机。

　　对这个人的怀念被我消沉的心情埋没了。情绪消沉其实时有发生，这一次未必特别严重，也许会如从前的每一次一样，安然度过。这一次情绪消沉的发作其实是长期积累，好像是积劳成疾。多年来，我的生活渐成规律，或是出门旅行，或是闭门写作。这种出门旅行和闭门写作在起初的阶段有一种强烈的对比的效果，动止结合。这两者起先安排得还不那么协调，互相有写影响，彼此侵犯了时间和精力。然后，节奏逐渐调整，一抑一扬，一张一弛。就在节奏协调的同时，我心里慢慢滋生出一种厌倦。这倦意其实与日增长。我无意地夸张我的快乐，意欲使自己视而不见。我有心制造喧嚣的空气，好掩饰内心的烦闷。我其实早就发现旅行渐渐引不起我的兴趣，近两次的旅行，我都来去匆匆，盼望早日回家。回到家又很无聊，写作日益成为功课。我倦意沉沉，且又忙碌异常。我好像已经进入轨道，脱身不去，身不由己。我一天忙到东，忙到西，心中却落寂无比。有时候，我会无缘无故地大发脾气，不吃饭，不睡觉，光看电视；或者相反，只吃饭，只睡觉，就是不看电视。我不看电视也不让别人看电视，这时候，我们家便寂静得象一座坟墓。好在那时候一切照常进行，没有哪一个关节受阻，我已具备了惯性，能够照常在轨道中运行。运行的同时又产生新的惯性。就这样，　节节推进。情绪消沉的事件发生于一件小事，这样的小事时有发生，屡见不鲜。在往常的旅行的季节里，我照例去旅行。我其实从心底里不愿作这次旅行，盼着早去早回。我不知道为什么，心里总是很急躁的，好像有什么东西在追赶我，使我马不停蹄，欲罢不能。我很不耐烦地提了一个箱子，箱子里马马虎虎放了几套裙子和几本签名本。这次旅行遭到了受阻的命运，原因是交通堵塞。在我生活的这个大城市，车辆增多，道路狭窄，行人大多数不遵守交通规则，喜欢乱穿马路，交通堵塞是日常事件，完全不足以大惊小怪。在我后来的回想中，这一个堵车事件越来越带有象征的含义。它意味着我的生活面临一次受阻与中断，它意味着我的旅行和写作相继的节奏被打乱了。　惯性将我冲出轨道,我变成一颗离轨的行星,粉碎成无数的陨石,散失在宇宙之中。从此,我的生活漫无轨道,迷失了目标。我应当去哪里?做什么?我每天都问自己好几遍,得不到回答。

　　堵车事件是我长期以来的一个真实的新经验,我重新一次地从实际中而不是从小说创作中体验了迷茫与消极的心情。这时候,对这个人的怀念还没有破土而出,它被许许多多俗事压埋着,见天日的一天还没来临。对这个人的怀念在黑暗中等待着我的寻找,我其实有几次险些儿摸索到了它的温暖的手臂,却又万分之一毫米之差地错过了。它很耐心地、宁静地、不出一声地等待着我的发现,而我总是发现不了它。这时候,我是多么多么绝望,我以为这世界上没有一桩事能拯救得了我了。我奇怪我这么多年忙忙碌碌,欢欢喜喜地过着没有目标的生活,我奇怪我这么多年　自以为很有目标其实没有一点目标,我还奇怪这么多年有目标的生活却象一场梦一样转瞬即逝,睁开眼睛才发现那目标是一个梦境,　这个梦境醒来之后甚至没有留下一点记忆。我有时候还不明白为什么一次普普通通的堵车事件竟会对我的处境有这样致命的破坏力,它几乎将我瓦解,难道我竟是这样脆弱,不堪一击,就好像一棵外表完好、内部已经蛀空的树,霹雳一声,便将它拦腰击断。按照概率的原则,在我们这个人口日益增多,交通日益发达,因而日益拥挤的世界上,平均每个人都　应当遇到一次或两次的堵车事件。所以,我的堵车事件并非偶然,而属必然了。这是我命中注定的安排,我无法回避,无论我怎样强调客观原因。因此,堵车给我造成的延误时间与改变线路,无疑是循了我的命运的轨道。这是我不应该埋怨的,我总不能把概率分配给我的堵车机会推给别人,而侵占别人的畅行的机会,这是不公平的,并且带有强权的色彩。我想,要度过这个难关,首先是要承认和接受受堵的命运,然后向命运挑战,这是唯物主义者的人生态度。

　　这一个认识命运的过程相当漫长,我为此去作了一次国内长途旅行。我找一些极其荒凉的地方去,乘坐了班车,在崎岖的山道上颠簸。汽车盖满了黄色的尘土,　破破烂烂,摇摇晃晃,汽车里挤满了灰尘扑扑的农人。车从山的狭缝中穿行,忽高忽低,忽左忽右。在这一时期里,黄土地成了人们热情向往的地方。那些在城市里,被社会责任和生活琐事折磨得身心交瘁的人们,背了简单的行囊,穿了牛仔服和旅游鞋,来到这里,希望寻找到人生的真义。在开春的季节里，漫山遍野就响起了信天游的的歌声，人们一手扶犁，一手扬鞭，驱策着耕牛，在贫瘠的土地上播种。然后，信天游的悠扬的歌声便回荡在每一个山坳里。信天游是一种上下句题的民歌，上句起兴，下句立题，唱的大体是爱情。哥哥和妹妹是它们对情人的称谓，体现出人类早期婚姻爱情的状况，使得城里来的文明人非常感动。如果是在正月里，便可领略到闹社火的热烈风光。人们在草也不长的山坡上，打着腰鼓，举着伞头，你唱我合，你问我答。这种质朴的欢乐可使人的心灵得到一次简化和纯化。人们在这歌声中不由会想：我们已经离人类的初衷走开得多么遥远了呀！艺术家们还到这里来寻找艺术的发源。他们收集剪纸，将剪纸中朴素雅拙的造型与现代艺术中的抽象和变形联系在起来。他们收集民歌，赋予现代的摇滚节奏，在艺术上走一个大回头的步伐，顿时抛下了许多人而独占鳌头。人们丧失目标的时候，最好的办法是回到出发地再作第二次远足。怀了这样的想法，去黄土地的人群日消夜长，源源不绝。我是去黄土地的人群中的一个，我也背着简单的行囊，穿了牛仔裤。在寻找初衷的行为下，还暗暗藏着做一个现代人的念头。寻根行为的本身其实就表明了对现代人立场的坚持。"寻找"这一桩行为是在"失去"之后才发生，我们特别要强调寻找，也就是特别在强调失去。

那时侯我还并不明白我去黄土地是为了找寻什么，我也不明白我为什么找了黄土地作我的旅行之地。踏上黄土地后我心情压抑。那时灶火已经闹过，春耕还未开始，田野里静悄悄没有一个人，没有一头牛，也没有一声信天游的时节。满目黄土沟壑，岩壁上没有一星绿意。风沙很大，遮天蔽日。汽车"笛"一声过去，有时可见绵羊如肮脏的棉球匆匆地滚下路边的干沟，一个牧羊人站在呼啸的灰沙里，头上扎了黑漆漆的白羊肚手巾，背上系了一个小包，里面大约放了中午的干粮。他睁着眼睛，木呆呆地望了我们的班车过去。这沟壑土地使我的心情沉闷，尤其当我站在黄河边，望着对岸大片大片的黄色丘陵，如同凝滞厚重的波涛，如同波涛的化石，它们压迫着我，使我透不过气来。这全然不是另人愉悦的风景，它使身在旅途的人更感到孤寂和郁闷，而且心生畏惧，那黄土随时都有可能波涛涌起，化作黄色的岩浆，把一切卷走，无影无踪。据说，黄河总是给人怀古的心情，可使人想起列祖列宗以及列子列孙，变成历史中的承上启下的一环。而我那时站在黄河边, 却感到从未有过的孤独, 我觉得天地恒古只有我自己, 没有人陪伴我, 没有人帮助我, 谁能帮得了我呢? 历史在书本上还可见声色, 到了黄河边上, 一切尽入茫然之中。我那时侯发现, 到黄土地来寻根真是一句瞎话, 纯是平庸的艺术家们空洞想像与自作多情。而我的选择又盲目又带有趋时的嫌疑。我顿时变得无根无底, 象个没娘的孤儿。为了寻根, 反而失去了根, 这难道就是我黄土地之行的结果? 后来, 有人建议我去抽签, 抽签就象是剧情的预告, 这使命运变得象戏剧。我觉得不可不信, 也不可全信, 但这确是一个不坏的旅游项目, 所以也就欣然前往。

那是去佳县的日子, 那天的印象至此已经混淆, 什么是前, 什么是后, 我有些动摇。不管怎样, 关于佳县这地方, 我想来个内容简介。据志书载宋元封五年, 北宋王朝在此修筑佳芦寨, 以防击西夏入侵, 这便是今天的佳县。它矗立于山头, 四面悬崖峭壁, 高临黄河。从此, 宋、夏、金在此激烈争战一千年。这里的风景确实壮观, 它唤起人们对古典战争的悬想。在古代, 人们利用天然的屏障为战争的工事, 因此, 所有被选择作战场的地方全都雄伟险峻, 气势凛然, 现代的战争再不会留下如此壮观的舞台了, 现代战争也不再有浪漫主义的气氛了。在佳县的那一日正是个大风天, 风声叫人想起了铿锵的兵器声, 黄沙漫卷, 遮天盖地, 想像战争场面激动人心, 热血沸腾且确保安全。我至今已记不清看城墙和抽签谁先谁后, 这两桩事合在了一起, 变成了同一桩事。只记得看城墙是在回头的路上, 我们走下佳县居高临下的街路, 走到黄河边上, 去的时候我们没有注意, 我们是穿过了城墙, 墙洞犹如深长幽暗的隧道。我们走出城门去看黄河, 这是无数个看黄河的日子里的最后一个。当我们从黄河边回来, 转身的那一瞬间, 佳县的城墙陡地出现在眼前, 就在这一刹那好像有雄浑无边的悲歌在耳边响起, 血流成河的场面好像出现在了眼前, 我忽然无比清晰地想到一千年的战争, 一千年这个漫长的数字跳上我的脑海, 战争这个宏伟的名词跳上我的脑海。一千年的战争是什么意义哪! 我问着自己, 我望着黑压压的巍峨的城墙默然无语, 城墙与天空联接的那一刹另人激情涌动, 城墙与峭壁联接的那一刹也另人激情涌动, 悲歌动天感地, 绵绵不绝。这时候, 我似乎已经抽过了签, 签上的文字在这一时刻响起在耳畔。那是在黄河崖腰上的一个宋代荒寺里, 一个看寺的老人为我摇着签筒，他嘴里喃喃地说：这是远道来的客，这是从很远很远的上海来的客——他的声音忽然使我自感孤零，我想我是个逆旅中客，我想人的一生其实都是在逆旅中而且是很远很远的旅途。老人让我跪在案前，那是一个很小而偏僻的寺，临了黄河，风声呼啸，老人的呢喃带有一股宿命的悲怆的意味。他说：这是远道来的客，有什么不懂规矩的地方请多多宽谅。我顿觉自己成了孤独无依的孩子，真正的孩子，我这个孩子在这世上艰难重重，一步一个坑，我的眼泪充满了我的眼睛，佳县的城墙陡然竖起在了眼前。我忘了抽签和城墙谁先谁后了，城墙的上空，足有成千上万只野鸟在飞翔，遮蔽了天空，杀戮声贴地而起，"一千年的战争"这一句话在我脑海里轰响，这是人类的命运吗？山河其实是战争的工事，它料定人类必定战争吗？

当我写着这诗篇的时候，海湾战争刚刚结束，这战争正合了一个十五世纪的大预言家的话：人类将为黑色液体而战。和平就好像是战争中的休憩，犹如山和山的缝隙。这时候，怀念已经充斥了我的身心，我心里已经平静下来，回到了以往的日常生活之中。表面上似乎一切如旧，实际上事情已经大不相同。在夜深人静的时候，是我思想飞翔得最为遥远的一刻，我会想起我有一位朋友，他写过一部诗篇。在诗篇中，他将一条河流作为他的图腾，以一个现实的故事作象征。我读了那诗篇横加指责，注意力全在那个现实的故事，说这写得不对，那也写的不对。其实这故事对不对是另一件事，重要的是这故事后面的图腾象征。而我这一个现代人完全不明白什么是图腾，图腾有什么用。那朋友从旁听来我的批评，这批评经人加工且又似是而非。从此，他就与我绝交。他想他从血管里流淌出来的诗篇竟遭我这样践踏；他想在这个实利的世界上，有多少人舞文弄墨，做着文字游戏，这些游戏这样五光十色，绚丽多彩，掩埋了真正从血管里流淌出来的诗篇。在这样的夜晚，我检讨着自己，可是也心生委屈。我想，并不属那些游戏的朋友，我也诊视血管里流淌的东西。可是血管里流淌的东西有浓有淡，有深有浅，有多有少，有的象火一样可以燃烧，有的却象水可以扑灭火。凡是从血管里流淌出诗篇的人都应结为伙伴，而不应互相误会，互相生气。我还想到图腾这一样东西，我想如何才能找到图腾？后来我明白，寻找图腾，只有一条途径，那就是：需要。我猜测这个朋友需要图腾开始于什么时候，我对他的经历一无所知，我不知道他经历了一些什么，这于我最终还是一个谜。他已经去了很远的地方，飘洋过海，留下一些诗篇今后还将再留下一些诗篇，这些诗篇包括有两种话题,一种现实的,另一种则不是现实的。非现实的那种隐藏在现实之中, 有些扑朔迷离。人们愿意接受那个现实的话题,因为它近乎情理,接近生活,比较好懂,而那个非现实的话题, 由于它超越了常人的理解力,比较艰涩,比较困难,而它的藏匿却为那个现实的话题增添了神秘的美感, 这一时期他的诗篇引起人们广泛的兴趣。人们争相解说,你说你有理,我说我有理,热闹非凡。他是那一个时期最最另人瞩目的诗人,关于他的诗篇有无数中阐释和理解,面对这一切,他的回答只有两个野蛮的字: "我操!" 后来, 他似乎有些按捺不住,那个现实的象征的话题逐渐简化, 而那个非现实的被象征的话题渐渐水落石出,最后, 那个好懂的话题终于退身而去,只留下那个艰涩的非现实的话题。他的诗篇失去了人心,人们觉得他丧失了才能,甚至他自己也觉得他丧失了才能。可我知道, 他的诗篇有无穷的才能,他的诗篇全是他血管中流淌出来的东西,装饰物几乎不存一点,那是可以燃烧的诗篇,所以那也是危险的诗篇。他的诗篇实在很不好懂, 那里全是他最隐秘的个人的事情。我研究至此,只有一点发现,那就是他的现实话题是母亲,而非现实的话题则是父亲,"父亲"是他给于那条和的最崇高最血脉相连的名称。这是我了解他为什么需要图腾的唯一线索。后来, 我也有了这种需要;后来, 我明白我去黄土地, 其实就是为了这个需要。可是我是一个在近代上海长大的孩子,我满脑子务实思想,我不可能将一条河一座山作为我的图腾, 我的身心里已经很少自然人的浪漫气质我只可实打实的, 找一件可视可听可触觉的东西作我的图腾。　我必须有一些人间的现实的感情作为崇拜的基础。　因此,我去黄土地基本可说是失望而归。回来之后,我的心情并未得到多少改善,甚至还更糟糕,我的郁闷、焦灼似乎更加强化与加剧,我变得很容易激动情绪忽高忽低。后来,我知道,其实这便是去黄土地的效用,这效用的内容是感动。这也是这一段落的题目。

　　我的心如同板结的地块,受到了震动。我后来回想, 黄土地给予我的感动其实又深又广。　感动这一情感已经离开我很久。生活在小说的世界里,我生产种种情感,我已经将我的情感掏空了,有时觉得自己轻飘飘,好像一个空皮囊。当我在现实中遇到幸或不幸,我都没有心情为自己做一个宣泄。我的心情全为了虚拟故事用尽了。我没有欢乐,没有悲哀,我有的只是一些情绪的波动,比如着急,比如恼火,比如开心,比如伤感,这只是生活的一些作料,不会伤筋动骨。现在,我内心渐渐地被一些不快的情感充实了。最初充实我心中的是不快的情感，是因为不快的情感具有极大的冲击力，它们可以冲破板结的地块。我轻松了许多，最初的充实使我感到不堪重负，我难免要夸张我的不快的情感。夸张不快情感使我心生怜惜，这是一个自怜自爱的可悲的小家子气的时期。黄土地的功迹在于击碎了我的这种蹩脚的自怜的情绪，它用波浪连涌的无边无际无穷无尽无古无今的荒凉和哀绝来围剿我的自怜，最后取得了胜利。至此，对这个人的怀念的一切准备，已经成熟。我们走过了"三角脸和小瘦丫头"，"看美国足球"，"做聪敏孩子"，"耶稣和信仰"，"感动"这样五个段落，来到了终结部分。

　　终结的部分又象是开头的部分，因为没有这部分，以上所有段落都不会存在，事情似乎就是这样开头的。有一天，记得冬天里一个作雪的阴霾的天气，有人打电话给我，说这人正在虹桥机场的候机室。他本来是飞往北京，由于天气关系，中途在这里降落，不知什么时候才可在这里重新起飞，他对那人打听我。那人为了找我的电话，花费了很长的时间，我感到一阵剧烈的心跳，想与他通话的念头忽然无比强烈。我立刻查询虹桥机场的电话，114查询台总是忙音接着忙音，我几乎绝望。我打电话给所有的朋友，问他们是否知道机场的电话，回答均是不知道，然后说帮我去打114查询台。 我所有的朋友在这一时刻一起在打114查询台，我们完全忘记了结果是大水冲了龙王庙，自己人犯了自己人。但这一刻一定是无比的壮观，几十个朋友同时在打114，114这一时一定如同开了锅。最后我终于得到虹桥机场候机室的电话，电话打去，回答说这个人的飞机刚刚起飞。我不知道这样阴霾浓厚的天空里是否还能飞行，也许阴霾之上竟是阳光普照。放下电话，我竟然很平静，我忽然想到一个问题，假如他在，第一句我应当说什么？从这日起，我一直在想，见了他，第一句话当说什么。我知道他十日以后还将来上海，那时侯，第一句话说什么？我感到这真是困难的一刻， 我简直有些知难而退。我想这一刻一定有些难过，还有些害羞。我记起我曾经托那个外国人带给他的一盒录音带，我在那录音带里说过想念他的话；他还写过关于我的文章，题目便叫做《想起王安忆》。一想起这些，便觉得见面的一刻困难重重，窘迫万状。可是，日子一天一天逼近，见面的这一即将来临。

　　相隔整整七年之后的重逢总带有戏剧性的色彩，在这戏剧性的一刻中，我应当有些怎样出色的表现，才不会辜负这重逢？我难捺激动的心情，一想到即将到来的重逢，便心跳加速，手足无

措, 这一刻所将发生的似乎不仅仅是重逢, 是比重逢更为重大的
什么事件, 那是什么事件呢? 我一无所知。　我一无所知。我只
觉得我等待这一时刻已经很久很久, 我积蓄起许多需要和情感
作这等待。我还觉得我切切不能失去这一刻, 即使困难重重, 我
也要于千钧一发之际攫住这一刻。　　等人是一件最另人着急的
事情, 它象火一样, 烤干了所有人的耐心和信心, 使人口干舌
燥, 坐立不安。关于等人有许多诗篇, 写道 "等待戈多" 终告完
成。"等待戈多" 最终是根本没有戈多这一个人, 将 "等待" 这一
桩苦事写到了尽头, 同时, "等待" 其实就悄悄消失了存在, 好像
负负得正。现代的观念常常走这样一条自圆或自封的道路, 走
到了绝处, 最终是回到了起点, 这也类似有就是无, 无就是有的
中国哲学, 而我的等待是古典的等待, 我所等待的确有其人, 确
有其物, 我也一定能够等待到他, 或它。因此, 我就能坚持不懈,
不屈不挠。

　　他到上海的那天大雪纷飞。上海是极少下雪的城市, 这又
是一个暖冬。大雪来得很突然, 接连十天阴霾天气过后的第十
一天, 早上, 睁开眼睛, 已是一个银白的世界, 太阳高照, 晴空万
里。这天早晨, 我忽然想起这个人所居住的岛上, 四季如春, 永
无下雪的日子。为了看雪景, 他们必走很远的路, 爬很高的山,
去看那山顶上的积雪。现在好了, 这个人可看见新鲜的雪了, 我
欢欣地想到。新鲜的雪就象鲜花一样, 转瞬即逝。可是这个人,
赶上了。从这天的早上, 一直到这天的深夜, 我一直在往他住的
饭店打电话。我这回采用的和上回万炮齐轰的打法不同, 是以
点射的战术。我每隔三分钟, 便往那饭店打一次, 开始是他没
到; 后来他到了, 可是去餐厅吃饭了, 还没有住进房间; 后来他的
行李进了房间, 人却出门了。这一天, 他的节目排得很紧, 有宴
会, 有记者招待会, 有参观, 有访问。后来, 我终于查询到了他的
房间号码, 于是, 我的电话每隔三分钟就在他的房间里响起, 他
的房间空无一人。我还知道了他们隔日就要离开上海, 留给我
们重逢的时间一分少似一分。而我铁了心, 我决心要于千钧一
发之际, 将这一刻攫住。这一刻对于我的重要性, 一分胜似一分
地呈现出来。午后, 太阳被新积的云层遮住, 又一层新鲜的雪飘
洒下来, 将夜间的旧雪盖住了。我守着我的电话, 裹着毛毯, 抱
着热水袋, 每隔三分钟地拨一次电话。接线员早已辨出了我的
声音, 一次一次地将我的电话接到他的房间。我有些恶作剧似
的好像一个秉性顽劣的儿童, 明知故问地, 一次一次给空无一人
的房间打电话。我每一次拿起电话, 心里就一阵紧张地想: 第一

句都应当说什么。 听见那铃声陡然地空荡荡地一遍又一遍响，我便松了一口气，因为这困难的一刻又推迟了至少三分钟。我一遍一遍地拨那已拨得熟透的号码时，我不由地想起那位绝交的朋友，几次三番，长途跋涉去看那条河的情景。我想，其实我们所寻找的东西是同一件东西，可是他的路程要浪漫得多，背着行囊，徒步行走，象一个浪迹天涯的游子。而我一遍又一遍拨着那七个号码，诗意全无。在这个熙熙攘攘，人头挤挤的城市里，寻找一个人是多么困难啊！

见面的一刻非常平常，犹如分手的一刻。我们很快就找了个地方坐下，他问道：说说看，分手以后的情况。分别的七年时间忽然凸现起来，眼泪塞住了我的喉咙，可使我觉得非常非常害羞，我强使自己做出平淡无奇的样子，却语无伦次。我想，这七年中的事情怎能说得清呢？那是说也说不清， 说也说不清的。对这个人的怀念，就在这一刻内，迟到地觉醒，充满在我的意识中，成长为一个理性的果实。他等我说完，就开始告诉我，他在这七年中的事情。他在这七年中做的事情里最新的一件是关于"花冈惨案"。在我们的《辞海》中，关于"花冈惨案"这样写道：

"抗日战争时期，日寇将大批被俘的中国士兵和强征的中国工人押至日本做苦工。1945年7月，在日本秋田县花冈矿山的中国劳工九百多人，因不堪虐待，起而反抗，惨遭杀戮，死560人。"

这个人说，当年亲历花冈事件的人还活着，他们分布各地，他们永生难忘那惨烈的场景，那惨烈的场景使他们这一生食不得安，寐不成眠，他们携带着这沉重的记忆度着余生。他们的儿孙不明白他们为什么总是这样郁郁寡欢，并且紧张戒备如惊弓之鸟。他们的经验越来越被时间隔离，他们开始还逢人就说，可是人们逐渐心生厌烦，使他们自觉得很象鲁迅笔下的晚年的祥林嫂，口口声声"阿毛"阿毛 老调常谈。他们渐渐地变得缄口无言，即使和他们最亲密的人，他们也沉默寡言，郁郁寡欢。没有人知道他们心中的那一个惨烈的场面，没有人知道他们怀了惨烈的记忆，度日很艰难。人们被几十年的和平景象冲昏了头脑，被和平的日子麻痹了心灵，以为世界大同的日子即将来临，一切可以既往不咎。既往不咎的一日是神圣的一日，人类进入这一日尚有漫长曲折艰苦的道路。那时候，人类将洗净污泥浊水，经过血与火的洗礼，敲响送旧迎新的钟声，那钟声响彻天宇。既往不咎决不是遗忘，假如要将既往不咎当成遗忘，那就铸下了大错，那就要走上了歧路、将真正的既往不咎的日子推迟，再推迟, 遗忘是多么可怕, 许多无耻与轻薄都来源于遗忘, 罪犯们就会趁了遗忘的时机, 在既往不咎的幌子底下, 躲在阴暗的下水道里, 篡改了历史。他们一步一步地来, 先在孩子们的教科书里悄悄地将"侵略"改成"战争"这类中性的词。孩子们将永远不知道他们的祖先的罪行, 以为世界上本没有罪恶二字, 有的只是光明。他们因没有黑暗做对比, 就无法懂得什么叫光明。他们的世界就象最初的世界: 地是空虚混沌。他们就再要将人类走过的犯罪与受罚的道路从头走一遍。"花冈惨案"留给他们的纪念。每当死去一个人, 他们就觉得自己少了一名兄弟。有关这事件的记载虽然进入了我们的近代教科书和《辞海》, 可是文字是那样隔膜, 那样表情漠然, 它无意地淡化了事情的真相, 人类的苦难全淡化于文字之中, 一件又一件, 这是多么危险的事啊!

  于是,对这个人来说,"花冈惨案"便成了一件十分紧要的事情。他将这一事件编成一部戏剧, 并且扮演其中的角色。他们自筹资金, 终于排练上演。他在台上, 看见台下有掩面的老人, 他们掩面而泣, 肩背抑制不住地强烈抽搐, 眼泪从指缝间一泻如注。他还看见有掩面的青年, 这时候, 他不觉也掩面了。他想, 这是希望, 他多么感激这些孩子呀! 我不知道这个人在舞台上是什么景象, 是不是有些象这人的父亲走上乡村教堂的讲坛。在这父亲宣讲福音时, 这儿子在宣讲灾难。无论是这父亲还是这儿子, 我都怀念。这父亲和这儿子讲说的其实是同一件事: 当人们在灾难前睁开眼的时候, 福音就到了, 好消息就来到了。我听他讲述他的事情, 心里很平静, 眼泪不在梗塞我的喉咙。那已是第二天凌晨, 零点的时候。再过六个小时, 他的飞机就要起飞了。我忽然想起了一句题外的话, 那就是: 我终于在千钧一发之际将这重逢时刻攫住了。我听他讲着"花冈惨案", 好像一个小学生在听历史课。我一点也没有感到奇怪, 为什么在分别整整七年之后, 在又一次分别之前, 这宝贵的时间里, 我们要说着这个陈年老调。"花冈惨案"是一整个抗日战争时期中的一个小事件, 它与这场战争的发起和结束都无关, 它还是我国与日本国一整个外交史中的小事件, 几乎没有一点经验和材料的基础。然而, 我们既没有重温七年之前在一起的快乐时光, 也没有诉说分别之后互相惦念的心情, 我们甚至提都没提那个在我们中间传递过消息的外国人, 我们还没有说彼此写过一些什么小说, 这些小说是否重要, 我们似乎忘记了我们是在海峡两岸的两个作家, 我们只说"花冈惨案"。在他走后, 我认真翻阅了材料，在《辞海》中找到了以上那个小条，我读着这几十个文字，却忽然想起这人的父亲在他远行之际对他的嘱托："孩子，此后你要好好记得：首先，你是上帝的孩子；其次，你是中国的孩子；然后，啊，你是我的孩子。" 我想，这大概就是一个人在一个岛上，却能够胸怀世界的全部秘密了。

　　我走出大门，门外是一个上海难得的寒冷的冬夜，雪已经停了，地面结了冰。我回身朝他挥了挥手，他忽然举起双手，握成了拳，向我做了一个鼓舞的欢乐的手势，我哭了。我不知道这个人所做的事情能否对这世界发生什么影响，我不知道这个世界能否如这个人所良善愿望的那样变化，我只知道，我只知道，在一个人的心里，应当怀有一个对世界的愿望，是对世界的愿望。眼泪不知什么时候流了下来，又冻在我的脸颊上、我知道这是欢喜的眼泪。我心里充满了古典式的激情，我毫不觉得这是落伍，毫不为这难为情，我晓得这世界无论变到哪里去，人心总是古典的。我想，我终于明白了我那朋友找寻的那条河的含义，那河就是他血管里流淌的东西，那河就是他血管里流淌的源源不绝的东西。我也终于明白了，我也正在接近与那朋友和河一样的东西。要说有所区别，那就是，那条河是过去，我找到的则是未来。未来其实也和过去一样给予人生命，与人血脉相连，给人以血管里流淌的东西。寻根已无法实现，我这一个孩子，无根无底，我的父亲和我的母亲都是孤儿，作了这现代城市的居民。我只可到未来去寻找源泉。我的源泉来自于对世界的愿望，对世界的愿望其实也发生于这世界诞生之前，所以，这愿望也是起源，如《圣经》所记："神说，要有光，就有光。" 我觉得从此我的生命要走一个逆行的路线，就是说，它曾经从现实的世界出发，走进一个虚枉的世界，今后，它将从虚枉的世界出发，走进一个现实的世界。我不知道我的道路对不对头，也许是后退，也许前边无路可走，也许走到头来又回到了原地，也许仅仅是殊途同归。我不知道命运如何，可是我却知道，无论前途如何，我也渡过了我的生命的难关，我又可继续向前，我又可欢乐向前。我还知道，无论前途如何。这是我别无选择的道路，我只可向前，而不可回头。我要上路了，我看见他举起双手，握成拳，向我兴高采烈地挥舞着，呵，我怀念他，我很怀念他！

1991年3月20日沪

1991年4月3日沪

忧伤的年代

当我站在黑洞洞的电影放映厅的入口，裹在紫红色的丝绒帘幕里，听见了那女人的压抑着的抽泣声。有一点光从我卷起的丝绒帘幕后面透过来，我正好能看见那哭泣的女人的侧影，她坐在最后一排靠门口的座位上，手里握着一个手电筒，这女人是领票员。这情景没有使我害怕，也没有惊讶，我甚至没有想，她为什么哭泣，我只是不自禁地，也啜泣起来。我的忧伤就在这一刹那，好像拨开了一个瓶塞，喷然而出，涌上心间。

这个电影院的名字叫"国泰"，在我们所居住的街道的西边。在东边也有一个电影院，叫做"淮海电影院"。这两个电影院虽然只相距两条横马路，情形却大不相同，她们各自代表了两种不同阶层的市民生活。"国泰电影院"在1949年以前，是一家专放外国原版片的电影院。在那时，它就有冷气设施。它有着华丽的大厅，大理石铺地，悬挂着电影明星的装了镜框的大照片。走过大厅，上两级台阶，便是用红丝绒穿在金属立架顶的铜球里拦起的检票口。检票口内还有一个厅，是栗色的打蜡地板，四周有皮沙发。日光照不太进来，就有些幽暗，但就是这种幽暗的情调，使它显得高贵。来早的人们坐在沙发上，等待着放映厅内亮起灯光，然后拉开紫红丝绒的帘幕，可以进场了。在这里，人们总是静静的，敛着声息。而"淮海电影院"则要嘈杂多了。它的门厅很浅，检票口离马路一步之遥，看电影时可听见马路上的汽车声和人声。门厅里也悬挂了明星的照片，可那照片似有些过时的。没有冷气，盛暑时就在检票处放一筐纸扇，检了票拾一把进去，出来时再仍回筐里。纸扇是用颜色艳俗的电影广告裱糊在竹片上的，大都已残破不全。一场电影从头至尾，都伴随着纸扇划动空气的沙沙声，就象蚕吃桑叶的声音。每个星期天，这里都放映早早场的儿童场电影，大都是战斗的故事，到了电影结尾时，我军向敌人发动总攻，全场便想起了合着音乐节拍的鼓掌声，整齐划一，好像有人在指挥。国泰电影院的票价要比淮海电影院高一倍左右，像儿童场这样的廉价场次，"国泰"是没有的，它显然是比较豪华，而"淮海"则是平民化的。

那时候，我十岁出头，父母们在忙着"四清"运动，有的下工厂，有的下农村。下农村的一周甚至两周才能回来一次，工厂呢，大都是离我这市中心遥远的城市边缘，大杨浦什么的，路上须换几部汽车，所以天不亮就走，天黑了才进家门。而我们也都到了能够自个儿去看电影的年龄。我们将零用钱用来买电影票，父母为了弥补无法经常陪伴我们的缺憾，给了我们较为丰厚的零用钱。我们都有一个钱包，是用玻璃丝编结的，里面珍藏着几张角票和一些分币。没事时，我们便整理和清点这些角票和分币。对于我们的经济状况来说，到"国泰"看电影是有些奢侈了，比较合适的是"淮海"早早场的学生场电影，可是我们不愿意和那些小毛孩子同流合污，那合着音乐节拍的整齐掌声特别叫我们害羞和讨厌，它有碍我们的矜持。而去"国泰"看电影，则使我们感觉良好。我们宁可多花些代价，去国泰电影院。

我们前一日买好了票，这一日早早地就来到"国泰"，检了票，在空荡荡的内厅里游逛，将打蜡地板当成溜冰场，溜来溜去。有时是单个儿溜，有时则一人蹲在地上，另一人拉着他的手，滑过地面。我们做这些时，总是小心翼翼地蹑着手脚，压抑着笑声，以免引起电影院职员的呵斥和驱逐，我们认为他们是有这个权力的，虽然他们看上去完全不关心我们在干什么。就这样，当我滑行到放映厅入口处，撞到那厚实柔软的紫红色丝绒帘幕上，丝绒的毛茸茸的光滑使我忍不住地将它裹在身上，然后将自己卷起来，卷起来，黑洞洞的观众席便展开一个角，于是，我听见了那个女人的抽泣声。

许多事情都是在这之前发生的。发生的时候，它们似乎并不是不幸的，它们只是叫我们着急，惊慌，扫兴，可却不是不幸。当时我们只顾着应付眼前的处境，无暇考虑是幸还是不幸。不幸的感觉被压抑着，在不自觉中一点一点地积蓄起来，然后遇到触发的契机，便一涌而出。这时候回想起来，不说别处，单是在这电影院里，就发生过不少不幸的事件。

就是在这光线幽暗的内厅，从里朝外看去，阳光烁烁下的马路，就象是另一个世界。国泰电影院正是在一个街角上，一面是繁华的大马路，一面是高尚的林阴道，两条马路相交而成城市的时尚的画面。它使我们向往，但也胆怯，意识到那里是有着一些危险的，而电影院内厅却要安全多了，它的华丽的幽暗有一种蔽身的效果。我们手里捏着电影票，脚步匆匆走过马路，到了这里，就放松下来。检票员撕去半截票，等于发放了通行证。放映厅还暗着灯光，电影开场早着呢，我们就在这里尽情地玩耍吧！由于空旷无人，我们轻轻的说话声都激起了回声，我们耳语般地交谈着，交换着对照片上的明星的看法。我们在打蜡的地板上滑行着追逐，以暗影作掩蔽捉迷藏。然后，人就渐渐多了起来，玩起来虽然不那么自由了，可却热闹了，有些回到人间的意思。因为邻近开映，内厅里亮起了灯光，这也叫人温暖。挤在人堆里，我们很安心。方才自个儿玩耍的情形，显得有些寂寞了。然而，这一次，就在临进场的时候，我们的电影票找不找了，那撕去半截的电影票是捏在手心里的，可不知什么时候却松了手，玩起来总难免忘形。我和姐姐脸色都变得煞白，我们先是不相信似的上上下下使劲掏口袋，期望它是躲在哪个口袋角里，然后则满地地找寻。我们在树林般的腿之间摸摸索索，手摸得漆黑。还是一无所得。人们都渐渐进场了，我们就留在了内厅悄声商量着。我主张去向领票员坦陈实情，看他们怎么说。姐姐不同意，说这样一定不会让我们进场看电影。我以为不进场回家也是一个办法，否则还能怎样？姐姐比我年长几岁，更有胆略，看电影的要求也更强烈。她说反正我们已经进了检票口，进放映厅不会再次检票，谁也不知道我们没有票，问题在于我们是否还能记得我们的座位号码。这实在是一个冒险的计划，万一半途查票，万一有人捡了我们的票前来看电影？这场电影我真的不要看了，这时候回家真是个解脱。可姐姐不由分说，她说她想起了我们的座位，拉着我进了场。

我们在姐姐说的座位上坐下，每一个人看我们的目光好像都存在着怀疑。人渐渐坐满了观众席，焦虑等待的事情却一直没有发生，那就是，有人拿了票过来，说，这是我们的位子，你们的呢？没有，没有人来。灯却暗了，银幕亮了起来，电影放映了。这一场电影从头至尾，如坐针毡，令人不解的是，这部电影每个细节竟都是记忆犹新。没有一场电影是看得这样滴水不漏的了。我们克制着恐惧不安的心情，强使自己将注意力集中到电影上，这实在很艰巨。电影的名字叫《自有后来人》，就是后来大名鼎鼎的革命样板戏《红灯记》的原型。电影的场景多是在夜晚，火车站，工棚，还有监狱和刑场，气氛阴沉。这气氛被我们此时此刻的心情扩张得更加浓郁。 故事到了悲情之处，我们都哭得分外伤心。 这场电影真实地引起我们的悲恸之情，谈不上是享受，而是经历浩劫。 直到走出电影院，还不能自已。 正午的阳光照得睁不开眼， 眼睛是红肿的， 脸上布着泪痕。虽然结果不错，安然无恙，我们显然是坐对了座位，姐姐的判断力和记忆力都属上乘，可是事实上，这次过失对我们造成了伤痛。这伤痛是以对这部电影记忆清晰来体现的。

遗失电影票到此还没有完，后来又发生了一次 ，也是在同一个电影院，事情的结局却要悲惨得多。要说，我们也实在缺乏吸取教训的经验， 居然会在同一个地点犯下同一个错误。这个电影院的幽暗内厅就好像是一个上演悲剧的舞台，布景华丽。

下一次夜场的电影，我和邻家的同龄男孩一起去看电影。我们的父母在同一个单位工作，是单位里发的电影票，他一张，我一张。这一天我过得很不顺心，和姐姐吵架，和保姆吵架，没有母亲来打圆场，事情就没有公平的了断。这时候，我总是感到不公平，由于不公平而生的委屈使我闷闷不乐。没有人安慰，只有靠自己给自己打气。晚上这一场电影无疑是一个契机， 可扭转这一日的局面。电影是个纪录片，名字就没什么吸引力，我便自己给它增添一些另人鼓舞的内容。我和邻家的男孩早早就出了门，我还带了一整只豆沙月饼，是母亲早晨出门前分配给我的下午的点心，我一直留到晚上。我一边吃着月饼一边走去电影院，加强着这趟出行的快乐。街上匆匆行路的人， 大都是在往家里赶，是吃晚饭的时候。想到人家将围坐在晚饭桌边，而自己则走在街上，不觉心生凄凉。天光还很明亮，却是暮色的光明，晚上单独出门， 总有一些大胆的反常的色彩。我不知不觉吃完了一整只月饼， 心情却没有明显的改善。邻家的男孩对单独出门要比我有经验，他熟悉这段路上的每一个商店和每个弄口，时常伫步，进去逛一圈，看看商品，或者进弄内小便池小便。他甚至还提议走过电影院， 到更远的街上走一走。出了门， 我举目无亲，就只有听他的。我们没有目的，却步履急促，远兜远绕再回到电影院前时，路灯亮了，使得本来还亮着的暮色沉暗下来。街上多了一些人，是吃过晚饭的人们，出来度他们的夜晚。人们的生活是那么正常和对头啊，而我们的，却总有那么一点不对头。路旁的商店也亮了橱窗，呈现出繁华的夜市景象。有些市声浮起，不夜城拉开了帷幕。我们走进电影院的门厅，厅里站了些人，或在票房等退票， 或在欣赏电影海报和明星照片。街上的繁闹漫进了电影院，使这里变得有些嘈杂。

来到了这里，心头的阴霾悄悄驱散了一点，略感轻松。电影院里的嘈杂，有一种暖意。由于时间不早了，内厅已亮了灯，有些灯火通明的意思。放映厅也开始放人，从帘幕后透出观众席里的灯光。人们或进场，或在内厅流连。可是我却丢了电影票。我的电影票，不知什么时候，又丢了。邻家的男孩是个处事老练的孩子，他带我去和检票员商量。为证明我确实有票，他拿出他的票，还有单位寄票来的油印信函。并且这一回我清楚地记得我的座位号码，就和男孩的挨着。因为有了前次丢票的经历，我认定记住自己的座位很有好处。男孩说，假如我的座位又来了新人，我就退出。检票员是个挺面善的妇女，她耐心听完我们的陈述和建议，说，我可以在这里等着，等到电影开场时，那座位还没有人来，我便可以进场。这样，邻家男孩就进场到他的座位上，而我，则站在检票口等着。男孩不时从场内出来报告，那位子还没人来。我站在检票口，紫红色的丝绒缎穿过金属立架顶上黄灿灿的铜球，连起来，在每两个立架之间，它优雅地垂成一个弧度，看上去华丽极了，也冷漠极了。我从来没有在这个角度看过内厅。棕色的地板蜡，在灯光下柔和地反光，有淡淡的人影，交错移动。人们不断涌入放映厅，川流不息。原来这里的气氛也是很熙攘的，几乎是甚嚣尘上。然后，高潮过去了，人都进了场，只有几个迟来者，零零落落地来到，进场。内厅渐渐冷清，灯光照在空荡荡的打蜡地板上，显得有些寥落。看电影的心情已经很淡，站在检票口，我感到及其窘迫，看不看电影我都无所谓，知识等待事情的结局，否则这一天就完不了似的。事情怎么结束，我也无所谓，该发生的已经发生，什么也扭转不了局面了。男孩终于带来了最后的消息，那座位上来了人，一个流气的中年人。男孩甚至上前问他，哪里来的票，中年人竟也回答了他，说是买的退票。事到如今，向来沉着的邻家男孩，也不禁惊慌失措起来。检票员同情地对我说，这就没办法了。她的同情也叫我窘迫。我和邻家男孩在检票口分了手，彼此都有些可怜。我一个人走下检票口的台阶，走出门厅，走到夜幕降临的街上，感到自己非常的狼狈。这狼狈的感觉压在心头，沉甸甸的，它遮盖了这一天下来所有的不顺遂，又将这一天的不顺遂推上了一个高潮，最终完成了着倒霉的一天。

很多年以后，我们早已经搬了家，离开了这个地区，有一次我又来到这个电影院。电影院的门厅一角开辟了一个餐厅，供应德克萨斯州的牛排。和所有的电影院一样，由于电影市场的不景气，它必须扩大经营范围。我在餐座上坐下，要了一份德克萨斯州牛排。已经过了午餐的时间，餐座上只我一个顾客，只这一角亮着灯，其他地方都暗着。两个小姐站在吧台里，轻轻私语，但在这寂静的空荡荡的厅里，声音却非常清晰，连说话的声气都一丝不漏地传进耳朵。餐座是在内厅的最深处，望出去，门厅外阳光下的马路显得十分幽远，那里的声息到了门厅里便偃止了，漫不进来了。因此，看起来就象是一幅无声的银幕。而内厅的中央则黑着，就象一个演出结束后的舞台，演员都退场了，布景在黑暗里沉默着，可是只需要一束追光，它便活了起来，戏剧又将开头，继续。可是追光没有亮起。倒是在黑暗和沉寂中，窸窸窣窣地上演着一些情节。

就在我吃着德克萨斯州牛排的当口，厅内的中央悄悄地摆起了一张长桌，然后聚拢了一些人，有瓜子糖果倾倒在桌面上的沙拉声，还有茶杯搁在桌面上的磕碰声，椅子从地面上拖拉过去的响声，人们说笑的声音。人们正常的音量的说话，反倒是有些虚飘，好像在空气中挥发了，传进耳朵的所剩无几。所以内厅并不因为这群人的加入而热闹起来，他们甚至是使这里显得寂寥了。切切磋磋的声响过去了，有一个声音独自响起，在做一段郑重的发言。原来，这是在欢送两位老职工退休。发言说，这两位老职工在这里工作了一辈子，现在到了光荣退休的年纪了。我望过去，看不见今日的主角，但猜测是在桌子边上最沉默的一角，那里机械地传来磕瓜子的噼啪声，而相比之下，别的方向，声音是活跃轻松的。他们应当是在我独自去看电影时候的放映员，检票员，或者领票员。在我那个忧伤的年代里，他们正是壮年，是电影院的主人，沉着，镇静，充满力量，对一个处在忧伤的成长阶段的小孩子视若无睹。就在这一刻，舞台上的追光亮起了，我好像看见了那孩子，初出家门，在这里茫茫然地滑行。这里是她在喧哗世界中找到的避身之处，这里的暗和光都是用来保护她的。成长是忧伤的，稚嫩的身体一点点地失去保护，所有的接触都是粗暴的。要通过多少日子，她才能触摸到粗暴的深处的那一点暖意。这暖意也并不是来自什么爱之类的情感，而是从你我他的生活的艰辛里，迸发出来的人之常情。可是，在最初的时候，什么都还谈不上，只有粗暴的感觉，尖锐地损伤着心灵。

一切又都处在无意识中，不知道什么是忧伤，不知道这就是忧伤。直到我卷在紫红丝绒门帘里，听见了放映厅里，女领票员的哭泣声，所有的郁闷才有了命名，我才睁眼看见自己的处

境。就象先前说过的,我的忧伤拨开了瓶塞,喷涌而出。我已经
忧伤了多么久了,可我一无所知。

　　我总是敏锐地感觉到不公平。这是由于所处的被动位置。我
没有能力决定某些事情,权力在大人手里,他们仅只是随心所欲,
便决定了我的快乐和不快乐。而且,在这个成长的时期里,另人
满意的机会似乎非常少,被我们严格地挑剔着,它往往是相对存
在的, 在比较之下才能体现出快乐的意义。这里含有着一种竞
争的内容,而我总是敏感到自己处于竞争的弱势,预先就为失败
的结果而愤怒起来,事后又为这丧失要伤心许久。于是,这不公
平的感觉便布满在这一时期里,成了阴影,遮住了少年时代的光
明。
　　事情总是围绕着电影发生。开头却是一场舞剧,是母亲单位
发的票,仅只一张。当然,隔壁男孩的父亲也得到了一张。这票
子是在舞剧开场前不到一小时的时间发下来的, 是夏天的傍晚,
姐姐和母亲带着弟弟在弄堂里散步,我一个人在家,什么都不知
道。只看见姐姐忽然冲进门来, 拉开抽屉换好衣服, 又冲出门
去。我听见她招呼邻家男孩的声音, 还有男孩蹦跳着响应的声
音。事情的发生猝不及防,等我追出门去,只看见他们快乐的背
影,在弄堂转弯处,倏忽消失了。我转而追问妈妈,他们去了哪
里。妈妈支吾了半天,实在被逼不过,道出了真相,他们是去看
舞剧《椰林怒火》。我顿时大怒,深感不平。这一回,我气得非
常厉害,很多天不能平静,不和任何人说话,生着闷气。有时气
得过不去了, 忍不住自己找着理由解脱。有一个很好的解脱的
理由,那就是母亲的允诺。她说下一次有票,一定让我去。当我
被生气折磨不过的时候,我就想着这个允诺。起初,连这个允诺
也安慰不了我,因为我总是顽固地抓住已经丧失的不放,而丧失
的是无法挽回的。这有些不讲理,还有些自己和自己过不去,可
我就是不能这样。我的思路非常狭隘, 我过于尖锐地感觉到丧
失的不可挽回,然后陷入悲愤不可自拔。然而,生气是那么可怕,
生活变得很难熬,四周一切都愁云惨惨,暗淡无光,天性又是渴
望快乐,不得已的,只能妥协。我最终接受了这个允诺,使自己
渐渐平息下来。
　　我敢说,母亲一定是忘记了这个允诺。因为有一些时间过去
了, 实现允诺的机会却没有来临。倒不是手母亲单位再没有发

票看电影和演出，而是，发两张电影票是无法体现这允诺的。两张票，正好我与姐姐同去，她还是比我多看一场。甚至有一次真的发了一张票，可是邻家男孩正好生病，他的妹妹很幼小，不可能离开大人去电影院，所以把票给了我们。姐姐依然比我多看一场。我们依然扯不平。可是这些票来票往却使人们忘了还欠着我一场，只有我记着。事情已经不止是看一场电影或者演出，而是要消除我的不平。　我的身心都急需要这次实现允诺来摆平，否则，这将形成严重的创伤。没有人明白这些，人们以为事情都过去了，已经解决了，一切都将从头来过。时机，就是在这种背景下来临的。

　　这一次，事情有着足够的准备时间，不像上一次，要看谁下手快，而我凡事总是比年长我三岁又神形机敏的姐姐，要慢上一拍。这一次，一星期前就收到了电影票。然而无济于事，时间带来的是不安和焦虑。由于这是一场招待会性质的电影，在放映电影前，还要演出几出小歌舞。其中有一出是舞蹈《洗衣歌》，由少年宫舞蹈队演出。姐姐班上有两个女生是少年宫舞蹈队的队员，平时腰里系着黑色的宽腰带，夏天人家穿裙子，她们则穿人造棉的练功裤般的长裤。所有的少女都特别崇尚舞蹈，可能是出于一种表现欲，表现她们刚刚觉醒的女性意识。这两个女生是姐姐崇拜的人，她们练功，排练，演出的细节，都使姐姐羡慕不已。所以，早在这张票决定给谁之前，姐姐已经和她的同学说好，这天一定要去看他们的《洗衣歌》。虽然，一切都是背着我进行，可姐姐向妈妈下的功夫，是可以想见的。票子依然是她的，还是她和邻家男孩去。由于时间充分，母亲回绝我的理由也很充足。她说我还小，她不能放心我与邻家男孩，两个同龄的孩子出去，因为这一回的电影院是远在南京路上的"大光明"。事情悲惨的就在，尽管有时间作改变，却一点也改变不了。我眼睁睁地看着，看电影这一天到来，不公平的事情再一次发生。

　　星期天的早上，姐姐和邻家男孩欢天喜地地出了门，我的生气已不是一般意义上的生气，它使我非常的压抑。我又开始不和任何人说话，同时则感到深深的孤独。谁都不知道在我顽强的沉默底下，身心遭受着怎样的折磨。有时真是受不了，就问自己，是怎么会到这一步的？于是，事情的来龙去脉就又在脑海里走一遍。事情重新上演一遍，心中的气恼就再添一成。这又是母亲早出晚归的日子，我的抑郁没有人注意到，谁能在意一个小孩子的心情呢？我抑郁地上学下学，在弄口看车水马龙的街道，直看到暮色沉暗，华灯初上。倒并不是说，绝对没有快乐的时候，同学们之间发生有趣的好玩的事情，和姐姐或者邻家男孩一同玩耍，我就努力地笑，以使自己从抑郁中脱身。可是笑过了，闹过了，抑郁还是如故。没有办法，我救不了自己。前面所说的，和邻家男孩一同去"国泰"看电影，就是在此背景下发生的。姐姐很大度地将这张单独的电影票让给了我，倒不是她还记得对我的不公平，以此作补偿，而是她对纪录片没有兴趣。谁对纪录片有兴趣呢？可使没有它就什么也没有了。即使是获得了补偿，我也高兴不起来。就象前边说的，我努力振作自己，收效甚微不说，还遗失了电影票，结果是，竹篮打水一场空。

我的抑郁终于引起了母亲的注意。在这么长久的抑郁之后，我的再一次陈述事实使她无法置若罔闻。可是，事情已经发生了，还有什么办法来补救呢？她问我。母亲的恳切之中，或多或少地带有成年人的狡黠，实际上是推卸了他们对事情应负的责任。她就这样问我：事情已经发生了，还有什么办法来补救呢？我回答不出，流着眼泪。这个问题还碰着了我的痛处，事情的不可挽回使我痛心棘手。这是个悲惨的痛处，事情就是这样，就是这样无可挽回地失去。失去了就再不会有了，没有补救的办法。母亲的问题真是问到了节骨眼上，她把事情最痛心的要害提纲挈领地拎了出来，但这也确是我此时此刻迫切需要解决的问题。我只能和母亲合作，几乎没有思考的，我提出要看一部电影。这个要求没有遭到反对，母亲一口答应，给了我超过一张电影票的钱，甚至没有规定我去哪一家电影院。本是带有挑战的意味，不料却立即被接受，事情解决得太过容易，反使我不满足，情绪并没得到缓解。我没有兴致走到很远的电影院，而是去了最近的淮海电影院。那里正放映故事片《生命的火花》，是由小说《军队的女儿》改编，而我刚刚买了一本《军队的女儿》，十分迷人。应该说运气不错，并且一切顺利。我及时地买到了票，临进场也没丢失电影票，电影且相当令人感动，整场电影，我都抽噎不止。走出电影院，是下午三点半光景，太阳正好。因是星期天，这条全市著名的商业街分外热闹，人头熙攘。我终于平静下来，不公平的感觉不再咬噬着我的心，抑郁也不在那么沉重压迫我。我只是感到十分孤独，经过的一切就好像砌起了一座高墙，将我和人群隔离开来。街上摩肩接踵的人群，与我相隔在两个不同的世界，太阳也是两个太阳。我们互相从彼此的影子上踩过，仅此而已。由于我没有认识和表达的能力，许多感受都处在无法交流的封闭状态，这就是我孤独的原因。

　　这是一个发展不平衡的阶段, 身心里某一部分因得了特殊的养料, 在疯长。而另一部分因养料不足, 几乎处于停滞。这种养料不均衡的状态即便是在短时间内结束, 但造成的不均衡的长势, 却还在继续发挥作用。苗壮的部分以强大的吸收力掠夺着养分, 瘦弱的部分则不因为养料匮乏而衰退生长的欲望, 甚至由于受到压抑, 它们具有着更大的动力。就这样, 你争我夺, 争先恐后, 形成了尖锐的冲突。什么都是不协调的, 难看而且痛苦, 由于盲目而深感绝望。有一种特别强烈的感觉, 就是觉得自己的多余。　这多余的感觉是由里及外伸延的。　自己的手脚首先是多余的, 不知往哪里安置才妥帖, 这已经足够使人变得笨拙了。然后是自己的嘴是多余的, 特别想表达得出色些, 叫人注意, 产生好感, 结果出来的不是废话就是蠢话, 或是招来不屑, 或是招来嘲笑。挺好的话, 一出口就变了, 就失了分寸, 有的重了, 有的轻了。最终是, 成了一个多余的人, 在哪里都找不到自己的位置。有时一群人站在那里, 满心渴望参加进去, 于是便向那里靠拢。可刚刚接近却发现人们都停了说话, 看着自己, 似乎是受到了侵扰或是妨碍。无论是多么蹑着手脚, 脸上笑开一朵花, 甚至于是有些谄媚的, 结果还是一个, 人们停了说话, 并不转身, 却用眼睛乜斜着你。自尊心和自信心便在这一刻, 被击得个落花流水。为避免这样的窘境, 便去找那些更小的孩子玩。和他们在一起是可以称王称霸。慑于年长和强力, 他们一律唯唯诺诺, 还很讨好, 可就因为此, 却再一次发现自己的多余。他们是好好的一伙, 眼光里全是默契。他们以示弱的姿态排斥了外来的入侵者。在这个时期里, 年龄的分界是极其细微的, 大一岁小一岁都隔着鸿沟, 有着本质的不同。所以就特别难找到同伴。内部生长的不平衡给我们带来的是, 外部关系的不和谐, 这使我们的处境相当困难。尤其是我们并不知道这只是阶段性的, 这个困难的处境就变成了我们生活的全部。一切都放大了。

　　这时候, 我的外貌变得很厉害。我的脸拉长了。原先那种儿童可爱的圆脸形不知不觉中消失了, 儿童的娇嫩肌肤也消失了。脸色枯黄而且粗糙。再要等上许多日子, 少女的光润的磁白肤色才会降临, 随之而来的, 还有少女的匀称结实的体格。而现在, 却形销骨立, 颜色暗淡。我的眼睛开始近视, 看远处便习惯地眯缝起眼睛, 鼻梁上堆起皱纹, 额上也全是抬头纹, 看上去就有些歪鼻斜眼的。我的牙齿参差不齐。气管炎使得我长期张口呼吸, 导致口腔狭小变形, 新长的牙又明显大于乳牙, 便前凸后凹。有一个时期, 我不得不整天戴着牙齿矫形器, 引来人们好奇的询问。于是我便与母亲讨价还价，今天戴，明天不戴，最终不了了之。我的发型也很糟糕。从小就是姐姐梳长辫，而我剪短发，这曾经使我象个日本娃娃。而这时头发变硬变多，七支八楞，很难修理服帖。像我们这样年龄的孩子，处在可爱儿童和美丽少女之间，似乎也很难引起理发师的兴趣。有几次，我的头发剪得完全像人们说的"马桶盖"。而我却不能自作主张留辫子，因为梳什么样的头发都是母亲决定的，虽然头发长在我们的头上。母亲的权威是不用怀疑的。我的胳膊和腿又细又长，每一件衣服的袖子都远远缩在手腕以上，胳膊肘以下。裤腿则吊在脚踝上一二寸的地方。那时还没发明化纤织物，棉布的缩水简直是雪上加霜。而且我的横和竖大大不成比例，够长的衣裤在我的身上就成了大布袋。我的身高已经不能穿童装，成年的女装于我要多不合适就有多不合适。最好的办法是量体裁衣，去裁缝铺做。可没等衣服做好，我又变了尺寸，不是这里长，就是那里长。好像我总是处在不安的变化之中，身体内的生长激素分外活跃和兴奋，不停地改变它们的作品。我时常对着镜子里的自己发愣，在我的眼里，自己的形象是不确切，不肯定的。我甚至怀疑人家眼睛里的我和事实上的我，是否是同一种形象。我对自己充满了犹疑。

最坏的是我的表情，总是动个不停，却显得十分呆滞。这就是紧张。事实上，我无意之中，一直在模仿着别人的表情。不是所有的孩子，都有着这样尖锐不调和的生长时期。许多孩子顺利地度过。他们协调系统特别完善，这使他们镇定自若。他们目光稳定，谈吐自如，而且表情生动。他们往往是我羡慕和学习的榜样，我不由自主地模仿他们的一招一式。其实那都是皮毛，实质是自我调节的功能，学是学不来的。这是一种类似遗传基因的素质，潜移默化在他们的行为中。这种孩子的各方面发展都呈平均水平，这是协调的保证。他们的智能一般是中等，可这决不妨碍他们在成年之后获得良好的社会成绩。而那一类有着折磨的生长过程的孩子，面临的危险则要大得多。他们的不平衡生长往往是因为暗藏着某一种特质，这种特质的活跃，打破了均衡的态势。它就象人体中某一种特别有生机的细胞，迅速地分裂繁殖，变异为异常细胞，前途不知是凶是吉。我模仿着那些幸运孩子的可爱的神情。在我眼中，他们都是天之骄子，无论动静都是美的。这种美来自松弛和心底安宁。他们还特别善于表现自己的个性，有一种天然的驾轻就熟。因此，他们就变得形象鲜明。而我却是模糊的。就像我不能确信自己的长相一样，我也不能确信我的个性。我不知道自己是哪一种人，具有什么样的性格，这使我对自己很不满意。我觉得我是"我"，是一件不幸的事情。

这时候，我认识了隔壁弄堂里的一个女孩。这个结交也得益于其时的"四清"运动，父母早出晚归，或者一周一回，根本顾不了我们的社交。我们才有可能去搭识邻弄的啊孩子。这是一条嘈杂的弄堂，居住的大抵是低薪水、多人口的小职员家庭。房子是进深而阔大的旧式楼房，有着大大小小难以计数的房间，住户甚多，于是就成了典型的"七十二家房客"。他们与我们的弄堂之间，本来隔着一堵墙，但是在大炼钢铁的时候拆除了，为了取那墙里的钢筋炼铁。从此，这两条弄堂就打通了。那条弄堂的孩子，就象放羊般的放养着，而我们的弄堂，孩子少，管得严，因此胆小如鼠，我们总是龟缩在背静的后弄里，悄悄地玩耍。这样，我们的宽阔的前弄堂，便拱手出让，被他们占领了。他们分为男孩和女孩两拨，男孩的游戏是踢球和打架，女孩的游戏却很新颖，是体操和舞蹈。她们吸引了我们的好奇和妒忌。有一个阶段，每到下午放学以后，她们便来了，而我们则站在阳台上，看着她们在底下的弄堂里蹦跳。她们的头是个面容秀丽的女孩，就是她带领了游戏。她是区少年体育学校体操队的队员，同时还是学校舞蹈队队员。这是与我们不同的另一所小学，一座民办小学。我们弄堂的孩子，都有办法不去那家小学，而去现在的重点小学。我们的小学没有舞蹈队，却有着全市著名的合唱队，用假声唱四部合唱。可就象前面说过的，这个时期我们都向往舞蹈。

这个女孩打动了我们的心，她身体矫健敏捷，姿态活泼美丽，而且很会说话。她极善表达，她的声音沙哑却不失润泽，口齿清晰。当她向你叙述一件事情的时候，真是有声有色，引人入胜。我们都对她着了迷。当然，最初时，这着迷是以仇视来表达的。后来，我们不打不成交，她成了我们的座上客。她对我们挺巴结的，这多少平衡了我们的心理。就这样，我们不再掩饰对她的着迷。而她也竭尽才能，做出最好的表现，回报我们。她跳舞给我们看，讲各种趣闻给我们听。她的学校生活显然比我们的丰富多了，她的阅历也比我们丰富多了，相比之下，我们真是白上学了。她的阅历大部分是和老师顶嘴，很有戏剧性。在她的讲述中，活脱出一个生动的形象：直爽，大胆，泼辣，且又妩媚。她实在是了不起，竟能和老师这样针锋相对，并且结局都不错，不仅获得和解，也没使老师对她反感。听起来，她的老师相当民主。这种经历十分令我们羡慕，她的个性也令我们羡慕。不知怎么，好事都落到了她身上了。其时，我们学她走路，学她说话，学她表情。我们的学习都是一是一，二是二的，不会举一反三。她怎么样，我们就怎么样。由于使劲太过，难免有些夸张和造作，可也顾不了许多了，我们多么急于变成和她一样的人。

这种渴望由于程度热烈，渐渐成为了一种幻觉。我们在想像中真的成了那样出风头的角色。比较起来，姐姐由于年长几岁，还保持着清醒。当我忘乎所以，特别引人注意地，以那女孩的方式说出一个词或者一句话的时候，姐姐便颇有含义地看我一眼。这一眼是心照不宣的，令我感到难堪，顿时面红耳赤。可我已经陷进去了，这样的提醒无济于事，更大的难堪还在后头等着我呢！

我开始向人讲述我在学校的故事。我甚至不懂得旧瓶装新酒，我的故事也是同老师顶撞。受顶撞的老师是一位教数学的男老师，他的数学在区里也排得上号，是学校的尖子。他衣着颇为讲究，头发梳得光滑，皮鞋擦得锃亮，呢料西裤的裤缝笔直的。他挺有风度的，态度矜持。他说话的声音是那种嘹亮的男高音，在脑门那里发出共鸣，美中不足的是，讲课讲到忘形，声音提到高处，猝不及防地，会破，发出尖锐的啸音。这种小小的失常放在别的老师身上算不上什么事，可他的行止是那么一丝不苟，无可挑剔，称得上完美，这点瑕疵就不容忽视了，它甚至成了个大洋相。小孩子是很喜欢看洋相的，越是他们以为不可触犯的人，越是热衷看他的洋相，这很刺激。所以，每逢此时，课堂里便一阵骚动，四处是压抑着的笑声。尽管他不动声色，一点没有停顿地把课讲到底，可依然透露出一点狼狈相。就是这个老师，成为我故事里的人物。他总是被我顶撞地无言以对，所有的口舌之战都是以他败下阵为结局。在这种虚构的胜利中，隐藏的是我对他特别的在意。像这样拔尖的老师，往往会对学生形成严重的挑战，他们以对抗的表现掩盖着内心的佩服，崇拜，还有羡嫉。其实他并不是一个心胸狭隘的老师，在教学中相当能广采博纳。有一回，他同我们讲解某种类型的题目，我举手提出另一种解题的方式，是他没有想到的，备课大纲上也没有。他沉思了一会儿，说你可以这样解。于是，我便以我的方式完成了作业。第二天，他把我叫到办公室里，让我解释这种方式的思路。我磕磕巴巴地讲着，他则不时从旁提示我，帮助我完善思路。终于等我讲完，他当着我面在我的作业本上画了一个五角星, 说, 很好。照理说, 我与他可以有相当好的师生关系, 可是不,我们关系紧张。至少在我这方面是这样, 这就是我方才说的原因, 我面临挑战。

他也是邻家男孩的算术老师。有一回, 男孩对我说, 这个老师在课堂上进行戒骄戒躁的教育, 以我们班上一位女生的活生生的例子作教训, 男孩听下来, 觉得他所说的女生特别像我。真的, 就是你, 他肯定地说。在这个老师的描述中, 这个女生虽然学习不错, 可是她很骄傲, 所以她永远得不到一百分, 当然, 她也不会是八十分, 因她学习还是不错的, 她就总是九十七, 九十八,甚至九十九, 可就是不到一百分, 永远功亏一篑。我听了顿时气得满脸通红, 我被他形容得如此糟糕, 而且倒霉, 不幸的是我又无从反击。他并没有当面说过我什么, 于是, 我只能在背后做小动作。

我的小动作很拙劣, 带有人身攻击的意思。我对班上同学说, 他的发型是"包头"。所谓"包头", 又叫"火箭式", 是将头发留长, 涂有发蜡, 用电吹风从额前高高翻卷上去, 梳往脑后, 直至颈下, 要说"包", 就是"包"在这里, 带有庸俗的资产阶级气味。我还将他名字中的一个字略改了笔划, 再读起来, 就是一个可笑的绰号。这两桩事一无遗漏地被好事者报告了老师。就是有那么多讨他欢心的人。于是, 有一天, 我又被叫到了办公室。这一回, 可不比那一回。要说, 这是面对面的时刻, 要反击就看着时候了, 可我却畏怯地哭着, 无法说出一句囫囵话来, 时机就这样贻误了。老师是真的生气了, 他非常恼火, 他甚至站起来, 转过身, 要我看他的头发, 说:"哪里包? 哪里包?"他又用手指敲着备课本上他的名字说:"这是家中老人起的名字, 老人是旧社会过来的人, 有封建思想也是正常的!"现在回想起来, 其实, 老师那时还很年轻, 也很天真。再有, 那"文化大革命"的前夕, 政治空气已经充斥着火药味, 我的出于个人恩怨的中伤, 弄不好会断送他的前途。而我的一点没有窥破他的虚弱, 反被他的发急的样子吓得要死。

这是一次非常屈辱的对峙, 我完全没有还击的能力, 尽是挨训。事后我有一百句一千句有力的回答, 可已经无济于事, 等于马后炮。比起我的失败, 那隔壁弄堂里的女孩更显得战绩辉煌。她怎么能如此节节胜利, 毫无损伤? 而我再羡慕她, 也只能在想像中扮演她的角色, 经历她的经历, 我没有她的魄力。这就是我向人讲述学校故事的由来。应当说, 开始时, 只不过略略夸张了一点，还没有大出格。可是我不由自主地被自己的讲述激动起来，我渐入佳境，我越说越多。别看我说的那么多，究其底全是鹦鹉学舌，将那女孩的一套直接搬了过来。我被自己的想像迷了心窍，我甚至不以为那只是想像，而是真实。起先，人们还有些怀疑，可到底是经不起我这样汹涌澎湃地说，便也认了，只是流露出缺乏兴趣的样子。因为在那女孩的讲述之后，再有什么样的与老师顶撞的故事，都有重复之感，没有新意。他们都企图转移话题，可我不让，坚持说我的。我的态度是那么凶狠，他们不得不老老实实地听下去。

然后，难堪来临了。学校开家长会，父亲在农村，母亲早出晚归，这事就交给了我姐姐。让大孩子管理小孩子其实是一件可怕的事情，他们过于热衷权力，免不了会滥施滥用。我们这些小孩子便在他们的权力欲之下，被任意地摆布着命运。这实在是相当危险的。

姐姐去开我的家长会了。她只不过是个初中二年纪生，自以为是个大人，在家长会上，不甘心只做个听众，而要与我的班主任谈谈我的情况。她以为她很有责任与我的老师合作，共同来教育我。她向老师反映情况，但事实只是为了揭我的底，同时引起老师的注意。她说我每天在家就很得意地说，如何与老师大吵大闹，不以为错，反以为荣。班主任对这个情况果然注视起来，她认真地说，倒没有听说过这事，她必须去调查一下。姐姐从家长会上回到家，劈脸就说：你们班主任说你在学校并没有与老师吵架的事情。她这一下可说是击中了我的要害，我顿时哑口无言，满脸通红。姐姐脸上便露出得意的神色。我猜想，她从来就没相信过我那些逞英雄的故事，只是没机会戳穿我罢了。以后的事情都很难堪。第二天去学校，班主任就找我谈话了，问我事情的究竟。我说不出一句话，班主任困惑又奇怪的眼光使我无地自容。她说：她已经调查过了，并没有这样的事情发生，到底是怎么回事？我回答不了，我也不知道是怎么回事，没有人能解释。那遭我编派的老师这次倒没有找我谈话，只是有一次，轮到我值日，去他那里领取全班的算术作业本，他淡淡地对我说了一句：以后不要瞎讲了噢。

这是一段乱七八糟的时间，千头万绪的，什么都说不清。就是说不清。在乱七八糟的情形下，其实藏着简单的原因。它藏得非常深而隐蔽，要等待许多时日，才可说清。但在这时，它就像河底湍急的暗流，制造出危险的翻船事故。我们看不见它的流向，做不到顺流而下，相反，我们常常顶着上，或者横着来，结果就是失败。生命的欲求此时特别蓬勃，理性却未觉醒，于是，便在黑暗中摸索生长的方向。情形是杂芜的。我们处在混乱之中，是相当伤痛的。而我们竟盲目到，连自己的伤痛都不知道，也顾不上，照样地跌摸滚爬，然后，创口自己渐渐愈合，结痂，留下了疤痕。等我们长大之后，才看见它。痛感间杂在种种莫名的感觉里，使我们不能突出地辨别出它来。这也好，免去了痛苦，这阵子，我们已经够难的了。

我们看不清自己的处境。　这处境有时候要借助别人的帮助，来进行认识。别人的某时某地的情形，如镜子一般照出了我们的。就象我在电影院放映厅门口，裹在紫红丝绒门帘里，看见了那妇女在哭泣的时刻。这很偶然，但总会有那样的时刻。还有一次，是母亲被分配到一个新单位参加"四清"工作，临去前夕，她做了一个梦，梦里她来到一个从没去过的地方，周围都是陌生人，心中很是害怕。母亲将这个梦讲给我听，我不由黯然神伤了许久，感到非常悲哀。这个梦在某个地方触动了我，锁在蒙胧中的抑郁世界似乎初露端倪，是不幸的端倪。原来是这样一无所助的，我们处在冷漠之中。其实早就是这样，而我们一无所知。沉睡的理性好像突然向我们眨了眨眼，再重又入睡，可就着这点倏忽即逝的微光，我们也看见了身体周围的一圈，我们孤零零的。其实这就是独立的最初状态，我们赤裸裸的，没有一点披挂和掩饰，任何时刻都会遭到袭击。

独立是极其孤独的。我们好像一下子与人群失去了联系，所有交流此时都中断了，这有些像幽闭症的处境。我们用闭关自守来抗拒危险，恐惧一触即发，犹如惊弓之鸟。弄口有一个街心花园，沿着马路。每天放了学后，我总是一个人来到这里，坐在铁栏杆上，看着街景。直到暮色降临，华灯初上。在暮色里，我感到很安全，它掩蔽了我，并且隔离了我与周围行人。路灯亮起的一刹那也很温暖，天光未灭，它们就显得有些微弱，黄黄的，一点也不刺激人。街上行人都模糊了身影，我也模糊了身影。此时，我好像获得了自由，身心都很解放。我放松了身体，任它在铁栏杆上扭曲成古怪的姿势。这姿势令我舒适。我的情绪也缓和下来。由于没了压迫，它反而变得很柔软，有一点点伤感，但温温和和的，一点不伤心。这一刻真的很享受，所有的焦虑都平息了。

　　这时候，我们的有限的户外活动都在后弄里进行。和所有的后弄一样，它很阴沉。阳光要到下午三四点钟，才照到这里，多半已是相当微弱了。所以它还很潮湿。就象前面说过的，我们弄堂与隔壁弄堂之间的墙拆除了，这样后弄就正对着隔壁弄堂的一面山墙。山墙已有了年头，墙壁剥落了，裸露出暗红的砖，有一些背阴的爬墙植物。和所有的山墙一样，它的顶部呈三角形，在那尖顶下面，有一扇永远关着的木窗。木头框子都朽了，是黑色的。窗玻璃积着成年的灰垢，也是黑的。山墙下是一块空地，没有铺水泥，是裸露的泥土，既不长东西，也没有人来。这小小的一块的空地，却将荒凉之气扩散开来，蔓延进我们的后弄。那扇木窗里有一些动静，是一种沉闷的空洞的声响，寂静中，突然地嗵嗵嗵一阵。倘若这时我们正走过空地，要拐进我们的后弄，就会惊得魂飞魄散，拔腿就跑。其实，那是一扇楼梯口的窗户，是腐朽松动的楼梯上的脚步声。

　　我们这排房子的后门对着一座高墙，高墙和房子之间的那条窄道，就是后弄。墙那边是一个辽阔的大院子，是党校的校园。那里原来是著名的震旦女子大学，1949年以后，震旦女子大学没有了，就由一所重点中学和这所党校分割了校舍与园地。后弄的高墙那边，正是属于党校的那部分地面。即使一分为二了，那园子依然很大。震旦女子大学是一所天主教会学校，所以，从楼上的后窗，可看见那建筑顶上，有一个小小的方形的拱廊，拱廊里有一座石雕的立像，一母携着一子，就是圣母玛利亚和圣子耶稣。也许是因为雕刻粗糙，它在我们远远的视线里，显得模模糊糊。但是，在那种空气澄澈的夜晚，它们的立在空阔夜幕前的静静身影，则变得边缘清晰。它们有一种寂寞的安详，另人感动。我们有时在后弄里打羽毛球，羽毛球很容易就飞过墙，从墙的那边落了下去，无影无踪。我们曾经壮胆去寻找我们的羽毛球，那就需要走出弄堂，走过一段马路，再走进另一条弄堂，那另一条弄堂的底处，才是党校的大门。我至今也弄不明白这地理位置，我们的后弄与党校的园子究竟是怎样的关系。好容易说通了党校的门卫，踏进党校的园子，却茫然起来，简直不知道该往哪里举步。我们在党校的园子里兜着圈子，寻找着那座高墙，高墙下的羽毛球。墙下长着杂树和杂草，相当茂盛，就象一个树林子。夕阳低低地斜照过来，树叶和草丛毛茸茸的，我们的羽毛球就停在那里。我们撒开脚步向它奔去，杂草在脚底柔软地倒伏了。这时，我们看见了高墙外的我们的房子。它变得面目陌生， 高墙也面目陌生。它们看上去陈旧而且灰暗。隔壁中学的下课铃声响起了, 在这隔成两半的大园子里游荡, 余音拖得很长。

这就是我们的后弄。它阴沉, 寂寞。可就是它, 成了我们小孩子的乐园。我们跳绳, 踢毽子, 造房子。形形色色的游戏磨损了它的地面, 使它布满裂痕, 并且高低不平。我们吃下的瓜皮果壳还会堵塞阴沟, 害得污水外溢。所以, 它就变得破烂和肮脏。我们就是喜欢在这里玩, 前弄其实宽敞明亮, 阳光普照, 可是它靠近马路, 生人较多, 不如后弄来得隐蔽和安全。看, 我们就是这样令人不可思议。我们龟缩在弄底, 高墙的投影笼罩着我们。我们一律面色苍白, 四肢细弱, 并且神经过敏。我们像惊弓之鸟一样, 老是自己吓自己。几乎不需要什么理由的, 我们就吓得个半死。我们的惊恐不是造作, 装腔, 人来疯, 全是实打实的。我们常常在后弄的转弯口, 突然飞奔起来, 压抑着尖叫, 直奔进家门, 心像擂鼓一样在跳。后弄的阴郁已经濡染了我们的心, 它对我们的迫害是很深刻的。可它就象我们的躯壳, 收藏着我们的灵魂, 像宝宝一样揣在怀里, 摇啊摇的。

不知道这是在成长的一个什么节骨眼上, 我们变得如此脆弱, 胆战心惊。有一阵子, 我们特别惧怕对窗的灯光。那一排窗距离我们很远, 是在我们房子的前面, 隔着另一所中学的大操场。我们用一条纱巾蒙着头, 透过纱巾, 那灯光就变得很诡秘。它的光涣散开来, 光的纤维飘荡移动。奇怪的事情在于, 那一排窗不知为什么, 只是这一扇亮着灯, 其余都暗着, 这使我们更有理由惊惧了。一到晚上, 我们将这条纱巾传来传去, 去接受那灯光给予的惊吓, 然后在惴惴不安中入睡, 让恶梦来侵扰睡眠。我们在这神秘灯光的惊怵之中, 沉溺了一段时间, 它给了我们足够的刺激。对, 问题就在这里, 惊怵给我们刺激, 它似乎是我们生长的需要。这是一种不甚健康的需要, 体内某一种腺素在活跃着, 在亢奋着, 要求着这种不正常的养料。夜幕中那一排黑洞洞的窗户里, 按时亮起的一扇, 向我们传送着一些晦暗不明的气息。楼房的暗影, 还有楼房与楼房间的空地, 都怀着沉郁的晦涩的表情。它浸淫了我们。这时, 我们怀着寻密探幽的心情, 我们放学不从大马路上回家, 而是在窄巷长弄里穿行。似乎, 所有的弄堂都有着蹊径别路, 它们四通八达, 将弄堂和弄堂结成一张网。真是想不到的发现, 忽然就走到一条背静的夹弄, 有时候则是相反, 一条背弄神秘地消失了, 怎么也找不到了。这就好像一团乱麻的一个线头，来无影，去无踪。即便是这样错综复杂的情形，它们依然保持有各自清晰的，不容混淆的面目，这面目来自它们各不相同的生活。那全都是离群索居的。我们也是离群索居。

这一条夹弄得自姐姐的发现，她吊了我们几天的胃口，然后在我们强烈的向往之下，带我们前往。这条夹弄其实算不上夹弄，它只是两座相连的楼房之间的一道狭缝，缝中是一条干涸的阴沟。我们只能分开脚，跨过阴沟，踩住沟的边缘，一步一步挪过去。墙就蹭着我们的肩，从这头走到那头，已经不成人样。身上是墙上的灰，脸上头上蒙着蛛网和小飞虫。阴沟散发出昏晦的气味，决不是臭，甚至连难闻都算不上，但却令人黯然。它给了我们一种晦涩的乐趣。我们来来回回地从狭缝中挤身而过，头顶上是一线天，我们就好像身居黑暗的蝙蝠。

这些晦暗不明的嫌恶的快感不知道暗示着什么，和我们的身体和精神的哪一部分有着关联，我们的好奇心变得十分怪诞，这是一个心理阴暗的时期。就好像白昼和黑夜交替，我们进入了黑暗。在日头高照的街道上，我们这几个小人儿就好像阳光里的阴影，勤勉地挪着脚步，走到哪里，阴影就到哪里，所有背弄里的，墙角背弄里的，墙角壁缝里的阴沉，都贯注进我们的身心，积蓄起来，驱散了光明。当这种阴沉达到某种程度，而我们的身心又处在一种极度薄弱的状态，它就会以某种形式爆发出来，那情形几乎是惨烈的。我们经受着怎样的折磨啊！生长的尖锐的激素咬噬着我们，痛楚是无可名状的，不确定的，不明所以的。寻找突破口，也是盲目的。

在这阴郁的背景上，凸现而起的是我们所居住其中的后弄。那后弄的拐弯一角，是我们的惊怵之地。那空地，空地上方的木窗，木窗里的楼梯声响，在我们心头布满了无尽的荒凉。天黑以后，从那里经过，是一件极其困难，甚至是不幸的事情。然而，怕什么就来什么，无论怎样躲避，厄运还是降临。

这时候，少先队的组织很健全，工作很积极。尤其我们学校，少先队的大队辅导员是一位优秀辅导员。她年纪轻轻，梳两条垂腰的辫子，眼睛黑黑的，令人敬畏。逢有少先队的节日，她便在颈上系一条红领巾，看上去很庄严。她富有想像力，且充满活力。她能够想出许多点子，活跃我们的学校生活，以及课余生活。我们的学校就在方才我说的街心花园前的，那一排民居之中，街心花园也是我们的校院。我们的富有生气的活动吸引了居民和路人。谁能想到，在这灿烂的花园背后，有着那样阴沉的夹弄。我们学校有一个电视室，倘若有好节目，便会给各中队发电视票。电视票不多，每个中队只四张，各小队一张。中队以班级为单位。和所有的学校一样，我们学校已经少先队建制了。这一张电视票发到小队，要进行讨论和推举。讨论是严肃认真的，花时很长，难免会有不快发生，但最终还是意见一致，口服心服。这带有一定的奖励优秀的用意，是一种荣誉。这种荣誉终于轮到我了。这晚的电视是电影《小足球人》。可是事情就是这样，不止是电视，而是，荣誉。我兴奋了一阵，紧接着便愁上心头。看完电视，我如何走进后弄，最终回家呢？学校和家只有一条弄堂的路程，可是却隔着后弄。这问题梗在心里，使我心事重重。然而，我不能不去，也不能让给别的同学，事情太不一般了，我只能硬着头皮，去看电视。

去的时候，天已经暗了。后弄里还有一两个人进出，后门碰响着。面对后弄的厨房也都亮着灯。我匆匆走过后弄，说不上有什么高兴，相反还有些凄然。人家都回家，而我，却走出家门。家人对我的夜晚出门都不以为意，没有人挽留我，叫我不要去，我只得去了。学校也暗着灯。白天喧哗的学校，这时变成了一座空房子，脚踏在楼板上，会激起了回声。只有电视室亮着灯，穿出些声响，却显得更冷清了。不过明亮的电视室毕竟叫人安心。老师们彼此打趣着，不像平日里那样严肃，而是有些随便。同学们则都拘谨着，互相不说一句话。情形似很反常，这时的学校，和平时的，竟判若两样。倘若是在白天，我们就会感到新鲜了，可是夜晚似乎对所有的孩子都有着压迫。此时，我们的兴致都有些低沉，还有些不安。小孩子天黑是不能出门的，出门的经历大多不那么愉快。后来，电视打开了，电影《小足球队》开映了。电视石里关了灯，街上的灯却映到了窗户上。霓虹灯变幻着，有些光怪陆离。人们都被《小足球队》吸引着，只有我，心不在焉。电影一开场，我就开始为回家担心。

我先把在场的同学扫视一遍，看看有哪个可与我哪怕同一段路。就是说，倘若是住在隔壁那条弄堂里的，也好，我也许可以厚着脸皮要求他送我一段。至少，有那一段同行，趁着一股子劲，我也可以冲进后弄，推开后门。可是，没有隔壁弄堂的同学。没有人与我同路。然后，我便展开了激烈的思想斗争。我是走后弄，还是走前弄？前弄虽然略微可怕得好一些，可是前门却不像后门，总是开着。它从里面拴上，与房间又隔了一个小院子。通小院子的门到了晚上，就锁上了。所以，走前弄就必须叫门，然后等着开门。最后才能进入安全的家。后门呢，就比较简单。走过后弄，直接就可奔进家门。可是后弄是多么阴森啊！我禁不住地打着寒战。走过后弄回家，几乎是不可能的。然而，前弄呢？要是家人听不见我的叫门声？即便听见了，我又需要在那里呆多久？一个人呆在黑暗的弄堂里，也是不可能的。在我反反复复的权衡比较之下，这两条弄堂被一遍遍寻根究底的掂量，不断地增添着阴森的程度。恐怖攫住了我的心，我渐渐失去判断力。一直到电视结束，走出电视室，我都还不知道走哪条弄堂回家。

这时候，即便是对于大人，也是个较晚的时刻了。街上的人不多了，街心花园里黑而寂静。我们这些看电视的小孩子，分散在花园里，一下子不见了踪影。我走进了大弄堂，街灯离我越来越远，我很快就不再看见自己的身影，眼前是一团黑。由于眼睛近视，这黑夜就更深了。我脚步越来越快，有一项决定也迅速地成熟，那就是走前弄回家。我转进了前弄。一进前弄，我就控制不住了，奔跑起来。此时，后弄的阴森黑暗如同洪水般从身后汹涌而来，前面则是，前弄里的空旷的黑暗。我惊恐地失声大叫，叫妈妈开门。我凄厉的叫声震惊了整条弄堂，所有的窗户，都在这一瞬间亮了。

幸而，肌体是健康的，而且，还是纯洁的。这些都给予了承受和抵抗的力量，平衡的机制最终将发生作用。尖锐的冲突达到濒临极限的时分，剧烈的疼痛便要求着和解。这不止是妥协和软弱，还是服从生长的需要。越是尖锐的冲突，和解的要求就越是强烈，和解的过程也越是艰巨。冲突之后达到和解，身心都将焕发和平的光辉。这是一种深刻的安宁，经历了残酷的斗争之后，终于获得。这一个过程其实极其正常，而且向上。它是在我们生命的初期，儿童的时代，身心还没有受到疾病与遭际的侵害，健康和纯洁都无损伤，一切处在自然之中。因此才能克服一次又一次的困难，去走向和解。

我们家的院子就只巴掌大，却是我的广袤的田野。就像我去绍兴鲁迅先生故居，看见那著名的百草园，我极其惊异百草园竟是这么逼仄，而且乏味，与鲁迅先生笔下的描写相去甚远。成年以后，我们再不会像儿童时那样，善于收获和播种快乐。就这样，我们家的小院子，成了我的大自然。院子里有两棵树，一棵是石榴，是保姆和姐姐有一天从菜场买回来的。另一棵是园林局统一来栽种的法国梧桐。隔壁院子显然要比我们的院子繁荣得多，单是依着我们这边院墙，就种了红白两棵夹竹桃和一棵枇杷树。到了春天，沉甸甸的花枝便垂到我们院子里来，还有，青枇杷也洒了我们院子一地。同时， 夹竹桃的有毒的香气也在院子上方弥漫开来。我们这边就萧条多了。我们的石榴树总也长不高，而且瘦弱，花朵稀稀拉拉，然而，却很醒目，是发亮的金红色。有一阵子，它甚至生了奇怪的虫病。虫是褐色的长条行，表面有着细细的节， 颜色与形状都与枝条一模一样。它紧紧地贴附在枝条上，很难发现。我耐心地用筷子一条一条地剥离，忍着恶心。我竟然一条不剩将它们全部剥离了。但这还不是转机，事情的转机出自我的一次农科实验。我从《十万个为什么》上面读到，在果树的根部截去一周树皮，可使养料更有效地供到枝叶部分，促进开花结果。于是，我便在石榴树的根部截去一圈圈的树皮。不想，来年春天，石榴开了满满一树花，好像挂了一树的金红小灯笼。可它还是长不高，也长不大，并且不结果。那一棵梧桐树，却飞快地长着。几乎没有人注意地，它长到了院子的上空。我甚至不记得它的树冠是什么样子的了。我从来没有照管过它，它在我们院子里，就象一个侵入者。大约七八年以后，已是"文化大革命"的中期，一场台风，将它刮倒，带起了一半的根。母亲叫上我，合力把它拔起，从墙上推了出去。母亲悄声对我说，自从来了这棵树，我们家就过得不好，这是一棵不吉祥的树。我虽然没这么总结过， 可我从来和这树不亲近， 视它于无睹。可能它对于一个小院子来说，太高了，它的树冠超出了视线，但它的树杆我也没有注意过。

除了石榴树， 我还在院子里栽种过玉米、向日葵、蓖麻和葱。我种的全是油粮作物以及蔬菜， 比如葱。因为那就是比较容易得来的种子。我特别细心地照料它们， 大大超过它们需要的程度。可是，一切都违反一分耕耘一分收获的原则，我几乎颗粒无收。而从来没有养育过的车前子， 却长得非常茂盛。在种植以外，我还热衷于架设藩篱。我用竹片编成篱笆，围住我的不得收获的庄稼， 又用砖块砌成花围边。我甚至于企图在院子里挖一口井。这项工程持续了好多天， 最终被大人阻止， 重新填平。这院子里埋藏着我的秘密。比如我蓄意砸碎的一个玻璃填纸。玻璃填纸里的小鸟始终困惑着我，我问所有的人，所有人都回答我， 那是一整块彩色玻璃。而我坚信那里有一只完整的玻璃鸟，我必须把它取出来，不这样就不得安宁。结果自然是失望，除了一摊彩色的碎玻璃， 还有就是闯了祸的恐惧。我将碎玻璃埋在院子墙脚下，以为这就没事了。我在院子了掘了一眼行军灶，像电影里的那样，然后烧火点炊，结果当然也是不成。即便是在这忧伤的年代，我的抑郁也没有濡染过这个小院子，它总是温暖我。脚下是温暖的泥土，还有茂盛的车前子，头顶是人家院子的夹竹桃和青枇杷。这是个美妙的小世界。是我的庇身所。

这时候，这城市还有许多柔软的泥土，它们零散在各处，倘若聚集起来，对一个城市来说，还是可观的。这些泥土还有着足够的养分，它们滋养了一些树木和花草，与此相依并存的，是一些昆虫，它们形貌不同，益害也不同，可这就是生态平衡。在各种昆虫中，有一种名叫"洋辣子"的，我们叫它做刺毛虫。它一般歇栖在柳树和梧桐树上，夏季时繁殖最盛。到了那时，它们身上的茸毛便随风而去，满天地飞扬。这茸毛细小得肉眼几乎看不见，可事实上它不是茸毛，而是极尖锐的刺，它一旦落到皮肤上，立即就鼓起了红包？又疼又痒，弄得人手忙脚乱，无所适从。唯一的办法是用肥皂水洗，以期肥皂水能将毛刺从皮肤里滑出去，可结果也很难说。被刺毛虫刺上，可真是夏天里不幸的事情。现在，这城市里再也没有刺毛虫了，没有刺毛虫的危险威胁我们，刺毛虫成为历史的遗恨了。

这一年的夏天，所有的不顺遂似乎都发生过了，人已经处在消极的状态，有一种心灰意懒，对什么都提不起劲。生气，惊怵，抑郁，都消融在夏季的慵懒之中，还有经历折磨的疲惫之中。事情该告一个段落了，可是，就是结束不了。不知身心内的哪一部分起着抗拒，不让事情就这么了了，似乎还期待着，期待着一个有力的结尾。结尾部分空白着。这骚动不安的时期，需要一个特别有力的结尾，否则就结不了。还有一些燃料没有消耗，一些冲突没有平衡。在慵懒和疲惫之下，有一些惧怕和等待压抑着，不知所以的，盲目的，其实那将来未来的，是一个打击，带有彻底的消灭的性质，它将把一切都推入过去，一无遗漏，永不返回。后来的岁月将重新砌起一个年代，完全不同的内容。

事情的起因极其简单，没有引起一点注意刺毛虫的毛刺落在了我的晾晒在院子里的内裤上，内裤是翻过来晒的。它刺伤了小孩子难以启齿的部位，我无法同人诉说，我甚至不知道发生了什么事情。惊恐和痛楚又一次袭来，却和以前的全不一样。它是贴近而且具体的。每时每刻，无法回避。开始时还能忍受，心里一觉醒来，就能过去。可是事态却在发展，一天比一天严重。红包被擦破了，并且感染了。我不知道该怎么办，没人能帮得了忙，我还得强颜欢笑，装作没事人一样，和大家一起玩啊、闹啊！痛处与恐惧与日俱增，我自己一个人，趁人们午睡的时候，悄悄地去到药房买消炎药片。药房就在那家平民化电影院的隔壁，中午时分，街上少有行人，蝉在响亮地鸣叫，阳光从梧桐树叶下洒下，闪闪烁烁的，叫人睁不开眼。柏油马路在汽车轮胎下软软地起伏。我赤脚穿一双凉鞋，齐膝的花阁子裙里的折磨，只有我自己知道。我走进药房说要买消炎片。心下紧张地盘算着，假如别人问我是什么地方发炎，我将怎么回答。不过那店员什么都没问，卖给我的是"强的松"，这样小小的，白色的药片，不敢指望它能解决我的什么痛苦。我的痛苦是那么巨大，任何措施都无济于事。可不指望它又指望谁呢？

　　人们香甜地午睡着，我吞下了"强的松"。这不敢指望的指望。我还是指望睡眠来拯救我，我不能放弃幻想：事情也许会在睡眠之中缓解好转。可这时候，睡眠已经变得不那么容易了。一半是刺痒和灼痛，一半是恐惧和忧虑。我在凉席上辗转反侧，默默地吞着眼泪，等着睡眠和"强的松"发生效应。而所有的折磨，在夜深人静时则变得分外尖锐，生病已经够苦的了，又是生这样糟糕的见不得人的病。我一心以为这是见不得人的病。炎症和焦虑使我开始发起低烧，并且迅速消瘦，可是谁也没有注意，我依然要应付人们，应付得滴水不漏。

　　小孩子是相当能受罪的。他们的承受力和柔韧度简直无法限量。倘若没有这样的能耐，他们如何接纳他们的敏锐的感受？他们娇嫩的身心能感觉到疼痛的最深刻，最细微。倘若没有力量承受后果，他们怎么行？所以，他们既是娇嫩的，又是坚强的。孩子的坚强，意义要更重大一些。成人的坚强有一半是麻木，是身心打上了坚硬的茧子，隔离了体验。

　　事情似乎不能再拖下去了，可我依然顽强地捱了下来，一天又一天。直到了有一天的晚上，母亲很晚回来，看我还醒着，问我怎么了。就在这一瞬间，我软弱了下来。我的意志崩溃了。多日来，以极大的毅力维系着的自尊自强，全崩溃下来。我泪流成河，从家里哭到医院里，在治疗台上清洗创口时，我大哭大叫，不让医生护士近身。这样暴露在众目睽睽之下，我觉得天都塌了下来。这正是最羞于自己身体变化的时候，连自己都不敢正视自己的身体。而就在这一刻，帷幕拉开了。七八个医生围着我，按住我的手脚。门口还挤着看热闹的病人，住院的日子是无聊的，难得来这么一场好戏。人们都在笑着，对我的痛苦抱着轻松好玩的态度,在我的哭叫挣扎中,有一位头发花白的医生挤进来,对我说:你这个孩子怎么这样,我告诉你,我的女儿在新疆……我一时上理解不了她的女儿在新疆和我有什么关系,可她严肃谴责的神情却震住了我,我不由止住了哭声。接下来,事情就变得简单了。那就是,清创,消毒,敷药,然后住进医院。事情就是这样简单,只是一次受伤和感染,需要的是治疗。

我住进了医院,换上肥大的病员服。由于我受伤的部位,我是在妇产科就医。在我这样的年龄,出现于妇产科病房,是十分招眼,并且惹人非议的。时常有人好奇地到我们病房门口来看我,然后窃窃私语。而我其时就像儿歌里唱的那样:我们都是木头人。我已经成了个木头人,不会说话不会动。我躺在床上,不理睬任何人。我不梳头,不洗澡,一切都等下午妈妈来探视的时候,替我完成。我的头发长了,母亲把它们扎成两个结结实实的牛角。先用玻璃丝在根上扎牢,再编几股辫子,最后扎成辫梢。因为扎得过紧,我的眼梢都吊了起来,瘦尖的下巴更成了个锥子。心里觉得这样的牛角辫不是我的年龄合适梳的,可这时什么也不在乎了,随妈妈怎么处置。我吃饭只吃一两,人们就向妈妈告状,妈妈便嘱我一定要吃二两。于是第二天早晨,我就要了二两稀饭,满满的一大盆,又一次招来非议,再向妈妈告状,说我竟然吃二两稀饭。妈妈不得不详细嘱我,二两是指干饭,稀饭则只要一两。我这才调整了饭量。

我将自己严严地封闭起来,与外界隔绝了往来。妇产科病房是个嘈杂的病房,人来人往很多,新鲜事也很多,可这一切都与我无关,引不起我一点兴趣。我终日躺在床上,脸朝着天花板,看着太阳光如何从天花板上走过去。心中无喜也无悲,空荡荡的,什么也没有。只在每天上午,大约九点钟左右,有一个小护士来叫我去坐盆半个小时。那护士个子小小的,端着一大盆消毒液,脚步很利索地走过我的病房,并不停脚,只是侧过头脆脆地叫我一声,在继续向洗手间走去。她总是把我的名字叫错一个字,我也能听懂。等我从床上爬起,走到洗手间,她已不见了身影,坐盆架上搁着那盆热腾腾的紫红色的消毒液,边上搭着一方干净的纱布。我就坐在消毒盆上继续发愣,时间一点不留痕迹地过去,我一点不操心计算时间,只等着那小护士脆脆地再喊我一声,便起身走回病房。有一天,我已经走到我的病房门口,忽听身后有人喊"喂"。走廊里没有别人,这一声"喂"又分明是冲着我背后。我惊奇地回过身去,想是谁老熟人一样地叫我,与我相邻的病房门口，站了一个女孩，梳着两条垂肩的短辫，她指着我说：本来是我最小，现在是你最小，是最小的病人。我愣着，不知该怎么回答她，她已经闪身进去，不见了。

这天傍晚，吃过晚饭，我走到了阳台上。我们的病房在七层楼，可看到城市很远的地方，无遮无挡的天空显得很辽阔而且贴近。那时侯，这城市还没有现在这样多的高楼，空气也比较清澈。太阳下去了，天空铺满了晚霞。楼下街道上已经有了黄黄的灯光，在树丛里隐现。我又看见了早上喊我的女孩子，她也在阳台上，但与我隔着围栏。她在阳台上拉手风琴。我方才想起，每天傍晚时的手风琴声，原来是她在拉呀！她眼睛看着远处，一点没有注意我。我就趴在水泥围栏上，静静地听着，直到夜幕降临，笼罩了我和他的身影。这时病房里开了灯，所有窗户都亮着，最后的探视者也都走了。病房里很安静，整个城市都很安静。风是凉爽的，一阵阵吹来，将白昼的暑气一扫而光，那女孩已经回了病房，琴声止了，而我却孩子阳台上，心里有一丝喜悦升起，是安宁的喜悦。我在阳台上一直呆到同病房的大人来叫我进去物睡觉。由于妈妈的嘱托，这里人人都觉得有责任管我。

第二天傍晚，我早早来到阳台上，等着那女孩出现。果然她来了，拖着椅子，挎着手风琴，朝我一笑。我还来不及回她一笑，她已经转过头，坐下，拉开了手风琴。她随着手风琴放声唱了起来，歌声和着琴声，在天空下散得很开。晚霞渐渐在头顶铺开，一直到极远的天边。晚霞下的绿树和红瓦顶，看上去很美。街心里有小小的玩具般的汽车爬行着，也是美丽的。在渐渐暗下去的天光里，她拉手风琴的轮廓是美丽的。她的发辫因刚洗了头散开着，披在肩上。唱歌的嘴一开一合着，手风琴的风箱也一开一合着。手在键盘上移动。歌声和琴声都消融了，消融在这一片黄昏美景之中。

我开始渴望与她搭话。我生出了一些虚荣心，心想，倘若我能与她做朋友，该是多么骄傲的事情。每天傍晚，我总是早早地在阳台上等她，寻与她说话的机会。而她在与我招呼的最初的热情过去之后，就对我熟视无睹了。我一点不觉得有什么不对，她美，她成熟，她会拉手风琴，还会唱歌。我呢？难看，丑陋，没长熟，头发梳得那么怪，而且乏味无趣，她凭什么要对我有兴趣？由于我巴结得很紧，她后来还与我说了几句话。她告诉我她是音乐学院附中的钢琴系学生，也是受外伤来住院治疗。她的外伤是这样发生的。有一天她正骑着一辆男式的有前梁的自行车，忽然身后有同学喊她,猛地一下车,撞到了前梁。她受伤的情形光明磊落,来龙去脉清楚分明,立即便被人们接受认可。而当人们来询问我时,我却无法这样明朗地叙说,所以就总是沉默。人们就再进一步问:　是骑自行车的缘故吗?自行车的妇科外伤已为大家确认无疑,除此以外,似乎再想不出有其他受伤的原委。我摇摇头,人们便用怀疑的目光看着我,走了开去。我知道我在人们眼中,已成了个不光彩的角色,可我不在乎。在经历了那么些之后,还有什么可在乎的呢?

我还是不说话,可内心却活跃了许多。我躺在床上除了看太阳光外,我还悄悄地照镜子。这是一面小小的,可以藏在手心里的镜子,背面是歌片,边缘包了一条红色的塑料胶皮。是姐姐留给我的。她到医院里来看我,就给我留下了它。其余,就是大吃我的水果和零食。我看着她吃,心里很少有的一点不生气,还为自己的慷慨生出喜悦。白天我就用这面小镜子审视自己。它只能照见我的局部,一只眼睛,一个鼻子,几缕散发,脸上的某一部分皮肤。这些局部都显得那么陌生,好像不是我,而是另一个人,是谁呢?在此同时,我开始注意房间里的动静。

我们的病房,有五张床位。三张是并排抵东墙而放,另两张是沿西墙头尾相接地一顺放。我就是西墙顶头靠窗的一张,阳台的门就在我的床头柜旁边。在门那边正对着我的病床上,是一个川沙乡下的农妇,有许多农人模样的男女,川流不息地来探望她,说着难懂的川沙话。她的病不重,眼看就要出院,却总是愁眉不展,时常叹息。忽有一天,她绽开了笑容。下午她的女儿来看她,也是笑容满面,前来探视的亲友则都向她道贺。她不善言语,只是笑着,几乎合不拢嘴。原来她的病因检查出来,是血吸虫引起,而凡属血吸虫病范围,都可由当地政府担负医疗费用。这才明白,这多日来,她愁的是这个。现在好了,问题解决了,病也治好了,她欢欢喜喜地出了院。出院那一天,亲朋好友来了一大帮,用各种手法溜了进来,前呼后拥地将她接走了。她的病床空了不到半天,就来了新病人。这是个年轻妇女,长得很文静,梳两条长辫,戴一副白边眼镜。她是一个人住进病房,却显得熟门熟路。安置好自己的东西,在床沿铺一块白布,然后坐下来吃荔枝。她铺一张纸在膝上,放荔枝的壳与核子。她一颗接一颗地吃,吃了一会儿,就起身检查身下的白布。只这一会儿工夫,白布上已染上了血迹。她一直在流血。可使她很镇定,毫不慌乱地再又换上一块白布,坐下来,继续吃荔枝。

当我开始注意我周围的情形时，东墙下那另两张床上，各有一个做剖腹产的孕妇。在我看来，她们的年龄都过于大了，似乎不该只是婴儿的母亲。她们从手术室出来，就一直闭眼睡着，床前有人日夜守候，主要是她们的丈夫。在我看来，也是大得可怕的年龄。其中有一个是白白胖胖戴眼镜的。有一天午睡时，我看见他悄悄地1，狼吞虎咽着产妇的西瓜。他大约是想把旧的西瓜消灭掉，好让产妇吃新鲜的西瓜，可情景看起来总有写滑稽。我不由偷偷地笑了。这是入院以来我第一次笑。这两个产妇生的都是女儿。护士长说，两个女儿都长得特别像妈妈。护士长还对其中一个说，她的子宫非常难看，这我就不懂了，子宫还有什么好看和难看？好看和难看又意味着什么？而这两个产妇无论护士长说什么，都无动于衷，却是一副如释重负的表情。似乎是，反正已经过来了，别的什么都不要紧了。她们和她们的丈夫看上去都是，疲倦，可是轻松。这境遇可能是与我的有些相似，所以我便领会至深。

邻病房的音乐附中的女孩，这时候已经彻底不理睬我了。她生性活泼，喜欢串病房。可是即便串到我们病房来，她也并不搭理我。甚至看都不看我，好像没我这个人。她手风琴不离身，在各病房里拉琴唱歌，也在我们病房拉琴唱歌。可她就是不理睬我。我一点不在乎，一如既往地喜欢看见她，听见她的声音。我，崇拜她。

我的外伤其实很简单，经过简单的敷药与消炎，便立即好了起来。疼痛和羞耻都是在入院第一天消除的。那清洗创口的惊心动魄的一幕，最终有力地解决了我的折磨，一些新的类似于快乐的东西在不知不觉中滋长着。我的身心进入安宁。这是真正的、和平的安宁。出院那一天，我和妈妈下了公共汽车，走过弄堂口的街心花园。我发现，我的肩膀已经和妈妈的一般高了，而我却还扎着那样可笑的牛犄角似的小辫，在地面投下奇怪的影子。

阳光明媚，过去的那一段时间，忽然沉陷进了阴晦的暗影里。

1997年12月9日
1997年12月25日

女作家的自我

我必须要着重强调女性作家在新时期文学里的极其关键的作用。

《爱,是不能忘记的》,在人们中间所引起的激动情绪,至今历历在目。我们还不会忘记,在这之前,关于什么样的题材可进入社会主义文学殿堂的问题,已由《伤痕》掀起的热潮解决;而爱情在人们社会生活中的位置, 也以刘心武雄辩的演论争取到手。那么,这一篇迟到的爱情故事,又是以什么理由来激起人们如此热烈的情感?这一个委婉美丽的故事决没有与社会方面产生的冲突, 纯属个人生活中的一件小事。私人的小事成为一篇公布于众的小说, 这已经夺人眼泪了, 而事情有远远不止这些。重要的在于这一桩私事并没有与社会政治去凿通关系, 而仅仅是与个人的情感发生了联系。 多年来我们的文学在一条"集体化"的道路上走到了极端,人人忘我,"个人"仅在受到批评指责的时候方可上升为"主义"。人们再不曾有这样的准备: 那就是去接受一桩仅属于个人的心情。这大约是多年以来, 个人的、私有的心情在文学中的首次出场。假如说,《爱, 是不能忘记的》, 其中还有一些关于择偶原则的训诫。还可与社会的集体意识、公共思想挂上钩, 那么紧接着出现的那一篇小小的《拾麦穗》,则是更加彻底地属于个人的了。在此应当坦白,我是在读了《拾麦穗》之后, 才觉得做一名作家于我来说是有可能的。之前, 我对文学充满了畏难情绪。在我心里蓄满了许多情感, 我就努力将这些情感与社会的、使命的共同意识去打通关节,结果事事难成。那时, 我绝大多数的文学创作便是日记和书信。因此, 我曾有几次说过这样的话——"过去我把日记当

185

小说写，如今，我把小说当日记写。"而一部《冬天的童话》固然表达的是个人的东西，但我们无法判断这就是作者自身的故事，我们只能认为这是两个创作的故事。然而《冬天的童话》却是一部真正的作者个人的故事、一部私小说，将文学的个人性推向了极至。再往后，就有了《在同一地平线上》，在此，"个人"终于上升为"主义"，而这才真正唤醒并触怒了一些纯洁的集体主义者。被触怒的人们并没有觉察到这部作品中的个人主义与那时候其实已经走到很远的女性作家作品中的个人意识联系起来，他们用"达尔文主义"、"存在主义"等等深奥的批评指向它。实际上，应该发生的一切都已经发生了。

在男性作家挥动革命的大笔，与官僚主义。封建主义等等反动、落后、腐朽的势力作着正面交锋的时候，女作家则悄然开辟着文学的道路，将战壕一般隐秘的道路，一直挖到阵地的前沿。这时候，中国的文学便呈现了崭新的却也是古老的面目，不再仅仅作为宣传的工具和战斗的武器，已被允诺了宽限的时间，与已在发生的事情拉开距离，迟到地表达个人的意见与心情，并且日益走向独立，却也失去了狂热的欢呼和显赫的光荣，越来越感到寂寞——文学回到了它本来的位置上。我想说的是，在使文学回归的道路上，女作家作出了实质性的贡献。

抑或是由于社会性的原因，抑或更是由于生理性的原因，女人比男人更善体验自己的心情感受，也更重视自己的心情感受，所以她们个人的意识要比男人们更强，而男人们则更具有集体性的意识。一个失败的男人才会沉溺于爱情，而女人即便成功了，也渴望为爱情作出牺牲。女人比男人更有个人情感的需要，因此便也更有了情感流露的需要。文学的初衷，其实就是情感的流露，于是，女人与文学，在其初衷是天然一致的。而女人比男人更具有个人性，这又与文学的基础结成了联盟。因此，在新时期的文学中，涌现了大量的女性作家。这些女性作家一旦出现总是受到极大的欢迎。她们在描写大时代、大运动、大不幸大胜利的时候，总是会与自己那一份小小的却重重的情感联络。她们天生的从自我出发，去观望人生与世界。自我于她们是第一重要的，是创作的第一人物。这人物总是改头换面地登场，万变不离其宗。她们淋漓尽致地表达个人的一切，使作品呈现出鲜明的而各不相同的世界观、哲学观、情感与风范。也许这一切这一切在中国表现得尤为特异，因中国的女人比别国的女人更长久地被禁锢在狭小的天地里，而中国的男人又比别国的男人更具有为政为道的人生理想。于是，中国的女人的自我意识越加强烈，而男人们也更强化了集体意识。

　　然而，接下来的问题却是，女性作家赖以发生并发展的自我，应当如何达到真实。我们都知道，唯有真实的才是可贵的，完美的，真理性的。我们大约都读过鲁迅的《幸福的家庭》，尚记得文中的作家是如何描绘他想像的幸福家庭：
自由结婚的夫妻，男着洋装，女着中装，一人一册《理想之良人》，餐桌上铺了雪白的布，厨子送上菜——"于是一碗'龙虎斗'摆在桌子中央了，他们两人同时捏起筷子，指着碗沿，笑眯眯的你看我，我看你……"然后说出一串洋文，同时伸下筷子。那贫寒交迫的作家所设计的幸福家庭，纵然很幸福，却谬误得可笑。有些作品中的自我表现，会使我想起这个幸福家庭。

　　一个人，是非常容易将自己想像成另一种形象的，而女人又更加倍地多了这种误入歧途的危险。

　　女人比男人更爱惜自己的形象，或者说是男人比女人更多一种恬不知耻的勇敢。还因女人更重视更能体察她的自我，因而也更爱护自我。她们如同编织人生的理想一般精心地编织着自己的形象，弄到头来，她们竟瞒天过海，将自己都骗了，以为那编织的自我，就是她们的自我，而事实上却不是。一个纯朴的、未受过教育的女人，因没有头脑与智慧设计自己，倒也许还有几分可贵的真实，她们无力抑制她们的忌妒、贪婪、凶恶、自卑、丑陋的私心和下流的情欲，却因而能够直率地表露。然而，一个有智慧，有头脑，有教养的女人，犹如女作家那样的，又可能回怎么样地对待她自己的形象？她有没有可能不对自我进行修饰和检点？写到这里，我不由想起了美国犹太作家辛格的小说《女妖》，其中那一位美丽的女人，因为爱护自己以致在做爱时都不能放纵自己了，最后衰竭至死。

　　我应当说，在我们新时期文学的初期，女性作家们是下意识地在作品中表达了自我意识，使自我在一种没有完全觉醒的状态中登上了文学的舞台，确实带有可贵的真实性。同时也应正视，在这一时期里的自我意识，因是不自觉的状态，所以也缺乏其深刻度，仅只是表面的，问题是发生在觉醒和深入之后。

　　女人希望被人欣赏，被人娇宠，被人爱慕的要求是那样强烈，她们无法忘记她们的观众，她们要求自己出场的时候，表现得好一些。她们下意识却又清醒地根据传统的根深蒂固的审美习惯抑或是时下流行的样式设计着自我。从这一个被谬误与聪敏改造过的自我，能够出发到什么样的境界呢？是更高尚，更深远，还是平庸与浅薄？这是最值得讨论，　　却也是最难于讨论的地方。我在前面已说过，　自我是作品中的第一人物，却也是不出场、或者改头换面出场的人物，那么我们究竟到哪里去找他？如果找不到他，又如何判断其真伪，由其真伪联系作品的成败而推断出讨论的答案。不过我想，我们可以从成功的作品里溯源而上地推论其自我是真实的，还是谬误的，而这真实还是谬误的自我在作品中起的作用又是如何。我在此能够提供的只有以我的偏见所承认的一些篇目，那就是《呼啸山庄》，《伤心咖啡馆之歌》，《方舟》也可算作一篇。写到此时，我才发觉我将自己带入了绝境，便只能再回过头去说了。

　　由于具有多愁善感的特质，　女人还会有一种将其自我意识扩大的本能，　这也是几乎所有具有浪漫气质的人所容易有的本能，　是一种近乎妄想症的状态。如梁实秋在其三十年代所写的文章《现代中国文学之浪漫的趋势》中所刻薄讽刺的——"离家不到百里，便可描写自己如何如何的流浪"。而女人又比讲究实利的男人更具有浪漫和幻想的气质。她们对外界的参预，要大大少于男人，她们时常地沉浸在自己的内心世界，当她们将自己的心情和体验咀嚼遍了，再回头去重复咀嚼的时候，难免会嚼出一些本来没有的滋味；当她们其实和男人同样蓬勃的创造力被约束在一个比男人小得多的天地里的时候，她们难免会无中生有地创造出幻想；而在她们狭隘的生活场景无法提供她们更多的体验的时候，她们也难免在少量的内容里掺进一些水分。在此，我更深地感到悲哀的是，如今有许多男性作家也越来越多地陷入这种困境，使得我们新时期文学越来越具有女性化的趋向。也许我们陷入的理由不同。例如，男人虽不是像女人那样希冀被人宠爱，而他却更渴望被人尤其是女人崇拜、仰慕，时时处处感受到他们是雄伟的男性。　当他们确信可以获其一切时，便滋长了虚荣性，这虚荣心使得他们虚枉的幻想更接近真实。他们的生活原本是开阔的，可是成为一个作家的命运却使他们走进了虽然不是厨房，却也是同样封闭的书房，这甚至比厨房还要单调和乏味，连普通的家务琐事都被关在了门外。而清洁的书房却更可以供他们海阔天空地幻想。当男人们将他们过人的蛮力从外部世界转移到内部来的时候，创造谬误的自我便得到了非凡的效果。

在批判了自我的谬误之后，我要进行的批判则是对于自我的不进步。就是说，假如我们已经保持了自我的真实性，接下来的问题则是对自我的提高。真实的自我与提高的自我之间，我以为应有一个理性的距离，也就是审美的距离，或者说是判断的距离。梁实秋在以上提到的文章中有这么一段话，大约可帮助解释："真实的自我不在感觉的境界里面，而在理性的生活里。所以要表现自我，必要经过理性活动的步骤，不能专靠感觉境界内的一些印象。"困难的也是矛盾的就在于什么是经过理性活动而表达的自我，而什么又是谬误的自我。又似乎是，真实的自我，必须经过理性活动的步骤，否则，便是不真实的了。那么，理性活动中我们应当做些什么？

我们已经听过了不止一个的"做女人难，做出了名的女人更难"那样不幸的故事。我们先假设这是一个真实可感的作品，作者在其作品中表达的自我也是真实的，结论也是真实的。然而，我们就要提问：做女人难，做男人还难不难呢？做一个出名的女人难，做一个不出名的女人还难不难呢？如果，我们宽容地承认做男人也难，做不出名的女人也难，甚至更难，那么再回过头去考察那万般为难的境遇，是否可发现一些并非由于性别和名望而形成不幸的原委？一些源于其个别的自我本身所造成不幸的原委？这一个造成自身困境的不善的自我，是否更具有真实性，并更高尚。而自我的真实里面毕竟还应当含有真理的意义。真理这个词在我们今日看来，竟是古典得近乎迂腐，而我以为万变不离其宗，古典主义因离我们的出发地最近，也许更接近了事情的本来面目，我愿意保持真理的观念。我们是不是因此可以这样说，如不与自身以外广阔的世界及人生联系起来，对自我的判断也会堕入谬误。在一方面是对自我真实的体察与体验，在另一方面则又对身外的世界与人性作广博的了解与研究，这便可达到真实的自我与提高的自我间审美的距离，理性的距离和判断的距离。这距离应在真实的自我与深刻的世界观之间建立并拉开。

在一个自我面前，还要有另一个自我的观照，这个观照的自我站得越高，那一个本体的自我便更真实更清晰。而这个观照的自我的提高，则有待于我们理性活动的步骤。自我与观照却寄存于作者一人之身，这是一个伟大的困境。

而女人们过于沉溺在自己的情感中，往往身不由己，为感觉所左右, 而脱不开身去, 拉开一段距离, 冷静地审视自我, 这便又一次地使其自我陷入谬误的困境。

在此我要说明, 我也是一个女性作家, 以上所说的一切, 我都摆脱不了干系, 而我将努力去做我已经意识到的一切。当我坐在空白的洁净的稿纸面前, 我要努力忘记我的观众, 我要强迫使自己陷入孤独的绝境, 这样我方可自由, 我方可静静地面对自己。

1988年9月15日

CORNELL EAST ASIA SERIES

CORNELL
East Asia Series

Order online at www.einaudi.cornell.edu/eastasia/publications or contact
Cornell University Press Services, P. O. Box 6525, 750 Cascadilla Street,
Ithaca, NY 14851, USA.
Tel: 1-800-666-2211 (USA or Canada), 1-607-277-2211 (International);
Fax: 1-800-688-2877 (USA or Canada), 1-607-277-6292 (International);
E-mail orders: orderbook@cupserv.org